FINANCE
MONTER

HOW MASSIVE UNREGULATED BETTING BY
A SMALL GROUP OF FINANCIERS PROPELLED
THE MORTGAGE MARKET COLLAPSE INTO
A GLOBAL FINANCIAL CRISIS

HOWARD B. HILL

*FOUNDER OF THE SECURITIZED
PRODUCTS DEPARTMENT AT DEUTSCHE BANK*

ISBN-10: 1503012409

ISBN-13 978-1503012400

A Note to the Reader

The world of finance has its own language, with specialized terms and frequently employed acronyms. These are highlighted with an asterisk when they first appear in the text, and defined in an italicized sidebar as well as in the glossary on page 229.

The term Finance Monster, which, in plural, serves as the title of the book, is my own.

FINANCE MONSTERS

Table of Contents

Introduction

While a lot has been written about the financial crisis and its roots in mortgage finance, no one has yet told the whole story. Because no one telling the story was actually part of the story.

I was, from the beginning, back when mortgage bonds were an innovation rather than a commodity. I invented half the bonds they call "toxic waste." Over a period of 25 years, I analyzed nearly every new bond structure that came to market. I worked on the "sell side" at some of Wall Street's biggest firms and on the "buy side" for important institutional investors.

I believed in this business, and had a painful ringside seat as it imploded.

In the pages that follow, I'll take you inside Wall Street's securitization business for an in-depth look at how it began, how it grew, how it worked, what went wrong, and the people who made it all happen. Some of what you read may surprise you.

The capital markets are complex, so it's easy to oversimplify them. Unfortunately, when it's time to explain what caused the financial crisis of 2008, oversimplification is common, either because writers think that readers won't be able to grasp something if it's too technical, or because the people they talked to on Wall Street oversimplified it for them. It's possible they didn't understand it either. Some of this stuff is hairy.

I'm going to open the "black box" and try to make it easy to understand, not by oversimplifying it but by taking you through it, step by step, layer by layer. You'll understand how mortgages become bonds, how they trade, who buys them and why. And I'm going to show you how betting on market events rather than investing in mortgage-backed bonds had a pivotal role in the financial collapse.

I didn't come to Wall Street as an intern, I came as a computer geek. I'd been part of a small company that wrote computer models to make things work – real world things like hydraulics and office management tools for physicians. I was one of Wall Street's original "rocket scientists," back in the day when mainframes had rooms of their own and I had to fight to get "mini" computers on our desks.

It was those early computers that helped us model and "carve up" mortgage cash flows into multiple classes of bonds. I built computer systems that analyzed the behavior of mortgage borrowers, how they paid (or didn't), and how those payments could be structured into bonds. It was a lot like designing hydraulic control systems but instead of actuators, valves and servos handling hydraulic fluid, our raw materials were principal, interest, losses, insurance, and reinvestment cash flows.

Over the next decade, I invented about half of the new mortgage bonds in the market, including the first bonds built from apartment building mortgages, the first bonds that hedged against mortgages paying off faster than expected, and the first bonds that financed Argentine mortgages. I enjoyed designing individual bonds to fit the needs of different investors, with different risks and ratings, and making them all fit together like a puzzle cube, without a "bad bond" in the bunch.

My job was fun. The money was good. But there was also genuine satisfaction in doing something that I thought benefited society. By making bonds out of mortgage cash flows, I was making the American Dream more accessible to more Americans than ever before. When mortgage lenders could sell us their mortgages in a pool, they lowered their risks, so they could lend at lower rates to more people.

It wasn't a hypothetical advantage. One deal I structured with a new kind of bond lowered the interest rate for the entire mortgage market by about 30 basis points. Put in terms we can all relate to, that one deal structure put roughly $40 a month back into the pockets of anyone buying a house, and gave millions of borrowers a reason to refinance.

By the time I had worked on the Street for a decade, my technical "jets" and sense of where to look for more efficiency in the financing markets made me the choice when Deutsche Bank decided to enter the securitization business. In 1996, I left my position as head of the Securitized Products Department after building the business from the ground up, and started a small structured finance boutique focusing on state-of-the-art technology.

It was hard to compete with the big boys, even with a smarter computer system, so in 2002, I went over to the "buy side," working first for a Dutch bank managing several new CDO (Collateralized Debt Obligation) funds, and then for one of my first and most loyal clients back when I was a junior analyst.

As a Managing Director in the Quantitative Management group at Babson Capital, a subsidiary of MassMutual, it was my job to help the firm assess the risks of mortgage deals and the mortgage market as a whole. Even though the structures of the deals had been standardized, it still took time to analyze the mortgages and how the future cash flows from those loans might feed the bond structure.

Naturally, I assumed that the raw data for our analysis – the description of the mortgages themselves provided by the Wall Street dealers – was accurate. But when the mortgage market become so "hot" that deals sold out before we had time to complete our analysis, I got worried.

Not long after we began to invest in the "down in credit" subprime mortgage market in 2006, the slide toward catastrophe began. First a few lenders and dealers failed, then more, and then enough that the even high quality mortgage loans, whole industries, and the entire financial world was on its way to a disastrous nose-first landing.

When the financial crisis really took hold in 2007, I was unwinding the small subprime stock and bond fund under my management. Unlike the big money players that got famous for their bets against the market,

I was sitting at a conservative insurance company that had a culture of betting with America, not against it.

We weren't the only losers or the biggest. The biggest losers were the American public. And the winners were the hedge funds. It's become popular mythology that hedge funds are the heroes of the financial crisis. They saw it coming, and made the right bets at the right time. But it wasn't that simple. Because their bets nearly bankrupted the world economy.

The tool that turned a market sector correction into a global catastrophe was a favorite of the hedge funds – Credit Default Swaps (CDS). CDS is a form of insurance that covers losses when a bond or loan defaults. The big banks – the ones "too big to fail" – wrote these insurance policies on subprime mortgage bonds, and the hedge funds bought them up. When those buyers demanded payment as the insurance came closer to kicking in, the world economy was held hostage.

The first ransom was paid when the government saved AIG, Fannie Mae and Freddie Mac in September 2008 and paid all their debts. An additional round of ransom got paid when the TARP program invested directly in the big banks a few weeks later.

During the crisis, over $20 trillion in credit support was pledged for US banks and big corporations. The Federal Reserve started lending money to domestic banks at zero interest, a policy they intend to continue until at least 2015.

This is the story about the people, policies and systems that created the subprime mortgage meltdown, and how a market correction grew to become a global financial crisis with a little help from some very savvy traders – the finance monsters.

CHAPTER ONE

Panic

Like a good trader, Wall Street has a short memory.

Just ten years before the financial crisis of 2008 and ten years after the Savings and Loan crisis, the hedge fund known as LTCM – Long Term Capital Management – was on the brink of collapse. LTCM had $100 billion in positions, mostly borrowed. Having paid billions of dollars in margin calls* over the previous month or two, LTCM was down to its last billion dollars.

One more big margin call and they were done. At that point, their holdings – $100 billion in U.S. Treasury Bonds, government bonds from other nations around the world, and various other stock and bond positions – were going to have to be swallowed by a nervous market that was already developing a terrible case of indigestion.

*Margin Call – a call for additional capital to protect a lender that has financed a stock or bond. The owner of the asset that is "on margin" is asked to deposit additional cash when the value of the asset falls so the lender is not exposed to a larger fraction of the value of the asset than they agreed to when the asset was financed.

William McDonough, President of the New York Federal Reserve, took a page from financier J.P. Morgan's playbook to prevent the crisis from subjecting the world's financial markets to an untimely death.

In response to the Panic of 1907, J.P. Morgan had invited a group of fifty bankers to his home on Murray Hill in New York City. He locked them in the library, and wouldn't let them out until they agreed to provide the New York Stock Exchange brokers with the credit they needed to buy up the stocks that were being dumped on the market. By the next morning, the bankers came up with an offer of $25 million in credit. That stopped the Panic of 1907 dead in its tracks.

Before that fateful meeting, the failure of one bank, the Knickerbocker Trust Company, had led to a run on banks and brokers throughout the country as people and businesses all attempted to get their money out at once. More than two thousand financial firms had already shut their doors including thirty national banks and one hundred state banks. No wonder they called it a "Panic."

Proving that human nature and emotion don't change, ninety-one years later, fear once again took hold in October of 1998 during the LTCM affair. McDonough followed J.P. Morgan's lead when he strong-armed a consortium of banks and Wall Street dealers to invest new money into LTCM to keep it afloat. The panic was avoided.

In his testimony before the U.S. House Committee on Banking and Financial Services on March 3, 1999, McDonough described the situation as follows:

"...I believe the LTCM episode and the supervisory response to it is fundamentally about two things: leverage* and good judgment. Leverage is a fact of life in our financial world, and is a key part of the risk-taking necessary for the creation of wealth. But sometimes banks go too far in extending credit to their customers and counterparties."

Leverage – Investment where the purchase is made by using some of the buyers' own money and the rest by using borrowed money. Often expressed as a ratio, a buyer paying 10% and borrowing the remaining 90% of the purchase price is said to have 9 to 1 leverage.

Even though a trader needs to forget his last trade when entering a new trade, lenders should have long memories, which is just another way to describe good judgment.

During the housing and securitization* boom that preceded the "mortgage meltdown," it was hard to find good judgment anywhere.

Securitization – The process of creating new securities by combining a pool of similar financial assets into a trust or other legal entity, which then issues the new securities. Especially common for residential and commercial mortgages, but used for almost any asset that has predictable cash flows, such as car loans, bonds, building or equipment leases, or even legal settlements or royalty payments.

We allowed ourselves to be driven by emotions, without paying attention to the facts. In the final surge of the post-9/11 housing boom, the key facts about borrowers' ability and willingness to pay their debts were simply ignored.

Greed drove the markets until "starter" homes were no longer affordable for people with "starter" incomes. Fifty years without a nationwide decline in housing prices convinced us that house prices would always go up. A few market participants actually thought it was safe to lend the full price of a house to borrowers who never proved they had the income they claimed on their applications.

We responded to an extended period of easy money that followed the attacks of 9/11 by giving highly levered mortgage loans to anyone who could fill out an application with the numbers we wanted to see.

As greed blinded investors to the reality of inflated home values and the poor or nonexistent credit histories of the people that wanted to own them, Wall Street took the mortgages and applied even more leverage through securitization. Fund managers who saw what was going on and refused to join the rush underperformed and lost their jobs, so fear drove those managers to buy as well.

The financial cycle of greed and fear is an old one. And when fear took hold in 2007 and 2008, any securitized debt was suddenly suspect. Investors rejected any and all bonds that had subprime mortgages as part of their underlying "collateral." The investing public believed that none of the subprime mortgage bond buyers knew what they were buying, and that the facts were being hidden from investors. Commentators and investors everywhere started to call all subprime mortgage bonds "worthless."

If anything, the panic that took hold was even more extreme than the greed that preceded it. In early 2008, actual credit losses in securitized subprime mortgage pools were below 3%. About 75% to 80% of all subprime mortgages were paying on time, a decline from the historical average of 85% to 90%, but not nearly as bad as the market prices of subprime mortgage bonds implied.

The panic made things worse, and no wonder. When investors stopped investing in mortgage bonds unless there was a government guarantee, lenders stopped lending, and houses that were already dropping in price went begging for buyers. Some borrowers could no longer sell their homes for more than their mortgages even if they were "good" or even "prime" borrowers.

Most people have trouble relating to large numbers, and it doesn't help when the financial press doesn't stop to check the numbers when they report on the economy. In the interest of making a story more exciting, they sometimes leave out facts that might make the fear a little less extreme.

For example, the reporters were correct when they said that prices declined by a "record" amount in the S&P Case-Shiller index of twenty metro area home prices. They just didn't say that the records for that index only consisted of only seven years.

Even the Chairman of the Federal Reserve didn't seem to have a handle on the numbers. In his testimony to the Senate Banking Committee on July 19, 2007, Chairman Bernanke responded to questions about the size of the subprime credit problem by saying it could reach $100 billion.

Just six months later, in January of 2008, he told the House of Representatives Budget Committee that the losses in subprime mortgages might have already reached $100 billion, but assured the Committee that they couldn't go any higher than half a trillion dollars.

As he explained, that was really a safe bet, because there were less than a trillion dollars of subprime mortgages outstanding at the time. Even if every one of those mortgages were foreclosed and the houses sold for half price, the losses couldn't realistically go past Chairman Bernanke's limit. When Bernanke estimated an absolute top limit for credit losses at $500 billion, he was imagining a scenario in which every single subprime borrower would default, and recoveries from selling their houses would average less than half the amount of the mortgages, or 35% to 40% of the appraised values..

When Chairman Bernanke was being grilled about the subprime mortgage problem, he was looking at the facts at the time, which weren't nearly as bad as the public perception. All subprime mortgage bonds were worthless if you believed hysterical press reports and ominous pronouncements from star hedge fund managers who stood to make better returns the faster and farther those subprime bonds fell in price.

Total realized credit losses from subprime foreclosures were still under 3% at the time. Loans delinquent by two months or more had popped up to low double digit percentages of the total, and the analysts at the Rating Agencies* were scrambling to deal with how to project losses with no historical data to compare. They raised their lifetime loss expectations for 2006 and 2007 subprime mortgage pools to a relatively modest 20%, which was nearly four times the original expected loss levels.

Rating Agencies – The companies that independently judge the credit quality of debt issues. The ratings range from "triple A" (AAA) through D for default, with gradations in between. Some of the Rating Agencies vary in the system of letters and symbols they use.

If every foreclosure results in recovery of only half the mortgage balance when the house is sold and expenses like taxes, commissions and servicer advances are repaid, 40% of the borrowers would have to lose their homes for a bond deal to lose 20% of its balance. So even if Ben Bernanke's worst case came to pass, and every subprime borrower defaulted and every home owned by a subprime borrower was foreclosed, the recoveries from selling all those houses would still pay back half the subprime mortgage bonds.

That's how securitization works (even in a meltdown).

A securitization is structured into multiple tranches* and priorities of payments are set up among the tranches. When the most senior credit-protected bonds – the AAA bonds – are formed, they are usually the largest group of bonds in the deal.

Tranches – Bond classes, from the French trancher, to cut. In a securitization, tranches are prioritized (cut) by maturity, allocation of interest, or in order of credit priority.

In a typical subprime mortgage deal, these AAA bonds comprised 75% of the deal. When the AAA bonds were further cut (tranched) into sequential bonds, several of those bonds are set to be paid in full as time goes on. These sequential AAA bonds from deals that are a year or two old can be among the safest and most profitable investments for the careful investor.

This is especially true when panic takes over. As a top priority bond, a "front pay" AAA subprime mortgage bond gets all the recoveries from foreclosure sales. A rise in foreclosures can help pay off the bond sooner than it would pay off otherwise. Buying bonds like these at a discount can create unusually high returns if they pay off quickly, with the greatest risk being a sudden slowdown in foreclosures, which lowers the return.

For subprime borrowers, there was a glimmer of good news to offset the predictions of doom we read about every day in the paper, assuming those borrowers kept their jobs. Rates were coming down. They came down so far that subprime borrowers were paying a lower interest rate when their loans reset in 2008.

As house prices declined under the weight of foreclosures, the average house became more affordable for the average income borrower. That is, if the borrower could get a mortgage. That seemed like additional offsetting good news to bond professionals that used the facts of history to make their buy/sell/hold decisions.

What the professionals in the bond business didn't know was that the real "checkmate" move for the mortgage bond business was to make sure that the mortgages weren't available for buyers. And that was happening in a completely unregulated, undisclosed business called "Credit Default Swaps," or CDS*.

Just nine months after Bernanke's testimony, the private mortgage lenders were virtually all bankrupt and Fannie Mae and Freddie Mac were in conservatorship. The world's largest AAA-rated insurance company (AIG) was bankrupt (without even being in the mortgage business) after taking hundreds of billions of dollars in losses from those undisclosed "side bets" on subprime mortgage bonds.

* CDS – Credit Default Swaps. A contract executed using standard swaps documents that specifies one party will pay regular payments equal to the yield spread of the bond, in exchange for the other party paying credit losses on the same bond.

Taxpayers kept bond holders from losing any money while the banks were paying off on the CDS. The CDS payoff was estimated at $50 billion on the day Fannie Mae and Freddie Mac were taken over, even though bond holders never lost a dime in actual credit losses.

Naturally, Fannie and Freddie made it much harder to get a mortgage after the fall, and the private lenders were just plain gone.

The Fannie/Freddie payday was peanuts compared to the CDS payoffs on billions of dollars of formerly investment grade subprime mortgage bonds. On many of those bonds, there were more than a hundred dollars of CDS claims paid for each dollar of credit loss the bond investors were taking.

The new financial instruments known as Credit Default Swaps not only accelerated the collapse but made it very profitable.

The best way to understand how it all happened is to go back to the early days. The mortgage securitization market had been declared dead more than once, and long before Credit Default Swaps buried it.

CHAPTER TWO

The Party's Over – Again

During my time on Wall Street, the mortgage market was declared dead and buried more than once. In 1995, I was interviewed for an article titled "Death of the CMO* Market" which appeared on the Bloomberg Professional news service. In that interview, I talked about two prior near-death episodes, the first in 1986/87 and the second in 1989/90.

Each time, the mortgage securitization market suffered. Each time, it came back after adjustments were made. And each time, we could look back and see that it took a period of rising asset prices and lowered losses to drive the market to a point where it was vulnerable again.

* CMO, or Collateralized Mortgage Obligation – a multi-tranche mortgage bond deal that distributes the cash flows from pools of mortgage loans or MBS to the bonds according to a set of rules for that distribution. The mortgage loans or MBS are said to "collateralize" the bonds.

Once the market had built up expectations that trends would continue in a positive direction, relatively small changes in the environment triggered a cascading negative reaction that caught most participants by surprise. As with most panic reactions, the correction was typically more violent and destructive than the round of optimism that set the market up for its decline.

Usually an entire sector of the market doesn't die in a single day, but there are a couple of days when participants in the mortgage market certainly felt that way. One of those was the day in 1994 that led to that pronouncement in 1995 that the market was "dead."

It was a day that will be remembered by mortgage market participants, but not the general investing public: March 31, 1994.

It happened to be my last day at Daiwa Securities America. In fact, it was the last day for our entire mortgage group, which was being shut down, so it was doubly significant for us. We'd had an amazing run at Daiwa, especially when we were buying the CMO residuals* that the Resolution Trust Company (RTC) was selling out of the portfolios of insolvent thrifts.

*CMO residual – the additional mortgage cash flows, usually excess interest, that is left over after the CMO bonds are paid their principal and interest.

March 31, 1994 was also the day David Askin's Granite Fund was dismembered by the Wall Street community that lent it money to hold mortgage bonds. I saw one estimate at the time that the sudden liquidation of Askin's fund was equivalent in market impact to the U.S. Treasury selling six months' worth of ten-year Treasury Notes in one day.

Over the course of that day, prices on Askin's bonds dropped by more than ten points. The selling frenzy even moved the cost of U.S. Treasury Notes by as much as five percent.

At Daiwa, we'd known we were all going to be let go on March 31, and I had been working eighteen-hour days to try to clean out our inventory and transfer more than twenty deals' worth of customer-owned bonds to Nomura Securities for financing.

The month of March had been tough. It seemed like every day I found a new problem to solve. For example, there were option contracts on prepayments tied to specific CMO deals. Not only were these contracts unusual for the time, they had been separated from the bonds they referenced and recorded in different accounts, including accounts that weren't even at our firm.

David Askin, whose fund was blowing up, had the same job running the research and structuring team as I did in the mid-80's at Prudential Securities, except he was at Drexel. After Drexel imploded, he got a job as the head of fixed income* investment for Daiwa Asset Management, sister company to the securities firm I worked for. Askin worked alongside

*Fixed Income – the generic name for all bonds. In spite of the name, adjustable rate and floating rate debt is also the territory of the Fixed Income Department.

Harry Markowitz, who had won the Nobel Prize in economics a year earlier for his work on portfolio theory.

At the time, Daiwa Securities was a brilliant marketing organization, capable of selling almost any investment product in Japan through a corps of Japanese housewives who worked part-time, kind of like our Avon Ladies or Mary Kay Consultants.

Askin and Markowitz had put together funds that appealed to the enormous retail investment market in Japan, a market that seemed insatiable until the Japanese real estate "bubble" began to unwind in the early 1990's.

By 1993, Askin had struck out on his own to set up a market neutral CMO fund that invested in various bonds in CMO structures, roughly balancing out the bonds in the portfolio with bullish characteristics and bearish characteristics. Then he used leverage to target a double-digit return for his institutional investors.

He soon became the favorite of a number of bond salesmen around the Street, because he was willing to buy the bonds that were difficult to analyze. Those were the ones that were tough to sell and which were called "toxic waste" by the people who didn't understand them.

Unfortunately for Askin, the Fed reversed their easy money policy and began raising rates in February of 1994. With rates going up, homeowners were no longer eager to refinance. Market participants felt that this was the beginning of a trend. Prepayments would slow down and keep slowing down, so the bullish Principal Only (PO) bonds lost value very quickly. At the same time, prepayments had been very fast for the prior two years, which drove down the price of the bearish Interest Only (IO) bonds.

In short, it was the worst of both worlds, since each kind of bond got priced on its own, and there was no rule saying that the bonds needed to be priced consistently with each other.

Askin had borrowed using "repo*", a financing method in which the lender holds the bonds, lends lots of money against the bonds, and has the privilege of repricing them nightly. With Askin's bonds plummeting in value, he suddenly faced a huge margin call he couldn't meet.

Bear Stearns was his biggest repo lender but all the vultures on the Street swooped in and seized the bonds, assigning whatever price they wanted for them. Askin's fund had been worth $600 million a month earlier. Now it was worth nothing.

* Repo – Sale and Repurchase Agreement. The holder of the bond sells the bond to the Dealer and simultaneously agrees to buy it back later at a higher price, with the price increase being the interest charged for the financing. The Dealer only advances a portion (often 90% to as much as 97%) of the value of the bond. Every day the Dealer can determine the value of the bond, and make margin calls for cash if the value of the bond has dropped.

The Street made a killing on the IO bonds, and in at least one case, sold PO bonds the same day so cheaply that other customers were willing to buy them with a big markup just hours later, even though, rationally, they should have gone down in price.

So there we were on Thursday March 31st, our jobs eliminated and our business killed the same day. Nobody wanted to touch a CMO after the Askin affair. It took more than a year for the CMO market to recover from that single day.

Another day that was memorable for securitized bond traders and hardly noticed outside their world was Columbus Day, 1998. On Wall Street, Columbus Day is unusual because the stock market is open but the bond market is closed.

On Columbus Day, 1998, everyone in the mortgage market was at their desks. The event that drew all of us into the office was the sale from Mike Vranos' Ellington Management fund. It was said to be half of a $4 billion portfolio. Vranos was forced to sell but he didn't want to be another Askin, so he held a fire sale of his own, giving customers an opportunity to buy bonds from him directly.

The lists came out, and there were some really great bonds. The name of the game was how to buy bonds with available cash, knowing that the LTCM aftershocks from three weeks earlier could make it almost impossible to get financing.

* CMBS - Commercial Mortgage Backed Securities. Pools of loans secured by income properties provide the cash flows to pay these bonds.

A number of investor groups stepped in and bought AAA rated CMBS* at yield spreads 200 basis points (2%) over LIBOR*.

That was five to ten times the spread those bonds paid a month earlier. For bond investors, it was home run territory.

Less secure bonds also traded at extraordinarily low prices and high yields. In fact, as the next ten years played out with a consistently strong commercial real estate market, anyone who bought even junk-rated CMBS that day or at any time during the remainder of that year didn't withstand a penny of losses on their purchases.

* LIBOR – London Interbank Offering Rate. Set each business morning at 11 A.M., London time, it sets the interest rates at which various top-ranked banks lend to each other for terms of one day to thirty years.

By the end of that Columbus Day in 1998, $2 billion in bonds had traded hands, with the trades waiting for the banks to open the following day for execution. Vranos and his Ellington Management team survived to fight again another day and the Wall Street dealers didn't get to feast on that portfolio all by themselves.

Having been a major player on the Street himself, Mike had known full well what the Street would do if customers didn't get to compete for the bonds. It was a bold and brilliant move to spread the opportunity beyond the dealer network.

Everybody who was in the business at the time remembers the Columbus Day when Mike Vranos beat Wall Street at its own game, but the rest of the world surely didn't notice.

The general market knew about the LTCM near-meltdown in 1998 and the extraordinary efforts of the New York Federal Reserve to get fourteen of the leading Wall Street banks and securities firms to invest more capital in that over-leveraged hedge fund to keep it from failing.

The market was less aware of the collapse of the securitizers. The late 1990's were not good for these companies, a few of which collapsed even before the LTCM episode. In 1997, Jayhawk Acceptance, a subprime auto lender and securitizer collapsed. It was followed in 1998 by the largest subprime auto lender/securitizer, Mercury Finance.

The same tightening of credit conditions that put LTCM in dire straights in August and September of 1998 spelled doom for FirstPlus Financial, which was happy to lend homeowners 125% of the value of their houses, and whose TV commercials featured Hall of Fame quarterback Dan Marino making the pitch.

Subprime mortgage lenders Cityscape Financial and ContiFinancial also failed as part of the fallout, as did several banks that had been buying subprime mortgages and securitizing them. The failures of the First National Bank of Keystone, WV and Pacific Trust and Loan of Woodland Hills, CA in 1999 and Superior Bank, FSB of Chicago the following year were all tied to aggressive subprime lending and inappropriate valuation of the retained residual classes from securitizations.

To round out the representative list, we have to include Criimi Mae, the largest holder of junior tranches of commercial mortgage securitizations. Criimi almost suffered the same fate as David Askin – asset seizure and liquidation. As a public company, it was able to seek bankruptcy protection when Wall Street hit it with huge margin calls in October of 1998, the same time that Ellington Management Group was fighting for its life.

Though it survived, Criimi Mae was forced into a series of distressed asset sales over the next year, and emerged from bankruptcy protection a few years later with a total market capitalization that was down 99% from its pre-LTCM level.

Fast forward ten years into the 21st century. As the subprime meltdown became the credit crisis and then the Financial Crisis, it seemed like every every month brought another of those signature events that people could point to as "The Day."

Certainly, this time the party went on longer and was a lot wilder than all the others put together. Now the hangover is worse, as well.

CHAPTER THREE

The Best Thing the Government Ever Did for Us

A hundred years ago, banks lent only 50% to 60% of a home's value for only three to five years, and then required the entire balance to be repaid or refinanced. Right through the 1920's and into the 30's, that's how mortgage lending worked in America. As a result, most people rented if they weren't fortunate enough to inherit their homes.

The issue came to a head in the 1930's, when borrowers couldn't afford to pay off their mortgages when they came due. Houses had declined in value as deflation took hold of the economy, and banks weren't willing to lend the same amount to the borrowers as a refinancing.

In the depths of the Depression, as banks were failing, the Dust Bowl grew by thousands of acres each week, and millions of Americans became homeless refugees in their own country, the National Housing Act of 1934 created the Federal Housing Administration (FHA). That agency of the U.S. Government changed U.S. housing finance permanently, and most would agree, for the better.

The biggest change was that Americans could now borrow money from banks to finance their primary residence at a fixed rate with fixed mortgage payments over 25 years, owning the house free and clear after the term of the loan.

Under the FHA program, homebuyers could borrow up to 90% of the value of the house, and banks had the safety of a government guarantee if borrowers defaulted.

In exchange for this guarantee, the government took a small fee. In modern times, this system of FHA guarantees and its Post WW II "sister," the VA loan guaranteed by the Veteran's Administration, have given millions of young families the means to buy their first home with as little as 3% of the house price as a down payment.

Throughout the history of these programs, they have turned a profit, in some years totaling in the billions of dollars. While there are years in which the FHA program showed a deficit (2007, for example), the retained operating surpluses still add up (over $20.5 billion at the end of fiscal 2007).

The government's role in supporting its citizens' home ownership aspirations expanded in February of 1938 with the establishment of the Federal National Mortgage Association (Fannie Mae or FNMA).

Fannie Mae invested in the FHA-guaranteed mortgage loans, and issued bonds and notes in the credit markets to fund those purchases. Since the interest rate at which the bonds and notes were issued was lower than the mortgage rates, Fannie Mae also turned a profit while providing capital for home ownership.

This came just in time, since 1937 was the year in which private banks failed in larger numbers than at any other time in our history.

In 1954, Fannie Mae's debt was no longer directly guaranteed by the U.S. Government and the path was set for the U.S. Government to gradually sell out its ownership in Fannie Mae to private holders.

That handover was completed in 1968, when Fannie Mae became a fully privatized entity and its housing assistance function with a Government guarantee was split off into the newly-created Government National Mortgage Association, also known as Ginnie Mae, or GNMA.*

* GNMA – Government National Mortgage Association. A government agency that issues and guarantees mortgage securities based on pools of underlying mortgages insured by the FHA (Federal Housing Administration) or the VA (Veteran's Administration). GNMA mortgage securities are the only mortgage securities that enjoy the explicit credit guarantee of the U.S. Government.

At that time, Fannie Mae was given the power to issue and guarantee mortgage pass-throughs*, which would bundle together a pool of mortgages and give institutional investors the option of purchasing them with the Fannie Mae Guarantee.

Modern mortgage-backed securities (MBS) were born.

In 1970, Ginnie Mae began to issue guaranteed MBS backed by FHA/VA loans. Fannie Mae and Freddie Mac (the Federal Home Loan Mortgage Corp.) began to issue and guarantee MBS backed by conventional mortgage loans, which were not insured by the FHA or the VA.

Like the predecessor program of FHA guarantees, the GNMA program

* Mortgage Pass-Through – A security that takes the monthly principal and interest payments from a pool of mortgage loans and pays them out each month to the investor. For guaranteed mortgage pass-throughs, the guarantor pays the monthly payments when they are due even if the borrower is late, and pays off the principal balance if the borrower defaults.

of fully government-guaranteed MBS has been a real moneymaker for taxpayers. In 2007, Ginnie Mae had only seventy full time employees, and it generated net revenues of more than $700 million, a level of profit surpassed every year from 2002 through 2007.

When Fannie Mae and Freddie Mac became privately held mortgage pass-through issuers, there were concerns that they might be at risk of losing their financial strength. Congress gave each of them credit lines with the Treasury, and supervisory authorities were created to ensure that the newly private companies behaved responsibly.

The Department of Housing and Urban Development (HUD) maintained control over Fannie and Freddie by requiring them to follow HUD-approved limitations on the characteristics of the mortgage loans they would purchase or "pool" into MBS.

Other measures over the years included installation of a federally appointed overseer known as OFHEO, the Office of Federal Housing Enterprise Oversight. OFHEO was the regulator for Fannie Mae and Freddie Mac until the financial crisis in 2008. Then, it was merged with the Federal Home Loan Bank Board, itself a creature of the Reagan-era crisis in the Savings and Loan industry.

The success of the MBS pass-through programs under government sponsorship led banks to issue their own MBS. The Bank of America began to use the technique in 1976, issuing the first of the modern-day "private label" mortgage-backed securities.

In order to make up for the lack of a direct or indirect government backing, the Bank of America MBS bonds were created with two classes: the senior class, representing 95% of the principal, and a subordinated class, which started out as 5% of the deal and would take the first principal losses from the entire pool.

Ginnie Mae, Fannie Mae and Freddie Mac provided credit enhancement to their MBS by acting as insurance providers. All three of these "Agencies," as they are called, collected guarantee fees to pay for this insurance, and insured every dollar of the mortgage balance in each MBS pool. The Bank of America senior-subordinated* structure substituted the subordinated, or junior, class in place of the guarantee to provide credit protection for the top-rated AAA senior class.

*Senior-Subordinated –
The technique of creating two or more levels of credit safety in a securitization. The senior bonds only suffer credit losses if the subordinated bonds have absorbed enough losses to be completely written off.*

If a mortgage loan goes into default in a guaranteed MBS pool, the Agency pays the MBS holders for every dollar of principal still owed by that mortgage, and then handles the foreclosure and selling of the house. If a loss occurs upon liquidation, that loss is taken in as part of the Agency's overall profit and loss.

"Private Label" or "Whole Loan" MBS - MBS or CMOs that have mortgage loans rather than Agency guaranteed mortgage pass-throughs as their collateral.

For the "private label" MBS* issued as senior/subordinated securities, a loan that goes into default will also be foreclosed and the house will be sold, usually at a loss. Before the credit crisis crushed the value of houses, a typical loss might have been 30% of the balance of the mortgage. The 70% of the balance of the mortgage recovered from selling the house would be paid to the senior bond and the other 30% of the balance (the loss) would be allocated to the junior bond. The junior bond would then have its principal balance reduced without any cash payment, in what is referred to as a "write-off" or "write-down."

Since defaults on these types of traditional mortgage loans with bank customers typically ran less than 1% to 2% over the life of a pool of loans, the 5% subordination* of these early, privately issued MBS gave more than enough coverage to get top ratings (AAA) on the 95% senior bond. In a typical case, only 1% of the loans went into foreclosure over the life of the pool, and the losses assigned to the junior class amounted to three-tenths of one percent, or 30 basis points.

Over the thirty-year history of these privately issued senior mortgage bonds through 2006, there was never a credit loss, or even a late payment to the MBS holders. No doubt investors in the AAA rated Bethlehem Steel bonds that were issued in the 1970s wish they had a similar experience.

Subordination – Credit protection for securitized bonds created by allocating loan default losses to the lowest rated bond in the "credit stack" and allocating recoveries from the sale of the underlying loan to pay additional principal to the highest rated bond in the stack.

The track record of rated mortgage-backed securities was better than any other type of bond. And it's all the more impressive when you consider that private label prime mortgage pass-throughs were a larger asset class than almost any other investment class, with thousands of issues totaling trillions of dollars.

The MBS market of the 1970's was virtually all pass-through securities*, and remained a narrow specialty both for the Wall Street dealers who created and sold them, and the investors who bought them for the additional yield they could provide.

Pass-Through Securities – The simplest form of securitization, in which a pool of financial assets is created and each investor gets a pro-rata share of the principal and interest payments on each payment date.

These investors liked the credit strength and extra yield of these MBS, but they didn't necessarily like the uneven monthly payments of mixed principal and interest that went on over a thirty year period. These bonds were much more unpredictable in their cash flow than the simple corporate or Treasury Bond that pays interest every six months and then paid all of the principal balance in a lump sum at the end.

Some investors that would have liked to invest in MBS couldn't because the thirty-year maturity was longer than the time frame in which were allowed to invest, or because the variance in the average length of time to repayment was difficult to predict. For example, a bank that issues Certificates of Deposit needs its principal back on its investments in time to pay its CDs at maturity. A pension fund may have to pay its pensioners beginning in twenty years, so its investment shouldn't mature too early.

This variance in time to repayment, or "maturity risk" prevented a large segment of the potential investor universe from participating in the first fifteen years of the modern mortgage securities market.

Starting in 1983, the maturity risk in MBS was redistributed with the development of multiple classes of bonds called Collateralized Mortgage Obligations (CMOs). By combining hundreds of separate MBS pools comprised of thousands of mortgages and by dividing the resulting cash flows into sequential maturity tranches, investors that had traditionally avoided mortgage securities investments were able and willing to participate in this developing market.

Car loans and credit cards followed residential mortgages into the securitized pass-through bond market. The 1980's also marked the spread of securitization around the world, beginning in most countries with residential mortgages as collateral.

In the 1990's, when the Resolution Trust Company took over the assets of more than a thousand failed Savings and Loans, it took over huge numbers of mortgages on commercial properties that were housed in those portfolios. Commercial mortgages didn't have nearly the same uniformity as residential home mortgages, but they still had value, and the RTC needed to unlock that value as quickly as possible.

To see if the same securitization technique that had been used for residential mortgages would work for commercial mortgages, tests were devised by the Rating Agencies to analyze the ability of the underlying properties to pay their mortgages. The properties were also studied to see what they could be sold for if the mortgages had to be foreclosed.

The results were added up, and subordination levels were set that provided credit protection for the most senior bonds sufficient to withstand the expected loss from a deep and protracted depression. To get the AAA rating, for example, pools of RTC-owned commercial property mortgages often had subordination levels of approximately 30%.

With this kick start, the Commercial Mortgage Backed Securities (CMBS) market began. Soon, commercial mortgage loan terms and documentation were standardized so that new commercial mortgages would "fit" into CMBS deals.

Fannie Mae and Freddie Mac were especially influential in this trend, because they had mandates to use a percentage of their capacity to support affordable housing. By creating documentation and credit standards for apartment building loans and guaranteeing the safest part of senior-subordinated pass-throughs for bundles of these loans, Fannie and Freddie opened up the market for apartment building securitizations.

"Conduits*" were created for the express purpose of making loans to sell into securitized deals. Wall Street began to sponsor conduits to provide financing to various kinds of property owners. Apartment building owners would work with one CMBS conduit, nursing home owners another, industrial property owners another, and office building owners yet another. A few conduits even offered loans on all types of commercial properties, and sold the resulting CMBS bonds to investors who felt it was an advantage to have the diversification of multiple property types.

* Conduit – A legal vehicle formed to buy financial assets for the purpose of selling or financing them shortly thereafter. Used as "warehouses" for loans before securitization or as off-balance-sheet financing vehicles, conduits are sponsored by banks, lenders, or Wall Street dealers.

Through the 1990's, more and more types of debt were bundled and turned into securities: corporate bonds (CBOs), bank loans (CLOs), infrastructure project loans, small business loans, fast food restaurant mortgages, student loans and boat loans.

Other sources of cash flow that weren't even debt were also being securitized, like tolls from bridges, medical insurance claims and box office receipts from movies. Financial assets that could be securitized seemed limited only by Wall Street's imagination, which is to say, hardly limited at all.

By the end of the 1990's, equipment leases, restaurant franchise fees, mutual fund fees, legal settlements, taxi medallion loan payments, music royalties, participations in multiple hedge funds, portfolios of preferred stocks and even whole businesses like brewery-owned pubs in the UK all became fair game for securitization.

When friends in the investment business criticized the securitization movement as some kind of "smoke and mirrors" scam, I used to point out to them that corporate bonds and stocks and municipal bonds were securitizations of company cash flows or tax receipts. In a way, those traditional investments were just inefficient securitizations that didn't have bankruptcy-remote trusts to protect the investor or the rigor of detailed cash-flow modeling and stress testing of the assets.

CHAPTER FOUR

The Roots of the Subprime Meltdown

Just as the seeds of future collapses are planted in the excesses of the growth period that precedes them, so the seeds of the next growth phase are planted in the crisis that precedes it.

The subprime crisis had a series of important problems preceding it. The LTCM collapse, the Y2K panic, the dot-com bubble bursting and the response to the 9/11 attacks all created an environment that convinced the Fed to lower short term rates to 1% and leave them there for nearly three years. That more than revived the mortgage market; it sent the mortgage market flying.

Concurrently, on every level from the Federal government down to the single-income household, what it meant to be able to "afford" something changed.

The children of the Great Depression were uncomfortable with debt and believed that "affordable" meant you would be able to pay off the debt, in full, even if times got tough. The goal of having a mortgage was to have it paid off and own your home outright.

The Boomers had learned the lessons of inflation in the 70's and 80's, and came to believe that "affordable" meant being able to cover the payments. In a curious reversal of logic, the fact that mortgage interest became the largest tax deduction available to the average American, made it financially irresponsible to have a home without owing money on it.

A change in the Federal income tax rules in the late 1990's also initiated a tax-free $250,000 capital gain exemption on first or second homes ($500,000 for a couple), and allowed that exemption to be taken every two years, as many times as taxpayers wanted. That freed homeowners to take profits on existing homes at a faster rate than ever before.

Homeowners who had large embedded gains in their homes could trade up if they could get financing on their next homes. Given their large down payments (30% or more), the "Option ARM*" was offered to everyone with a good credit record, giving borrowers the dubious privilege of letting their loan balances increase by paying less than the stated interest rate (negative amortization).

* Option ARM (or Pay-Option ARM) - Adjustable Rate Mortgage that gives borrowers several payment plans: 1) Paying variable interest only for five or more years or 2) Paying principal and interest each month to pay off the loan over 30 years or 3) Paying a minimal interest rate and adding unpaid principal to the loan balance.

Lenders felt safe making these loans, because they knew it would take nearly five years of minimum payments before the loans grew to 80% of the value of the houses. The slightly higher stated interest rate also allowed lenders to make larger profits.

High-end homebuilders, prime mortgage lenders and affluent homeowners reveled in the new growth regime. In fact, with rates so low, some banks could even offer "teaser" rates averaging 4.5%, since CD's and bank deposits were only costing about 1% to 1.5% in the artificially low rate environment the Fed had engineered.

While they collected 4% teaser rate interest on their Option ARM loans and paid out around 1% on their deposits, the banks were comfortably cash flow positive. Even better, the stated interest rate was 6% or higher on these loans and lenders reported earnings based on that higher rate. Most of the borrowers took the option of making the minimum payment and allowing the balance of their loans to rise, or negatively amortize.

The only missing piece for a true mania was a flood of new buyers. They soon came in the form of first-time buyers for houses that were being sold by the trade-up buyers, and in the form of speculators who were looking to buy houses and quickly sell ("flip") them to other new buyers.

Along with the general rush on home buying, subprime mortgage teaser rates dropped to an average of 7.5% for an initial two-year period, making home buying affordable to a segment of the borrowing public that wasn't able to own a home when rates were higher.

These subprime loans were very attractive to lenders. Subprime borrowers pay 3% to 4% more than prime borrowers and subprime loss rates had averaged just 1% to 2% per year during the prior fifty years. The raw profits of 2% to 4% per year from this kind of lending were much better than the 0.5% to 1% per year in profit that the conventional, prime mortgage lending business provided.

Unwarranted confidence led lenders to take new risks when making loans to subprime borrowers:

1) "Liar loans," or mortgages without income verification. These were a small but growing minority of subprime loans, peaking out at close to 30% of all subprime mortgage loans in 2007.

2) No down payment loans. These were occasionally loans for 95% or 100% of the home purchase price, but were more frequently loans for 80% of the purchase with a second "piggyback" loan* at a higher rate for another 15% to 20% of the purchase price. Investors in the 80% LTV* (Loan-to-Value) first mortgages sometimes weren't informed that the piggyback second mortgage existed, which increased their risk.

Piggyback Loan – A second mortgage simultaneously originated with the same borrower on the same house for a borrower who did not have the 20% down payment.

LTV – Loan-to-Value. The amount of a loan expressed as a fraction of the value of the asset that secures the loan. For most US home mortgages, the standard was 80% LTV or lower until the housing bull market of 2001 through 2007.

3) Investor loans, sometimes classified as loans for "second homes." These also grew from less than 5% of the subprime universe to more than 10% for a few of the issuers of subprime mortgage debt.

4) Layering two or more of these risky lending practices into a single loan.

There are limited circumstances in which it makes sense to make a loan to a borrower who can't provide normal income verification. These loans have normally been made to people who run their own businesses or live off their investments.

These "no doc" loans were historically strong credit performers, especially when borrowers made meaningful down payments. The mitigating factor for these "non-conforming" loans without income verification was the fact that financing was limited to 70% to 75% of the value of the properties by most lenders. At least that's the way it was until the mania got into full swing.

Bank examiners never liked this kind of loan, and made it clear in their capital requirements and examinations that they preferred the safety and uniformity of mortgage securities or "prime" mortgage loans with full income documentation. The segment of the population that was a good credit risk but that desired non-conforming loans was served by non-bank lenders.

Unfortunately, once mortgage lenders outside the traditional banking system had seized on "no doc" loans as a popular option with borrowers, they cranked up the volume far past the limited pool of borrowers who were good risks for this type of loan.

These "no doc" loans drew out thousands upon thousands of liars, which naturally led them to become known as "liar loans." The big payoff? For virtually "nothing down," and a simple lie, borrowers were buying winning sweepstakes tickets. All they had to do was sell their homes for a nice profit a year or two later. At the rate that home prices were appreciating, it looked like that was a safe bet.

At a late 2007 conference, I met the owner of a company that does very thorough checks on borrowers using the information in mortgage loan files. He found that one large selection of files they reviewed included borrowers who had used Social Security numbers that were not their own, and this comprised more than 5% of the borrowers. Those borrowers took the concept of "liar loans" to a whole new level.

Some borrowers turned their 100% financing into a genuine economic benefit regardless of the fact that they ended up losing the homes to foreclosure and ruining their credit scores. They simply took advantage of the fact that it takes considerably longer to foreclose on a house than it does to evict a tenant.

In 2007, a number of lenders experienced a huge increase in the number of EPDs, or Early Payment Defaults*. These were mortgage loans that stopped paying in the first, second or third month. While it varies by state, in most states it takes a year or so to complete a foreclosure. Fraudulent mortgage borrowers could pay the equivalent

* EPD, or Early Payment Default – a loan that defaults soon after it was originated. Occasionally legitimate, as when the primary breadwinner dies after the closing, but more frequently a loan where the borrower never intended to pay.

of one or two months' rent in mortgage payments (or none at all) for a house they might be able to live in for a year or longer. It sure beat not paying the rent, and being evicted by the landlord a few months later.

Even for subprime borrowers who wanted to make their payments but weren't sure they'd be able to, there wasn't that much at stake. These borrowers already had lousy credit scores, so they weren't losing much if they chose to default on their mortgages and live in their houses for free.

For prime borrowers who spent years building a good credit record, the risk of lowered credit scores acted as a real deterrent to this kind of behavior, even if the mortgage loan balance might be equal to or greater than the value of the home in a forced sale.

The environment of mortgage lending in this era permitted a special class of unscrupulous borrower to borrow money from their lenders, and pay nothing in return. It may have been the fault of the borrowers themselves, the real estate agents, the home builders' salespeople, the appraisers, the mortgage brokers, rogue (or stupid) loan officers at the lenders, or a combination of the above.

The FBI pursued 1204 mortgage fraud cases in fiscal 2007, resulting in 321 indictments and court orders for $595.9 million in restitution.

* Mortgage Underwriting - The process a lender goes through before approving a loan to a borrower, which may include employment verification, credit checks, appraisal, clearing the title, searching for liens and lawsuits, and review of tax returns.

Typically, rings of fraudsters operated by selling the same houses over and over again, at ever-higher prices, increasing the value of many houses in the neighborhood simultaneously, so it was very difficult for loan reviewers and mortgage underwriters* to detect a problem when looking at individual loan files. The final act in the scam was to take out mortgages on a number of the inflated properties, and then disappear.

It didn't help that politicians, activists and reporters decided to unilaterally champion the cause of innocent homeowners losing their homes and assign all the blame to other parties. Unscrupulous borrowers got a free pass to allege they were tricked into lying about their income, claiming the terms of their loans were never disclosed and they were victims of predatory lending.

Were there predatory lenders? Of course. A few. Was it commonplace? The answer is no.

The fact is that most larger mortgage lenders have compliance rules and training programs designed to prevent their employees from making predatory loans. In the late 90s, too many lenders took large losses due to predatory lending lawsuits to behave any differently.

Let's not overlook the fact that loan application documents with "stated income" were sworn and notarized legal contracts. It does seem extreme that some politicians believe that several million borrowers were tricked into committing perjury, or somehow didn't understand that the ridiculously high number they furnished as income was a legal assertion that they truly earned that much money.

There can be bad apples in every basket. But when organized groups set out to defraud by creating loan files that meet a lender's criteria, complete with verifiable appraisals and comparable property sales, it is a stretch to blame the lender. Certainly some lenders were easier to fool than others, but this kind of fraud could only be prevented by eliminating the kind of financial mania and irresponsible activity that was engulfing the real estate and mortgage business.

CHAPTER FIVE

The Blame Game

As problems with subprime mortgages began to appear, attention zeroed in on mortgage brokers, banks, lenders, appraisers and mortgage borrowers. Certainly, they all deserve to take their share of the blame, if only for being overly optimistic.

But there were bigger players at work, those who created the "macro" environment individuals and smaller companies could take advantage of. They created the systemic demand that may have had more to do with the size of the problem than all the smaller participants put together.

In this macro category we can put the Federal Reserve, the investment banks, CDO* managers and other securitizers, portfolio managers, Rating Agencies, hedge funds, the Financial Accounting Standards Board (FASB) and the media. The government, the government-sponsored housing Agencies (Ginnie Mae, Fannie Mae and Freddie Mac) and state mortgage lending regulators also get to take partial credit for the macro conditions.

CDO – Collateralized Debt Obligation. A securitized bond deal that uses bonds or loans as collateral for a new multi-class bond deal.

Together, these macro players set the policies and took the actions that created an environment where the originate-to-securitize business model was terrifically profitable. Unfortunately, the macro players also provided the accelerant that inflated the housing "bubble."

The macro players set up the largely unregulated mortgage lending business that steered market share for subprime and non-conforming lending away from the banks, making it easy for the micro players so inclined to take advantage of lax oversight.

The Fed lowered rates to 1% and kept them there, allowing lenders to extend low rates to their borrowers, who could "lock in" those low rates for two or three years. Some lenders, especially the big securitization machines, offered loans with all the "innovations" – easy documentation standards, very low down payments and low initial rates with prepayment penalties that made those loans profitable even if they were quickly paid off.

When mortgage originator/securitizers started making and buying loans with very small down payments and no income verification, they were essentially betting that the value of the houses would rise so fast that the mortgages would still be paid even if the borrowers really couldn't afford to pay them. A house and its expected appreciation became a substitute for the true equity of a traditional down payment.

Only steady house price inflation could make such loans safe. To be fair, until 2007, this wasn't such a stretch, as there had never been a year since the Great Depression in which house prices in the U.S. had not gone up by at least a little bit.

With house price appreciation in the double digits, more and more lenders found they could be even more profitable if they sold their loans into securitizations. In this environment, making 20% "second mortgages," often as part of a home loan equal to or close to 100% of the home's value, didn't feel so risky.

Subprime lending was booming. By 2006, there were banks, Wall Street dealers, specialized finance companies, hedge funds, and even well-known companies like General Electric, General Motors and H & R Block all competing for pieces of the subprime mortgage pie.

Companies securitizing subprime mortgage loans were making equity returns of 25% to 40%, even after paying overhead. Wall Street firms were making more than 60% return on their subprime mortgage business before paying overhead and bonuses. Even if losses went back up to the 4% to 6% levels that accompanied the prior two recessions, these bulk mortgage purchasers would still enjoy a handsome profit from their securitizations.

In a unique case of unregulated madness, Wall Street firms provided credit to CDO asset managers to buy the lower credit portions of mortgage securitizations and provided credit to hedge funds to buy the unrated portions.

While Wall Street had to follow certain regulations, the entities it funded to buy its products did not. These entities ended up having an enormous impact on the events that unfolded, since they were instrumental in the expansion of securitization beyond sensible or reasonable bounds, with disastrous effects for the market as a whole.

It was the CDO managers who really drove demand (and prices) up for subprime mortgage bonds in 2005, 2006 and the first half of 2007. They were the largest buyers of subprime "mezzanine" bonds (the bonds rated below AAA and above junk) from existing securitizations

In putting together CDO deals, CDO managers typically purchased fifty percent subprime bonds, and built the rest of their deals from a mix of commercial real estate bonds, auto loan bonds, student loan bonds, and even CDO's from other managers.

The raw ingredients for a successful CDO recipe often came directly from the Wall Street dealers, who recommended and then sold the bonds to the CDO managers. The CDO managers then combined those bonds to create new bonds rated from AAA down through AA, A, BBB, and unrated.

What did they do with these re-securitizations? Why, they sold them to the Wall Street dealers who had supplied the raw materials to make them in the first place! Wall Street, in turn, sold the CDOs to investors, and sometimes to Structured Investment Vehicles (SIVs)*.

The SIVs which weren't under the direction of banks or other lenders were frequently created and controlled by the very same Wall Street dealers.

If the CDO managers didn't have the capacity to finance the bonds they used

SIV – Structured Investment Vehicle. A special purpose entity that buys very highly rated (AAA or AA) structured securities and issues short-term debt called Asset Backed Commercial Paper (ABCP) to fund 95% or more of the purchases. Additional debt with ratings of BBB supplies more of the funding, with only 1% to 2% of the investment put in as equity by the sponsoring bank or lender.

as raw materials while they held them, they were, in essence, captive entities of Wall Street. They got their raw materials from a Wall Street dealer who also supplied their financing, and they were obligated to have that same Wall Street dealer sell the bonds they would ultimately create.

The Wall Street dealers themselves were doing about a deal a week, and had access to the Rating Agency models, which would determine the credit rating of the tranches that came out of the deals.

The Rating Agencies had a forty-year track record of rating first-level securitizations with excellent results. It was all based on evaluating risk and the precept that the credit performance for one borrower in the deal should not be dependent on how other borrowers perform. In a successful securitization, bond builders attempt to isolate risk, so the poor performance of some borrowers in the collateral pool will have limited correlation to the performance of the other borrowers.

Unfortunately, the Rating Agencies had no track record to speak of when it came to evaluating re-securitizations that were structured as CDOs. When rating the tranches of these re-securitizations, the Rating Agencies felt they could model the probability of loss for a pool of CDO mortgage bonds the same way they could with any other pool of credits. They assumed that one BBB rated subprime mortgage bond would have distinctly different credit losses than other BBB rated subprime mortgage bonds.

They were wrong, of course. They had overlooked an important fact: If history showed that all BBB rated subprime bonds had behaved uniformly well in the past, it must be equally probable that they could all behave uniformly poorly in the future. Instead, the Rating Agencies chose to focus on the differences between lenders in quality control, servicing diligence, and regional marketing, and based their analysis on those factors.

With separate households paying their mortgages or companies paying their bank loans, this analytic approach works. But with BBB bonds from mostly similar pools of mortgage loans, the fact that each pool has thousands of borrowers actually makes the bonds more alike than different.

CDO managers acquired bonds from structured finance deals that had already stratified the probabilities of default among relatively uniform pools of loans. CDOs built from these bonds were essentially super-levered concentrations of credit performance.

In other words, all BBB bonds behave more or less like other BBB bonds. Ironically, this is what the ratings, which establish whether a bond is rated AAA or BBB, are based on. If you buy a BBB corporate bond, it is supposed to be just as likely to default as any other BBB corporate bond.

When times were good, all the subprime bonds performed better than expected. In fact, from 1984 through 2004, subprime mortgage bonds which were rated BBB performed about as well as municipal or corporate bonds rated AAA.

The new CDO managers were able to set themselves up in small offices and, within a short time, have billions of dollars in assets under management while they let the Wall Street dealers supply the raw materials, do the structuring and marketing, provide the financing for the assets during the warehousing period, and sell the CDO re-securitizations.

Even a senior management fee of as little as 10 basis points equates to $1 million per year on a $1 billion CDO. Once you get half a dozen deals under management, a "two guys and a Bloomberg" operation could make really nice money.

The best payoff was for the Wall Street firms, though. They quoted fees of $5 million for those $1 billion CDO deals, and they also made fees off the first tier deals that created the BBB bonds the CDO managers were buying. All the fees owed to Wall Street were paid up front, at the closing table for the deals. So that tiny CDO manager would have paid their friendly Wall Street dealer $30 to $40 million in fees by the time they had a half dozen deals.

Sometimes, CDO managers also held the first loss equity tranche of their deals, so they had capital at risk in a position that would take losses before all the other CDO investors. But even this investment paid healthy returns of 15% to 20% when all the bonds were paying, which almost all rated mortgage bonds did for at least a few years, even if they eventually take credit losses.

For the CDO managers, the biggest perceived business risk was not the credit risk. They had good reason to minimize that risk in their minds, because they were typically buying bonds rated BBB or higher. There had never been meaningful losses in those bonds in their lifetimes.

The real risk they saw was that the profit (the "spread") they hoped to capture would shrink before they could buy all the bonds they needed to make their new bonds. If profit dissipated (spreads "tightened"), the deal might not work any more. The anticipated returns to the first loss bond or even to the rated bonds in the CDO structure might disappear.

For this reason, CDO managers wanted to jump into a fully invested position as quickly as possible. Whenever they could get a few extra basis points by buying one BBB bond instead of another, it didn't take long to make the decision. Bonds that traditional investors would have bought only after lengthy due diligence were flying off the shelves.

Long-term investors that had been in the market for years suddenly found themselves outbid by CDO managers, on every deal, often within minutes of the deal being announced. The frantic rush to buy left no time for proper analysis of the bonds before a commitment had to be made.

The CDO managers made the business of analyzing and purchasing bonds more like a TV quiz show than a business transaction. Speed at putting in the buy order was the thing that separated the winners from the losers. Competition to get all the bonds quickly and grab a little extra spread eliminated any meaningful relationship between price and quality for bonds in the marketplace.

It was all made worse by the fact that some Wall Street houses had bought and securitized pools of subprime mortgages containing at least 20% to 30% of the riskiest subprime loans.

At the same time, mortgage brokers had learned how to submit a "clean" looking file to lenders, and borrowers were more than happy to do whatever was necessary to qualify for a loan. Generous appraisals became the rule of the day for appraisers who relied on referrals and knew the numbers needed to make the mortgage brokers and real estate agents happy.

At real estate closings, the mortgage brokers and real estate agents walked away with thousands of dollars. The mortgage bank walked away with several hundred dollars of profit on each loan when they sold them to securitizers, selling the loans in blocks of several hundred at a time. The securitizers also made several hundred dollars on each loan by turning the mortgages into bonds. And many of the mortgage bonds went on to be re-securitized into new bonds by the CDO managers.

Structured finance CDO issuance grew from a few billion a year in 2002 to over $200 billion in 2006. Several Wall Street shops were issuing or underwriting $40 to $80 billion a year of subprime mortgage bonds, and then selling pieces of the deals to fund managers to whom they offered liberal credit.

Wall Street had created its own customers.

In essence, a huge interconnected system existed to create mortgages, create mortgage bonds, and then to create new bonds from bonds that had just been made, all in very big hurry, with almost every entity along the line unloading the risks as they took home the profits.

A vast financial empire was being constructed on a very shaky foundation.

Shakiest of all was the fact that the customers for the highest-risk parts of the deals were beyond the reach of regulators, as nearly every CDO and hedge fund legally resides in a tax haven like the Cayman Islands, even though almost all the people making the investment decisions live and work inside a fifty-mile radius of Wall Street.

In 2007, the breaking of the bubble showed up initially in second mortgages. Securitizers like the Household Finance division of HSBC Bank had been ready buyers of "piggyback" loans. Early in 2007, HSBC was the first major bank to acknowledge large expected credit losses from subprime loans. It announced that it was reserving $9 billion for future losses in its portfolio of second mortgages.

Soon after, the market suffered repeated additional shocks. Subprime lender New Century admitted that it had overstated earnings for several years. H&R Block said their Option One division was taking a $100 million dollar loss on loans that defaulted in the first three months. While H&R Block's subsidiary experienced the worst of these early payment defaults (EPDs), other lenders were also seeing an uptick in early defaults.

At the same time, homeowners who had borrowed nearly the entire purchase price of their properties were going into foreclosure in unprecedented numbers.

The losses from early defaults on presumably fraudulent loans generally remained the burden of the mortgage banks (originators). At least that was the case until all the large independent mortgage banks went bankrupt. The servicing of those mortgages then had to be transferred, and the confusion factor was enough to cause more delinquency all by itself. Borrowers sometimes didn't even know where they were supposed to send their payments. Sometimes their payments were "misplaced." Greater delinquency gave us more borrowers in the hole, which led to more foreclosures.

The losses that hit hard in the bond market came first in the CDO market, as participants realized that the reversal of house price appreciation could lead to much larger losses than anticipated in the subprime mortgage pools backing the bonds CDO managers had bought. The bonds the CDO managers held started getting downgraded in anticipation of future credit losses.

Most CDOs have provisions that define a default condition if a significant fraction of the debt in the CDO gets downgraded. So even before there were actual losses on the loans that affected the subprime bonds in the deals, CDO deals were technically in default. Credit losses in the BBB subprime bonds used as collateral could result in credit losses even in the AAA tranches issued by the CDOs. Half or more of the 2006 vintage subprime BBB bonds were in danger of credit losses.

Managers of mutual funds heard that anticipated losses from subprime bonds were expected to hurt some CDO bonds that were originally rated AAA, and some jumped to the conclusion that no bond backed by subprime mortgages was worth anything, even if it was AAA. They reacted by selling the stock in any company that had any investment in subprime bonds, and the AAA rated small investor followed.

The knee-jerk reaction that categorized all AAA bonds with subprime exposure as complete junk propelled a massive sell-off. The lack of due diligence and inability to properly evaluate those AAA bonds was even more unfortunate given the fact that the AAA subprime mortgage bonds made up nearly 80% of the deals, on average. Most subprime deals had only 2% or 3% of the BBB bonds that were the problem.

Unfortunately, subprime mortgages weren't the only ones in trouble.

Things weren't looking so rosy in the alt-A mortgage sector, either, despite the media's early assertions that this sector was insulated from the problems plaguing subprime borrowers. Unlike the subprime borrowers, alt-A borrowers tend to have "prime" credit scores but they do not qualify as prime borrowers. This is most often due to the fact that they have their own businesses or work as independent contractors, and thus have no established salaries.

The alt-A mortgage loans certainly seemed better. They seemed better because of the high credit scores of the borrowers. But some deals were backed by pools of loans in which half came with no income verification. A few alt-A deals were composed entirely of no-doc loans.

The alt-A sector of the market tended to draw the most aggressive house-flipping investors. Pools of alt-A mortgages could be comprised of 80% primary residences with the rest of the pool comprised of "investor properties," while pools of subprime deals averaged around 5% investor loans.

Many of these investors never thought of themselves as landlords. They were not investing for income like traditional buyers of investment properties, but solely for price appreciation. They bought properties that couldn't rent for enough to pay the mortgage and maintenance, hoping to make a killing by flipping them. "Flippers" sometimes bought multiple properties at the same time so multiple lenders would not be aware that they had so many loans, since it would take time for their credit reports to update.

In 2007, alt-A borrowers took out nearly $400 billion in mortgage loans, not too much less than the $600 billion peak that subprime lending reached in 2006. In early 2008, some pools of 2006-vintage alt-A loans were performing just as badly as subprime deals of the same vintage. Without the extra structural protections built into the structures that subprime deals have, AA rated alt-A bonds turned out to be just as risky as single A or BBB subprime bonds, or even worse.

Once the credit issues became apparent in the alt-A sector, the leverage in the system worked in reverse, pushing home values down faster and faster. The inevitable result was to push even prime mortgages "underwater," so that those responsible borrowers were now one pink slip or hospital visit away from foreclosure.

The Fed seemed oblivious as this snowball of credit problems rolled over the housing market. In fact, the Fed kept raising rates until the middle of 2006, buoyed by a false confidence that a major correction in the largest asset held by Americans would somehow be "contained" in the realm of subprime borrowers.

During the bubble years, extraction of equity from American homes amounted to hundreds of billions of dollars every year. Some estimates say a full percentage point of our GDP came from the refinancing boom.

Construction, finance and real estate companies added millions of workers to handle the increased volume of new homes and the turnover of existing homes. A sudden reversal of the lending environment was sure to eliminate those jobs, but our policy makers pretended that couldn't happen, and kept tightening the screws so they could fight inflation.

In an ironic twist, foreigners holding U.S. mortgage bonds felt the losses as well, and they soon decided that the cornerstone of the United States' economic system was hopelessly fragile, so they avoided U.S. dollar investments.

When the dollar dropped as a result, inflation resulted from the currency decline in spite of any attempt to control it through monetary policy. In a sense, the Fed's attempt to be the Great Inflation Fighter led directly to inflation in all of the goods we import, which includes commodities and most manufactured goods.

Accounting standards adopted after the corporate scandals in 2001 and 2002 added more fuel to the fire. Those standards forced investors and other holders of mortgage bonds to realize market value losses as immediate declines in capital or outright losses, even if the bonds were still in portfolio.

The result of this short-sighted regulation was that when one weakened levered holder collapsed, that single event automatically led every other holder to take an immediate loss to capital. Each time the prices of the bonds declined, other bond investors who used borrowed money to finance their mortgage bonds were that much closer to being forced to sell.

Large supplies of high-quality mortgage bonds were being sold under duress into a market that was having real trouble absorbing them. Making new loans to securitize had become a money-losing exercise because the secondary bonds were being sold so cheaply.

Lenders couldn't lend if they had to keep the loans in their investment portfolios, which had to be "marked to market," resulting in a loss to capital the day the loan closed. With the securitization market effectively shut down, any loan that couldn't be guaranteed by one of the Federal mortgage Agencies would have to be kept in the lender's portfolio, resulting in an immediate loss in capital.

Homeowners who might have been able to refinance their adjustable rate mortgages when rates adjusted after the teaser rate were suddenly left with no refinancing options that didn't require an additional down payment, even though fixed mortgage rates had dropped far enough that many borrowers could have easily handled the monthly payments. As a result, millions of homeowners were left with only one option: to try to sell their homes, which just lowered prices further.

The macro player lenders added fuel to the fire by tightening credit standards far past where they were before the bubble in debt developed.

Other macro players like the press did their part to make the situation worse, coming up with frightening headlines like "House Price Growth Drop Fastest on Record." Reading that, it was easy for nervous homeowners or potential buyers to miss the word "Growth" and come away believing that prices were dropping, even before they had.

The Fed stayed the course with inflation-fighting high interest rates until September of 2007, when the collapse of the credit markets was all but assured. Investors avoided any exposure to any fund or bank that had any exposure at all to subprime mortgage bonds, no matter how small or how safe the investment might be.

Rating Agencies left their high ratings on subprime mortgage bonds until it was obvious that the problems were coming, and then they devised new and tougher tests, which suddenly ratcheted all the ratings lower.

Regulators and politicians began to announce investigations into mortgage lenders, accelerating lenders' downward spiral toward bankruptcy, as shareholders dumped their stock into a fearful market.

To complete the picture, hedge funds that wanted to bet against housing and mortgage bonds applied tremendous pressure, with leverage, to drive down the prices of mortgage bonds and the stocks of mortgage lenders.

What no one could know was that the dollar amount of pressure driving prices down was many times larger than the mortgage bond market itself, and that the CDS contracts which the largest banks and Wall Street dealers had written were allegedly reinsured by others, including the municipal bond insurance companies and AIG.

CHAPTER SIX

The Tribes of Wall Street

As with any man-made disaster, understanding the financial crisis has to include understanding the groups of people who created it.

There are "tribes" in every business. These groups form based on their job functions and they compete for power. Different companies in the same business operate differently depending on the tribe they come from and who their leaders are.

A clear example is the advertising business. Ad agencies are described as being "account driven" if they are run by the account people who handle clients and "creative driven" if they are run by writers and art directors.

In business, unless there is a major coup, the outgoing top management team nearly always replaces themselves with people from their own background, so the character of a given company can survive generations of changes among the individuals filling the top roles.

On Wall Street, the three main tribes that lay claim to power are trading, banking and sales.

Other smaller tribes include the research "geeks," systems, legal, risk management, compliance and accounting. Traditionally, the support groups, also called cost centers, seldom get the top spot at any Wall Street firm unless the firm has been shut down or nearly so, in which case regulators, major shareholders or other outside forces might put a lawyer, accountant or risk manager in charge.

At Bear Stearns or Salomon, the traders ruled and they often referred to Collateralized Mortgage Obligations as trades. No doubt when bonuses were paid at the end of the year, the bankers and sales people who did the structuring and placement were paid less than the traders, since they were facilitating the successful trades.

At Goldman or First Boston or Morgan Stanley, everything was a deal, and the bankers were the stars. Not coincidentally, their CEOs had nearly always climbed the ladder of success as bankers.

I remember a watering hole conversation with a friend in sales at Goldman who had the temerity to ask why he was paid such a low commission on bond sales compared to other shops. He was told that the firm's relationships were what made the difference, and that it was his chair at Goldman that was earning him half the money he was being paid.

At Merrill Lynch, Paine Webber (later the core of UBS), Prudential-Bache and Dean Witter, sales was king, and retail brokers* dominated the corner office for years after those shops made the transition to institutional business. At times, whole deals in the CMO market would make less profit than the commissions the salesforce expected, a fact that guaranteed frequent skirmishes between the tribes.

Retail Brokers – Stockbrokers in branch offices that deal with individual customers. They were paid an average commission of 40% of the firm's gross sales charge, while institutional sales people were paid 8%.

With their differing talents and jobs, the tribes of Wall Street have little incentive to understand each others' roles in detail or others' contributions to their success. Each needs to believe that they alone are the most important part of the machine if they want to get the biggest slice of the pie.

Members of the Trading Tribe need the unique ability to forget what happened ten minutes ago and be completely sure right now. That's not to say they don't know history or pay attention to details. But what they do need to do is forget the last trade as soon as it's over. If they can't, they'll second guess themselves into a kind of paralysis. Even though they can't be right all the time, and most successful traders are right barely more than half the time, it's still true that each time they make a bet, they believe in that bet.

Traders' confidence in their ability to make snap decisions can make it hard for them to think they need to understand the work that went into creating the bonds they trade. While working at the Union

Bank of Switzerland (UBS), one evening I was looking forward to
putting in a quiet night working on a deal structure* as the trading floor
emptied out. As I walked down the center aisle, a trader who handled
market-making in bond options was at her desk, waiting for the car
service to arrive to take her home.

As I passed her , she stopped me
and said "I have 20 minutes before my
limo gets here. Explain the CMO
business to me." It was one of the few
times I was completely speechless. I was
thinking of telling her that it generally
took six months to a year to teach a
Wharton Associate Professor enough to
be a useful member of my CMO team.

*Deal Structure – Payment
rules and bond class sizes that
determine how cash flows are
allocated to multiple tranches
of bonds. The tranches are
divided by maturity, interest
rates, principal payment
schedules or credit priorities to
divide the risks among different
types of investors.*

Truly understanding how the bonds worked was actually very rare
for the salespeople and traders who filled the trading floor. When Andy
Stone, who was building a new mortgage department at Daiwa invited
me to join him as his second hire, he asked me why I would consider
leaving UBS. I told him that he was the only person I had met on a
trading desk that "got it" when I explained how the cash flows from
the various bonds fit together in the deals I structured.

Even when a bond is designed for a specific trader's specialty, that
trader may not see what it is worth. When I invented the "super-PO"
as a cash-flow hedge for investors who have earnings streams from
mortgage servicing, Andy had me take it to the PO (Principal Only)
bond trader to get a price.

The trader knew his job was to price the bond, not necessarily to
understand it. Over my objections, he priced it to trade to a yield
higher than the thirty-year Treasury Bond, which translated into 14
cents on the dollar. By the time the deal closed a few weeks later,
technologically sophisticated customers had bid it up to twice that price
and within six months, bonds like it were being sold at yields less than a
third of the yield of Treasury bonds, and prices 50 cents on the dollar
or higher.

The Sales Tribe needs a different talent than the Trading Tribe, but
it requires no less ego. In institutional sales, where a single sale may

have a million or more dollars in profit attached to it, only a few sales per month will come through for each sales person. Successful salesmen still make dozens of calls every day, convinced that each and every call will be a sale. If you looked at their actual "hit rate," chances are that only about one in a hundred calls resulted in a sale.

Imagine having a job that involves being told "no" a hundred times in a row, yet somehow you keep believing in yourself and keep making the calls. On the other side of the coin, a good sales person that makes a dozen or two dozen good sales a year on Wall Street can get paid a million dollars or more for putting in a year of being told "No."

As I learned even before coming to Wall Street, sales fundamentally consists of only two things that have to happen – making the customer feel good about themselves while conveying to them the information they need to make the buying decision. Thankfully, most customers feel best about themselves when they like the people they are dealing with, though a dreadful few only feel better about themselves when abusing the salesman.

Some customers were willing to commit to buying bonds with some happy talk, football tickets or expensive dinners with their sales rep, but the biggest (and therefore most important) customers developed their own expertise. When the mortgage bond business became so technical that there were only about a dozen of us on the Street who really understood it, it became a matter of putting the structurer in touch with the smartest buyers.

One salesman I worked with got an award one day for having the most commissions for the quarter. By chance, he had two of my best buy-side relationships on his account list, and he'd had them before I joined the firm. As far as I know, they hadn't done much business until I started making specific bonds for those customers. It was kind of funny when Jorge got the award that day. Another salesman down the row blurted out, in a typical 100 decibel trading floor voice "You wanna see how Jorge gets his sales?" Then the other salesman picked up a phone, punched a bunch of numbers, held the phone up in the air and yelled "Howard!"

What that other salesman didn't realize was that Jorge had done the second essential part of the sales job: he got the customer the information needed to make the buying decision, while making that customer feel good about himself.

Members of the Banking Tribe have gigantic egos just like members of the Trading Tribe, but their justification for believing their contribution outweighs all others is rooted in relationships and expertise.

It wasn't unusual, for example, to hear a banker declare "I structured that deal" even though the investors decided what to pay for bonds based on yield tables that the banker might not even have seen.

To a banker, structuring was their work with the lawyers making sure the description of the legal structures, the bonds and the issuer conformed to an understanding they had reached with the the client on whose behalf the bonds were issued.

When we created brand-new companies to be issuers for our mortgage deals, a big part of the bankers' job – relationship management – had disappeared. Still, there is no doubt that traditional merger or takeover deals were landed by bankers with their relationships and they deserved the credit.

With rare exceptions, the leaders of the Wall Street tribes -- the traders, bankers and salespeople -- can "only" make $10 or $20 million a year even at the largest firms on the Street. Managers of hedge funds and private equity firms can make ten or even a hundred times as much. So if the door to the corner office at the Wall Street firm is closed, the most talented and driven members of the tribe take a detour.

Most hedge funds are headed by former Wall Streeters, with a heavy concentration of traders. Their talents and personalities suit the hedge fund world of big trades and big opinions.

Bankers are more likely to start private equity or venture capital firms and continue to do deals that take advantage of tax codes and financing techniques. When they control the companies coming to market with the financings they structure, bankers can become their own clients as fund managers.

The main skill of salespeople is getting institutional fund managers to commit money, so top salespeople can go in more than one direction, with partners from the other tribes.

Even technology specialists have gotten huge rewards by leaving Wall Street. Though the "geeks" never dominated an investment bank, Michael Bloomberg and the High Frequency Trading (HFT) hedge funds have proved that even members of minor Wall Street tribes can become billionaires.

CHAPTER SEVEN

Over the Transom

I came into investment banking "over the transom" without an internship, an M.B.A. or a Ph.D. Answering a classified ad in *The New York Times*, I applied for a job as a computer systems manager in the Mortgage Department at A. G. Becker. The year was 1984, and mortgage securitization was taking off.

My interview for that first job spanned at least fifteen hours, with most of that time spent in conversation with a brilliant mathematician named David Spear, who was a senior analyst in Becker's Mortgage Research Group.

When I arrived to begin my new job, I was told that instead of working for David, I would be working for Fred Mitchell, David's boss, with whom I had spent all of fifteen minutes during my fifteen-hour interview.

It turned out that my first assignment in my new job was to suck every bit of knowledge out of David, who had been let go and was leaving in two weeks. I also had to set up the computer system the Mortgage Department had bought and installed, but never used.

After several months, during which the business of Wall Street seemed less like a business and more like a daily adventure in a kind of organizational bipolar disorder, three-quarters of our department was called into a windowless conference room with a case of chilled champagne sitting on a large wooden conference table, which had been pushed to one side of the room.

Since we hadn't done anything particularly noteworthy that day or even that week, I really wondered what this was all about. Then our department heads toasted us as survivors, letting us know that the people who weren't in the room with us were gone.

Playing to a captive audience, our department heads then took turns painting a rosy picture of the future. We were told that the French bank Paribas, with its AAA financial strength, was now 100% owner of our company, and we were going to be building on our top tier strength in mortgages and commercial paper to become a major player in the market.

Even though Becker (now called Becker Paribas) had its AAA parent and its status as one of the handful of Primary Dealers* that the U.S. Treasury uses to sell its debt, no real infusion of capital had occurred after the takeover. Within weeks, rumors flew around the Street that Becker was a goner.

Soon thereafter, we watched as the crawling news ticker around the top of our trading room spread the news to the world that we had been sold to Merrill Lynch. We got the memos on our desks about an hour later.

Primary Dealers – SEC registered broker-dealers that provide the Federal Reserve with distribution for U.S. Treasury auctions. As of 2008, there were only twenty such Wall Street firms.

That day I got to watch the tribes of Wall Street turn on one of their own. We had a trading inventory of GNMAs, possibly the most liquid security there is after Treasury Bonds. We had to sell our inventory but we weren't in a position to buy anything. So the other Wall Street players immediately lowered their bids on our bonds by 2%, all the while trading with each other at normal prices.

Merrill Lynch, the firm that was taking us over, already had people who did just about everything we did, with the possible exception of the mortgage and commercial paper business, where we had a larger market share. All of us were looking at all our options.

The man who had almost been my boss at Becker, David Spear, had landed at First Boston. Firms on the Street were desperate enough for people that did what David and I could do that they had given him a business card with his name followed by the title "Rocket Scientist." I had an appointment to interview at First Boston that coming Monday.

The night before, I got a call telling me I should show up at Merrill's offices on Monday morning. I was glad my First Boston interview was set up for Monday afternoon.

I was greeted in the lobby at Merrill, and taken to meet the Head of Fixed Income Research. He asked me if I could program in APL, and said they had a CMO model that was 90% of the way there and they just wanted me to complete it. No problem.

Then came a set of interviews that were like a business version of speed dating. Merrill had set up a suite of offices, each with three or four senior research professionals scattered in chairs or leaning on credenzas, ready to grill us when we walked in and sat down. Every half hour, I and the other members of our little Becker mortgage research team would switch rooms for another gang interview, while the Merrill people shot questions at us as fast as they could from multiple directions. I made it out in time to catch the subway to head uptown to First Boston, wondering what lay in store for me there.

Rocket Scientist David Spears took me to a corner office to meet the head of Short Term Finance, the first female partner in First Boston's history. Her office was furnished in Louis XV style, and I was invited to sit on one of the delicate bergères upholstered in silk brocade. I'm built like an offensive guard, and I was actually afraid I would break the chair if I let all my weight down on it. Our conversation lasted fifteen minutes or so, and then a seven-hour marathon of interviews began. I recall as I left her office wondering which of us was stranger – her for caring what my SAT scores had been sixteen years earlier, or me for remembering.

Next, I interviewed with Craig Phillips, the Number Two person in the Short Term Finance Department. He asked me whether I thought car loans could be securitized into multiple classes of bonds like CMOs. I said, yes, and added that it wouldn't be too hard to model. Then he said I could have the job if I could tell him how to use the copy of the Flight Simulator computer game a friend had given him.

My last interview was with one of the senior traders. As David took me onto the trading floor I could tell, even after my short career on the Street, that the trader I needed to see was having a bad day. The trading day was over, but as I stood waiting at the side of his desk, he kept talking on the phone, and punching the keys on the keyboards on his desk, bringing up different screens of bond prices on a dozen or more TV monitors stacked on top of each other.

After about twenty minutes, he got up without a word and started walking to a small glass-walled meeting room at the edge of the trading room. A hand gesture gave me the clue that I was supposed to follow him into the fish bowl. I handed him my resume, and he zeroed in on a summer I spent doing graduate work in mathematics at UC Berkeley. He asked me which textbook I had for one of the analysis courses I took. I closed my eyes and visualized the book I had held in my hands eleven years earlier. I told him it was Michael Spivak's <u>Calculus on Manifolds</u>. The trader said that couldn't have been the book for that course, and walked out of the room.

The last hurdle of my interview took place at the bar at The Four Seasons, with David, the Rocket Scientist, and Diane, the partner with the Louis XV office. Diane turned to me, and asked me to complete a sentence for her:

"A year from now, Craig (Mr. Flight Simulator) and I are having a drink, and Craig says 'It's too bad about Howard. He would have worked out, except....'"

After a pause, the answer came to me: "...except he was hit by a bus."

I left, happy with the thought that I would be getting a job at First Boston working with my buddy David, who got to work at noon and had a card with the title "Rocket Scientist."

Except I didn't get the job. The reason given was that the trader who was so interested in my functional analysis textbook just didn't think I was the right guy.

A few days later, our job offers from Merrill came through. Only 5% of Becker's workforce was going to retain their jobs in the "merger." I was offered a research position as an analyst at a third of the salary offered to our twenty-year-old trading assistant, who ran the programs I wrote (in those days, some of the traders and salesmen hadn't gotten the hang of logging on to the computer).

I turned that one down and went to join the new investment banking effort at Prudential-Bache ("Pru"), which had been formed when retail broker Bache Halsey Stuart & Shields was bought by Prudential Insurance.

At Pru, we tried to build up an institutional business around our new strength in CMO's and mortgage securities. But the sales culture was so strong that we regularly had situations where a retail broker in one of our branch offices would call our CEO directly, claiming big retail commissions on trades we did with the banks, insurance companies, or other institutions that were our customers. According to these retail brokers, they should be paid for the sales because they played golf with the management at the banks.

Our firm had been an all-IBM shop for a number of years when they hired a new Head of Systems who had spent more than twenty years at IBM. In those days, IBM sold mainframes and was making a late entry into the PC business. Our firm's IT budget soon flew right past $100 million a year on its way to several times that amount only a few years later. That's when I realized how cost centers cement their power. In departments whose importance is defined by the number of people it contains along with the size of its budget and how much it can expense to the money-making parts of the firm, it's all about empire building.

I was young and brash in those days and as a lowly Associate, I took on the Chief Information Officer, who was also a member of the Board of Directors. It was my first Wall Street war. I'd been a computer consultant before coming to Wall Street, and I knew our Research Department could have more computing power for a lot less money if we used minicomputers instead of an IBM mainframe.

One night, as I logged off after a sixteen-hour session of debugging and testing my program, I saw I had used over twelve hours of CPU (Central Processing Unit) time on one of the parent firm's four mainframes. That meant I had used three-eighths of the total computing power of Prudential Insurance all by myself that night. If I gave the program to a couple of hundred traders and analysts, the company would never get to send out trade tickets for the brokerage, not to mention any life insurance bills.

It was clear that we needed our own computers. It made sense to me that instead of a $10 million machine that cost several million per year in maintenance and systems manager costs, we could use the computing power from one of the mini-computer systems sold in those days by Digital Equipment, Prime or Data General.

I was frustrated by our computer systems but even more frustrated that Pru didn't seem willing to do any deals as lead bank. So I went and got a job offer from Kidder Peabody, a firm that seemed ready to do deals as soon as they had models.

When I went in to give my two weeks' notice, I was told that Pru would match Kidder's offer. I answered that I didn't get a raise from Kidder. All they had promised was to do CMO deals and to buy a non-IBM minicomputer for my department.

That was my first big lesson in how the Street values risk takers. We did our first two lead-managed CMO deals in the next two weeks. In the process, I learned even more about how Wall Street operates.

We were structuring a $100 million deal for MDC, a builder in Denver that decided housing finance could be even more profitable than building houses. The traders at other houses on the Street knew we were a sales shop and didn't carry much inventory, so they delivered $100 million of GNMA 9s* to us that didn't match the characteristics we required to structure our deal. We couldn't deliver CMO bonds that differed from the advertised terms of the deal. The only choice we had was to buy another $100 million GNMA 9s for the first deal, specifying the characteristics we needed, while simultaneously pricing a second deal using the $100 million in GNMA 9s we had received.

> *GNMA 9 – Mortgage pass-through security (MBS) backed by 9.5% FHA and VA mortgages. Investors get all the principal and 9% interest, while the bank keeps 044% (44 basis points) to service the loan and GNMA takes just 6 basis points for its guarantee of principal and interest.*

Near the end of that year, Pru hired Andy Stone, a hot young trader from Salomon Brothers, to run our trading desk. We were on a roll. I was modeling every competitor's CMO deals to see how much money they made and could usually model their deals in less than an hour after they were announced. That fast modeling was a critical factor that helped Pru become one of the major players in the market.

Soon, my Financial Strategies Group had become the engine driving both stock and bond deals, and we had become a prize to be taken, as the Romans might have viewed Gaul. Our Julius Caesar was named Vinny Pica, a Managing Director at the firm who liked to quote Machiavelli.

I found out I was being eliminated one day when I attempted to log on to my computer and nothing happened. When I called the system manager, I found out my password had been changed. It was now "Vinny." Less than two years later, Vinny got hold of Andy Stone's trading empire, too. Machiavelli was a good mentor, even if he had been dead for over 450 years.

I used my contacts to arrange as many interviews as I could, telling each firm that I was going to accept offers on the last Friday in August. I got three offers on the specified day. Banker's Trust and L. F. Rothschild each wanted to get into the business. I ended up at UBS, the Union Bank of Switzerland. They had never done a public mortgage deal and they hired me as an investment banker to set up a new Mortgage Finance Group.

When I joined, an analytic group was already in place with twenty professionals and an IBM mainframe on order. But on the trading floor, we were permitted to buy our own computers, as long as they were PCs. So we stayed on the trading floor and that's what we used. We left the mainframe to the multi-year software development plan the team in place had proposed. With our PCs, we attained the number one spot in underwriting private label CMOs the very next year.

I'd learned some lessons about power and money at Becker and Pru, so before I took the job, I had made a deal with management that my group would get a quarter of the profit it made after expenses as its bonus pool.* My position at *Bonus Pool – The money Wall Street firms allocate to pay year-end bonuses that can be millions of dollars for top producers. Even clerks and administrative assistants can get six-figure bonuses, so "Bonus Day" is a yearly exercise in mass hysteria.* UBS made me an officer of a Swiss bank, and as such, I got detailed daily accounting of our profits in both U.S. dollars and Swiss francs. As we approached the end of our first year, the firm accounting showed we had earned close to $15 million.

I was feeling on top of the world when the day came when our bonuses would be announced, and no small sense of pride that I'd made a deal that would ensure that everyone in my tiny 4-person group would get a great bonus. As I sat with the Head of Fixed Income, he explained that my group with its three PC's had accrued over $12 million in systems cost from the mainframe. I argued that a deal was a deal.

That's when he came up with his version of the classic Wall Street bonus speech. That's the one where they say "For you to have a great year, you personally have to have a great year, your department has to have a great year, and your firm has to have a great year." We'd done all that. So he added, "And your industry has to have a great year."

I was outraged. "Are you saying that if Merrill Lynch loses money, I don't get paid?" That's when he gave me the honest answer. He said, "With people getting laid off in mortgage departments all over the Street, we don't think we have to pay you." He was right. It had been a handshake deal, so it meant nothing.

Eight months later, I took a job at Daiwa Securities, one of Japan's Big Four brokerage firms, and joined Andy Stone as the second person in the door to start their mortgage department.

My experience with the bonus pool at UBS provided me with a life lesson I didn't forget. It was embodied in a clause in our department's contract with Daiwa. We agreed to have a million dollars per year of our departmental profit paid to the systems department, but only if no systems person was ever allowed to touch our computers. We paid for, managed, and controlled our own systems and wrote our own software. And when we made over $150 million in profit our first full year, the Systems Department got exactly $1 million.

Later, when I headed the Securitized Products Department at Deutsche Bank, I had a very similar clause in my contract, but I took it a step further. We also had the ability to choose our own attorneys, and the right to interview and approve any person hired to oversee or assist our department in accounting, risk management, credit or operations. I made sure that our operations, accounting and other support professionals were the most expensive and experienced people we could find, because that saved us a lot of money. We were able to do our business with less than a quarter the number of support people assigned to other departments at the Bank, even those with relatively simple trading and accounting, like corporate bonds.

At Deutsche, I had the job of supervising traders, bankers and salesmen as well as the analytic team. I played referee while Tribal Warfare went on around me. Some days, my job seemed to consist mainly of listening to the salesmen say the traders were jerks that never took their customers' excellent offers for bonds, the traders complaining that the bankers were worthless because they never finished the documents on time, and the bankers asking why we had half a dozen analysts being paid so much, when we could get kids fresh out of school to do that work so much cheaper. Each group was convinced that I was short-changing them and paying the others way too much.

The contract I'd negotiated with Deutsche ensured that our group would get a full third of the profit we made for the firm. I had used this as a recruiting tool, and I tried to make our profits transparent to the members of our group.

Bonus numbers were due to be given out in January, so beginning in October or November, everyone started campaigning for their slice of the pie. By early December, when Bonus Madness set in, it would be hard to get anyone to concentrate on work. There were times when I thought we should just shut the department down, like a Wall Street version of summer vacation.

Of course, everyone knew exactly what they had contributed to every deal and considered their contributions to be the most important. Between the months of November and January, everyone attempted to ensure that I knew exactly what his or her fair share should be when it came time to divvy up the bonus pool.

In one very good trade, we had bought a bond from a deal that had been launched several years earlier at Daiwa. The bond was a difficult one, with no rating, based on loans against mobile home parks scattered all over America. We bought the bond for $30 million and sold part of it for $50 million. Everyone wanted a big piece -- if not the whole piece -- of pie.

There was the salesman, who had sourced the bond from a seller anxious for a quick sale.

There was the trader who bought it and hedged the interest rate exposure.

The credit analysts re-underwrote* every loan in the deal with a brand new credit review.

Credit Underwriting for Commercial Real Estate – Assessing properties for their current and future income potential, evaluating them in comparison to similar properties in the same area, and examining them for any deferred maintenance issues.

One of the senior bankers oversaw the valuation consultants who were paid $1000 a day to produce due diligence reports on each property, and went to a number of the properties himself.

The "relationship" banker obtained updated financials on each property and compared rental rates, market positioning, overall supply of mobile home lots in the area, maintenance issues, utility charges, amenities and other key characteristics for each of the fifty-four properties represented in the bond trust.

The programmers modeled the cash flows of the properties after that analysis, projecting out expected cash flows and several stressed cash flows.

Then the execution bankers took the results of the updated cash flow modeling and went to the Rating Agencies to get the level of subordination needed to rate most of a new deal BBB (investment grade).

The bankers, lawyers and analysts produced the supporting documentation and the models to create the new deal with a rated bond and an unrated bond, along with a "strip" of excess interest.

Another salesman sold the entire BBB bond to one account after several days of calls, with follow-ups of custom stress analysis from the analytic team and pricing negotiations with the trader.

All told, we spent about two months and nearly a million dollars in legal, rating, accounting and other direct expenses to do this single trade.

When bonus time came, the trader sat in my office and said he knew we had made $20 million on the trade, so he should get $2 million added to his bonus. The relationship banker told me that he should get $2 million added to his bonus. So did the salesman who bought the bond, and the salesman who sold the bond. The other bankers and the analytics team also made sure that I knew that they deserved to get paid handsomely for working on the deal.

When all the expectations of the team were totaled, it added up to around $9 or $10 million. Unfortunately, our very generous one-third profit share added up to only $6 million, and that was before we allocated some of our $20 million in annual fixed costs to that complex deal.

I listened as each person involved in the deal completely discounted the contribution of the other people towards our success. Even the financial wizards couldn't add up the numbers.

CHAPTER EIGHT

Innumeracy

According to the Random House Unabridged Dictionary, some time between 1400 and 1450 AD, the word numerate appeared in the English language, referring to a person who is able to use or understand numerical techniques of mathematics. In 1959, the same dictionary says the antonym innumerate entered the language, which means unable to use mathematics. From that adjective, we get the noun innumeracy.

Innumeracy is all around us and it isn't helping anyone understand what's really going on inside the world's financial markets. I'm showing my bias here, but I think that people in the financial press should know how to add, subtract, multiply and divide.

I heard a Pulitzer prize-winning financial reporter speak on National Public Radio about subprime mortgages. She claimed that she had talked to many people whose mortgages had reset from 4% to 11% in one year and whose monthly payments had more than doubled after the two-year initial low payment period.

A case of innumeracy. The reporter can only report what she was told, but it's pretty clear that someone (or a number of people) didn't do the math.

While it's true that subprime mortgages often did have lower fixed rates for the first two years, the lowest rates I heard of were around 7%, and the rate resets were capped at 2% or 3% on the first reset. That would mean that some people had their rates reset from 7% to 10%, not 4% to 11%.

For a typical $160,000 subprime mortgage, the payment after reset would go up from $933 to $1,333 for interest only loans, or from $1064 to $1,391 for a loan that pays both principal and interest. That's significantly different in dollars and cents from the reporter's example, where the payment could go from $533 to $1,467 for an interest only loan.

No matter how many times the rate resets, the monthly payment for a subprime mortgage will not double. Not on the first reset and not on subsequent resets, either.

In addition, since almost all subprime loans have initial rates of 7.5% or higher, and lifetime maximum rates that are typically 6% higher than the start rate, that equates to a lifetime maximum rate of 13.5%.

Reporters should be accurate about the information they convey, because people believe what they read (and hear). Would listeners (or readers) have felt differently about the subprime "meltdown" if they knew that this reporter's claims were innumerate?

Once this reporter grasps simple arithmetic, she can look up the reference interest rate and add the margin, the way the Adjustable Rate Mortgage (ARM) disclosure form signed by every borrower does.

The fact is that option ARM's – the loans that offered borrowers the option of choosing very low monthly payment amounts – were not made to subprime borrowers. They were made to borrowers who had good to excellent credit histories and who could also afford substantial down payments, averaging nearly 30%.

Despite what you might have read in the papers, if you heard about mortgage payments doubling when loans reset, they weren't subprime mortgages to begin with. Strangely enough, it became a common claim that subprime mortgages would have "payment shocks" that more than doubled borrowers' monthly payments.

One popular financial reporter who wrote a regular column and appeared frequently on CNBC set a high water mark in innumeracy when it appeared that he couldn't tell which was preferable: an asset that produced positive cash flow or an asset that produced zero cash flow.

This reporter wrote dozens of articles over a period of more than five years focusing on one of the subprime lenders, NovaStar Financial, which had a market share of approximately 1% to 2%. His common theme was that the company was too aggressive in its accounting and possibly overstating its earnings.

One of his articles claimed in its headline "Something undisclosed in earnings release." The article implied that something must be wrong because the company had just reported more than ten million dollars in cash flow and income from mortgage securities with no cost basis.

Of course, the very thing that this financial writer thought was a negative would be thought of as a positive by any investment professional. The company had already charged off the cost of buying those securities, and written them down to zero.

With a fundamental misunderstanding of what the numbers mean, this reporter also applauded the fact that intangibles which produced no cash flow whatsoever appeared as positive values on the balance sheet of one of NovaStar's much larger competitors.

He wrote several flattering articles about a mortgage company which attributed tens of millions of dollars of value to "assets" like the client relationships of its CEO and "goodwill*" from the CEO selling his asset management company to the public shareholder company. Both these "assets" showed up as part of the value of the company, but neither of them produced a penny of cash flow.

* Goodwill - An accounting entry put on a company's balance sheet to categorize acquisition cost for which no tangible book value is received, for example, a brand name. If the asset becomes impaired, as a brand name would if the product were no longer sold, then the goodwill entry is written off and charged against earnings.

In perhaps the ultimate irony, this innumerate reporter failed to focus on the largest publicly traded subprime lender in the business, New Century, a company with nearly ten times the market share of NovaStar. In fact, he only mentioned New Century a few times, and each time he held the larger company out as an example of conservative, "clean" accounting. Just months after his series of articles, New Century admitted that it had been improperly accounting for bad loans for years, and declared bankruptcy only six weeks later.

To be fair, it's not just reporters who are guilty of innumeracy. A specialized cottage industry that supplies expensive "independent stock research" has developed to support short selling hedge funds.

These companies bill themselves as the counterbalance to Wall Street's positively biased equity research. They often puff themselves up a bit by giving themselves the title "forensic accountants." Sounds pretty impressive, right? You'd expect them to be even more numerate than a Certified Public Accountant. But that kind of accountant at least passes an exam and submits to a licensing regimen, complete with professional ethical standards.

How independent are these stock research companies? Some of them may not be very independent at all. These research companies often give their subscribers the privilege of directing them to focus on one or two companies per year as part of the $20,000 to $50,000 per year subscription price. Add a zero or two in potential profit with a well-timed short position, and you can see what a good investment a subscription could be if it resulted in doubt cast on a targeted company.

Of course, when these companies issue their reports at the behest of one client, every subscriber gets the research piece when it's finished. If those other subscribers also sell short after reading it, the stock price is almost sure to go down. If the forensic accountants also generously provide their research to financial reporters a day or two later, chances are that individual stockholders will join the shorts in deciding it's time to sell, adding to the profit of the strategy.

The best part is that everybody has the cover of protected sources and independent research, so it's hard to prove collusion or market manipulation.

In a case of "what's good for the goose is good for the gander," a confidential source of mine sent me one such report to review. The report had a strong negative bias, and more than a few flat out mistakes.

While I can overlook the mistakes in the cash flow modeling and accounting for securitizations as a simple lack of specialized competence, I can't give the self-described "forensic accountant" a pass on basic arithmetic.

After going through a deeply flawed earnings model, this particular research piece ended with a seven-year projection of the company's performance. In the year that had already begun, they estimated $3.48 earnings per share for the target company.

At that time, there were almost forty million shares of common stock outstanding. There were also just under three million shares of preferred stock paying a yearly dividend of $2.225 per share.

In a spectacular display of innumeracy, the research piece then concluded that the company's common stock would only have $3.48 minus $2.25, or $1.23 per share, available to pay dividends to shareholders. Not only did they copy the amount of the preferred dividend incorrectly, they failed to adjust for the 11 to 1 differential in the number of shares.

The correct adjustment would be about 20 cents per share, not $2.25. In case you're wondering how the year actually turned out, earnings per share were around $4.20 after deducting the preferred dividend. A far cry from $1.23.

For the short seller that submitted the company as the topic of that report, things worked out just fine. The stock price dropped dramatically right after the piece was released, and it went down even further after a national reporter got a copy, and quoted the research company's innumerate CEO on the terrible prospects for the targeted company.

That's bad enough. But some financial reporters don't even attempt to make sense of the numbers. Why bother understanding when you can just label it all "toxic waste?" Over the last twenty years, the phrase "toxic waste" has become a perfectly acceptable synonym for any complicated securitized product that contains mortgages. It doesn't matter whether the market is loving them or hating them, they still carry the label.

As one of the "financial engineers" who created these products (we referred to it as "building bonds"), I prided myself on making good bonds, based on real numbers and thorough analysis. My customers were sophisticated institutional investors who wanted to buy the bonds I built for them and appreciated the detailed custom performance analysis available for every bond. I was shocked when I read that the bonds I built were being called "toxic waste," and I have to say that I'm disappointed the phrase has stuck.

I first read it in 1987 or 1988, when a colleague dropped a copy of a Forbes Magazine article on my desk. The gist of the article was that CMO deal structurers were working some like alchemists, pretending that base metal was gold, and investors buying CMO bonds were taking big risks.

When I was working at Daiwa in 1993, I was asked to spend some time with the same journalist who had written the article in Forbes. She was now at *The Wall Street Journal*, and my mission was to explain our business to her. I was sure that if I just explained our business thoroughly and clearly enough, she'd understand that dividing the risk among various bondholders was not an inherently nefarious occupation.

The popular bond structures at the time divided the prepayment variance of the mortgages, because a lower interest rate environment had sparked a flood of mortgage refinancing.

One popular CMO type was called a "PAC IO," or Planned Amortization Class Interest Only bond. By making a preferentially paid principal payment schedule (the "Planned Amortization"), some of the prepayment volatility was passed on to other classes. In other words, these bonds gave investors partial protection against early payment at a time when that was a concern.

Another popular CMO was called a "super PO," with the "PO" short for Principal Only. The super PO was a bond I had invented several years earlier, which sold for a deep discount because it had no coupon*. It was called "super" because it received a disproportionate share of prepayments if the borrowers paid off their mortgages faster than expected. By design, the super PO absorbed extra principal payments so the PAC bonds could be protected from early payment.

In my informal deal-structuring seminar, held one evening in our offices, I showed the WSJ reporter the analysis of a regular Ginnie Mae pass-through under expected,

* Coupon – The interest payment for a bond. The word comes from the time when bonds were engraved paper certificates that had small detachable "coupons" around the edge of the paper, each of which was cut off and presented to the payment agent to receive each interest payment.

fast and slow prepayment assumptions. It did exactly what the name implied; it passed through the cash flows from the mortgages in the Ginnie Mae pool to the MBS exactly proportionate to the way the payments came in from the borrowers. The reporter watched as I created a CMO structure from the Ginnie Mae's that included a PAC IO and a super PO. Both of these bonds qualified as CMO derivative*

bonds – the bonds the reporter was convinced were "toxic waste." I showed her how the combination of the two derivative CMO bonds performed nearly the same as the GNMA if prepayments came in as expected, but beat the Ginnie Mae bonds if prepayments came in either fast or slow.

*CMO Derivative – The tranches of CMO deals that had unusual characteristics that made them unlike the underlying mortgage loans. Examples included Principal Only (PO) and Interest Only (IO) bonds, inverse floating-rate bonds, and bonds that had special payment rules, such as the "jump Z," a bond that took a different place in the payment order for the deal if a pre-defined trigger event occurred.

The extra yield from the super PO in the fast payment scenarios more than offset the loss in payments on the PAC IO. In fact, if the variance was only a little faster than expected, or "pricing" speed, the PAC IO lost no performance at all, while the super PO had a nice yield bonus.

On the other end of the spectrum, the loss in the combined performance from slow prepayments was less than the loss in performance for the MBS, because I had structured the super PO as the last principal cash flows in the deal, which kept it from losing very much value if prepayments slowed down.

Whether she remained innumerate or simply didn't care, she continued to use the phrase "toxic waste" in her articles about derivative mortgage-backed securities over the years, vilifying an entire class of investments, regardless of their worth.

One day in October of 1993, the phone rang, and it was the WSJ reporter on the line. She asked me if I knew a particular state pension fund manager. He was an active buyer of PAC IOs and super POs, so of course I knew him. She then asked me if I knew how much money he had lost in his inverse floaters.* I replied that I hadn't created any inverse floaters for him, only the super POs, but she had no interest in knowing how much profit he had made on those.

I told her it was important that she tell the whole story in her article, explaining that he had other investments that made tremendous profits when the inverse floaters had losses. The next day, her article ran with no mention at all of the portfolio effect. It made the pension fund manager look like a dope, and slammed a small Houston brokerage as a fast-and-loose operation that had put a pension fund in a terrible bind with high-risk investments.

* Inverse Floater – A CMO bond that is paired with a floating rate bond in parallel so the combined interest on the two bonds equals that of a fixed-rate bond. Some call a recombined fixed rate bond the "parent" of the floater and the inverse floater.

Dow Jones and the reporter were sued for libel and the phrase "toxic waste" became even more firmly entrenched in the lexicon, as Dow Jones's attorneys used the phrase in their remarks to the jurors. The trial ended with a $222 million judgment against Dow Jones and a $20,000 judgment against the reporter, briefly setting a record for a jury award in a libel case, until the majority of the judgment was reversed on appeal.

Two years later at Deutsche Bank, I was in standing on the trading floor when the newly appointed Head of the Investment Bank used the phrase "toxic waste" to describe my department's trading portfolio. The fact that we were making a nice profit and that our hedging programs were working exactly as they were supposed to made no difference to him.

By 2007, the phrase "toxic waste" was so endemic that it even got an entry in the popular financial web site Investopedia.com, which defined it as follows:

A slang term referring to securities that are unattractive due to certain underlying provisions or risks making them generally illiquid with poor pricing schemes and transparency.

Mainly used in reference to CMOs, toxic waste represents the small portion of these products that are byproducts created as a result of providing the majority of CMOs with minimal risk. In effect, this small portion of byproducts is used as outlets for transferring a substantial portion of the underlying risks involved in making the obligations and then marketed to investors.

Investopedia says the phrase "toxic waste" represents "a small portion" of the products in the sector, but in common usage, we find it used in reference to all and any mortgage securities. It became an even more popular phrase as the subprime collapse unfolded.

The panic that arose as a result of this phrase can be easily understood if you believe that toxic waste leaches from its waste site and contaminates all the other investments in a portfolio. Of course, I don't believe that investments are contagious, but that didn't stop the collapse of Structured Investment Vehicles (SIVs).

In 2007, the bank-sponsored entities known as SIVs held hundreds of billions of dollars' worth of highly rated debt instruments, and issued Commercial Paper (CP)* to provide the financing for those investments.

CP, or Commercial Paper - Short maturity debt issued by a highly rated company or special purpose financing vehicle for short term funding. Typically bought by Money Market Funds, CP has to have maturity of 270 days or less.

Only 2% of the holdings of the SIVs were subprime mortgage securities, yet the world was quickly convinced that the holding of top-rated subprime mortgage bonds, albeit miniscule, had somehow destroyed the ability of the SIVs to pay their obligations. Innumeracy strikes again.

SIVs were now considered so infected that they might not be able to pay off their Commercial Paper, even though 98% of SIV holdings were completely unrelated securities. A whopping 43% of those holdings were very high-grade five-year to seven-year issues used by financial institutions to fund their own operations – bonds and CD's issued directly by insurance companies and banks.

Still, once some of the "toxic waste" in those SIVs had been detected, many reporters and analysts became convinced that the entire SIV must be worthless. Unfortunately, a lot of Wall Street traders went along with this ridiculous idea, and stopped buying the short-term Commercial Paper the SIVs had issued.

The result of this sudden loss of an important category of buyer for CD's from banks raised the cost of funds for those banks. Naturally, they passed along those higher costs to their customers. In this case, unnecessarily.

Ironically, the subprime holdings of the SIVs were only estimated at $8 billion, a tiny portion of the total subprime market. When the SIVs stopped buying subprime mortgage bonds, it made news but it made no difference to the subprime market.

A much larger portion of the SIV portfolios consisted of asset-backed securities backed by trade receivables from producers of commodities and other goods. These were much more important to their borrowers as a source of cheap financing. On a relative basis, collapse of the SIV market and its main funding vehicle, Asset-Backed Commercial Paper (ABCP)*, hurt a number of unrelated businesses much more than it hurt the subprime mortgage market.

ABCP, or Asset-Backed Commercial Paper – Short maturity (less than 270 day) debt sold in regular auctions to money market funds and other investors seeking safe places to hold cash. Secured by trade receivables and other assets, ABCP pays slightly higher returns than conventional CP issued by top-rated corporations.

As 2007 drew to a close, disclosing the fact that there were any portfolio bonds that might be tied to subprime mortgage loans in any way was enough to damage the stock of a bank or insurance company within minutes.

All impulsive acts, based on innumeracy.

CHAPTER NINE

Gunslingers

Financial reporters and analysts aren't the only ones that cross the line. There are plenty of characters among the Wall Street players that push the limits as well, or better, than their journalistic counterparts. We can thank the journalists for bringing them into the public eye.

The reporter who introduced the term "toxic waste" into the Wall Street lexicon wrote a profile of securitization heavyweight Mike Vranos for *The Wall Street Journal* in the early 90s. She'd gone to college with Mike, who was running the mortgage trading operation at the now-defunct investment bank Kidder, Peabody & Co. when she was at the Journal. He probably let down his guard while talking to his college classmate, and she scored with a great quote.

Mike made the Wall Street version of Warhol's fifteen minutes when he got one of those signature hand-drawn "hedcuts" and a center column on the front page of the Journal. Unfortunately, he also got quoted as saying "We look for the stupid customer" during Kidder's heyday as the number one investment bank in the CMO business. Kidder's owners at General Electric were probably not pleased.

Another fifteen minutes belonged to Andy Stone when he was Head of the Mortgage Department at Daiwa Securities. The cover story in the issue of Institutional Investor was "Daiwa's Mortgage Gamble Pays Off."

Some may recall a trading scandal at Daiwa Bank in the U.S. around that time. The two were never related. Daiwa is Japanese for "harmony" or "unity." Investors and authors who confuse the two are making the same mistake as saying United Van Lines was in trouble when United Air Lines was near bankruptcy.

The U.S. subsidiary of one of Japan's "Big Four" brokerage firms, Daiwa Securities had made huge profits from the Mortgage Department, which was then a little over a year old. When asked how he felt about working for the Japanese, Andy replied, "They don't have a clue what we're doing, but they leave us alone, which is fine with me."

I was working as the Managing Director for the analytic team in the Mortgage Department at the time this article appeared. When I read the quote insulting our owners and senior management, I knew we wouldn't get our contract renewed, no matter how much money we made.

Sure enough, at the end of Andy's three-year contract, Daiwa shut down the Mortgage Department. When they did, we had to do something with the hundreds of millions of dollars' worth of bonds we owned. Even more important was the billions in bonds that we were financing for customers.

We had launched a number of groundbreaking deals, including new types of CMOs and commercial mortgage bonds backed by apartment and office building loans, along with more "exotic" loan types never seen before in the securitization market, like nursing home loans and mortgages on mobile home parks. That made it difficult to hand our customers' positions off to other dealers.

When our Japanese management finally handed off our book of financing to Nomura Securities in a deal brokered in Tokyo, it was up to us in New York to make sure the Nomura team could correctly model and price the bonds.

There were serious holes and a number of bugs in Nomura's computer models when we first tried to match numbers*. They just weren't set up to model the cash flows from all the different kinds of properties and loans. They also had a relatively primitive CMO model that couldn't handle the new bonds we had launched that used existing CMO bonds as collateral.

Matching Numbers or Tying Out – When analysts at dealers, accounting firms, issuers or other transaction participants each run multiple sets of assumptions about the assets and liabilities of a deal structure through their computer models, and compare the outputs to be sure that all cash flows and calculations are identical.

Our analytic team spent most of its last month cleaning up our inventory, and providing cash flow runs to our competitors at Nomura so they could debug their models. They had to be able to model every bond correctly, so they could service the customers that had been ours, but were now theirs.

A year later, Nomura was on its way to becoming number one in the commercial mortgage backed securities (CMBS) business.

Ethan Penner, just 33 years old, ran Nomura's CMBS Department. Launching his new department with Daiwa's book of business, he was riding high. A couple of years later he was giving parties featuring headliners like Bob Dylan and Diana Ross, rivaling the famous Predators' Balls Mike Milken used to host for Drexel.

Flying around in his Gulfstream, Ethan was pulling down paychecks rumored to be as high as $45 million a year. Doing complicated real estate financing deals without a lot of due diligence can pay handsomely. Nomura had carved a niche for itself, removing all the hassle that commercial building owners went through with traditional real estate lenders like insurance companies and commercial banks.

Ethan had his chance to make friends with Nomura's management with an apt quote in *The Wall Street Journal*. Instead, he announced, "I'm a credit committee of one." Even if Nomura didn't like it, commercial real estate borrowers loved it. They could convince one person in a single meeting, rather than waiting for a committee to review a proposal.

By 1998, just four years after Nomura got a working CMBS computer model, senior management at the firm accepted Ethan's resignation and injected $530 million into their U.S. commercial mortgage subsidiary. That subsidiary, which had been created to hold the billions of dollars in commercial mortgages and mortgage bonds that Penner's group originated, showed a $275 million loss that year.

Andy, Ethan and Mike all embarrassed the firms they worked for, but that didn't mean the ends of their careers. Far from it. The securitization business was expanding. Everyone wanted to securitize anything they could think of – from the "Bowie bonds" that pledged cash flows from David Bowie's record sales to deals that securitized taxi medallion loans in New York City to deals that compensated electric utilities for canceled nuclear plants using the future increases in electricity rates as collateral.

Andy got another firm, Credit Suisse First Boston (CSFB), to take his knack for trading big risk to the next level in 1995. In a deal he negotiated with John Costas, Head of Fixed Income, Andy got a bonus pool set at 40% of the profit he made for the firm, with personal control over its distribution. In other words, they let him bet big with the house money, and keep nearly half the profit if the bets worked out.

The bet worked out bigtime. The first year, there was no profit to be split according to the formula Costas and Stone had worked out, because Andy's team had come on board close to year-end. Andy had the firm's regular 1995 pool to dole out between 140 existing employees and his newly hired lieutenants.

The traders and bankers who had been with the firm for years said they were "stiffed" on their bonuses for 1995 because Andy gave the lion's share to his new crew. Putting it in context, Wall Street style, that means that there were a lot of poor employees who only got $100,000 or $200,000 instead of a million, although rumor had it that several dozen were told they would get no bonus whatsoever for their prior year's work.

The old CSFB crew threatened a class action suit, and to prevent a trial that all of New York would have enjoyed watching, First Boston CEO Allen Wheat stepped in and created a second bonus pool. That additional pool was paid out to the pre-existing traders, salesmen and bankers in a successful effort to avoid a public spectacle. The sweetheart deal Costas negotiated for Andy cost him his own job within the year.

Andy survived at CSFB several years longer than John did. He invested the parent bank's money heavily in real estate deals, especially in and around New York City. When the market value of all those commercial mortgage loans plunged in late 1998, Andy helped set up an "outside" fund that bought $2.2 billion of the bonds his CSFB group had created. CSFB provided financing to the new fund and Andy negotiated a deal to get management fees paid to him as an "outside" manager while still inside CSFB.

When the whole series of transactions turned out to be a better deal for the new fund and its manager than it was for Credit Suisse First Boston, Andy was on his way out. He spent the better part of a year suing to get what they owed him for his final year – $80 million. In December of 1999, the industry press reported that he was would be collecting close to $100 million as a severance package.

Ethan Penner traded in his G-3 for a G-4 after leaving Nomura, and joined the Silicon Valley private equity gold rush that took place in the late 1990's. He still had enough left over after the dot-com collapse to become a principal in a Los Angeles-based real estate investment fund that specialized in buying properties in the $15 to $70 million range, and continued to take home a hefty paycheck.

In his opinion piece in *The Wall Street Journal* on March 25, 2008, Ethan described the scene at the Los Angeles Convention Center when 2,000 potential buyers each deposited $5,000 to gain entry to an auction of foreclosed houses in southern California. Expressing his faith in the long-term viability of the securitization market, Ethan demonstrated, just by showing up, that he believed some serious money would be made by buying while everyone else was selling. He'd been right before.

Mike Vranos got together with some of his former Kidder colleagues, and a former competitor from Lehman Brothers, and formed a hedge fund. With $100 million from a Harvard college buddy's family investment fund, Mike's Ellington Management Group became the leader among the very specialized bond hedge funds that bought the most esoteric pieces of mortgage deals, seeing value where others saw "toxic waste."

When most of the market values some investments as almost worthless or sky-high, a few "gunslingers" who see a different value can make fortunes and reputations for themselves by exploiting that difference of opinion and converting it into large profits.

One way to do this is to bet that the market prices will change. That kind of directional bet can win big or lose big. That's how the big CDS buyers won big. Some have since managed to lose big after winning with their huge bet against the housing market.

Another way to make money when there are huge gaps in perceptions of value comes from applying the techniques of finance. In the language of the bond market, we call that "capturing spread." A very successful career can come from capturing spread.

CHAPTER TEN

Spread

I've spent my entire financial career focused on one thing in many forms – spread. I'm not alone in this. Every bank, insurance company, brokerage firm, lender, borrower, bond trader and income investor does the same thing. We all share the same goal: To capture spread.

In its simplest sense, spread is profit margin.

Spread can be the difference between two interest rates. For most financial firms, those rates are the rates at which they borrow (also known as the funding cost) and the rates at which they lend (also known as the portfolio yield).

If you're a buyer or lender, and the funding cost is far below the portfolio yield, then management is happy and shareholders (if there are any) are happy. More spread is good if you're on the receiving end. If you're on the paying end, more spread is bad. That's especially true if you're borrowing money.

If you've invested when spread is "thin," and spreads get wider, that's bad, too. For example, if you own a portfolio of bonds or loans, and spreads widen, your portfolio just lost some its value, because any buyer will want more spread to take the investment off your hands. Since the terms of the loans and bonds you own can't be changed, the only way to make them pay a wider spread is to sell them at a discount.

A simplified example will demonstrate how this works. Imagine you own a 5% two-year corporate bond. You bought that bond when the two-year U.S. Treasury Note was paying 4%. We would say you bought the bond at a spread of 1%, or 100 basis points, over the Treasury yield.

Fast forward a bit, and now the market is concerned about corporate credit risk, or about the credit of the company that issued your bond. Now the market demands a spread of 200 basis points (2%) above Treasuries to take that risk. The only way to make your 5% bond pay out a 6% yield is to sell it at a discount of 2%. The bond that you bought for 100 (you paid 100% of its face value, or par) is now only worth 98. You can have a loss in value even though the Treasury rates, or interest rates in general, did not move.

For mortgages, the relationship is the same, but the math is a bit more complicated because loans pay principal and interest every month, and most mortgages pay off before their 30-year maturity. If mortgage spreads were to widen by 100 basis points, the effect on the value of mortgage loans could be a loss of 3% to 5%, or even more.

Spread is everywhere money goes. It comes in many flavors and from a variety of factors. Some of these factors are liquidity, uncertainty, expected maturity and complexity. All these factors are assigned values by the market, and end up being reflected in the spread.

Perhaps the easiest kind of spread to understand is credit spread. If you have good credit, you pay a lower rate; if you have bad credit, you pay a higher rate. A prime mortgage borrower, for example, usually pays a 2% to 3% lower rate than a subprime borrower. The extra spread paid by the subprime borrower compensates the lender and investor for additional credit risk.

Similarly, most banks have good credit and don't pay very much to borrow money. The bank's customers, businesses or individuals, however, could run into difficulties paying back the money they borrow. It certainly happens to them more often than it does to the banks. So customers pay a higher rate to borrow money than their banks do.

The typical spread between banks' borrowing rate and customers' borrowing rates might be 3% per annum. If a bank loses 1% to credit losses each year in its portfolio of small loans, it ends up with a profit of 2% above its own borrowing costs. The bank has captured a spread of 200 basis points in its lending business.

Another common spread that investors try to capture is maturity spread. For most of the last half century, short-term interest rates have been lower than long-term interest rates, even for the same borrower.

The best example of this is the U.S. Treasury, which borrows money for as short a term as three months, and as long a term as thirty years. Every three months, the U.S. Government funds its needs through auctions of its debt obligations, with a mix of two-year, five-year, ten-year and thirty-year debt.

We call the Treasury debt obligations "on the run Treasuries" if they are among the half dozen Treasury issues that the government sells in its regularly scheduled auctions. We chart their yields on graphs and call the resulting graph the "yield curve*." The chart below shows the yield curve in the midst of the crisis, using data from the US Treasury.

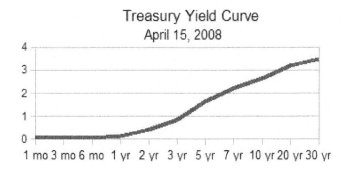

Treasury Yield Curve
April 15, 2008

More frequent auctions handle the short-term cash needs of the government by issuing three-month and six-month Treasury "Bills" or "T Bills." The two-year, five-year and ten-year obligations are called Treasury "Notes." Only twenty-year and thirty-year maturities are called Treasury "Bonds."

* Treasury Yield Curve – The family of tradeable obligations (Bills, Notes and Bonds) of the U.S. Treasury that span the range of maturities from three months to thirty years and are regularly auctioned to fund the U.S. Government's current deficit, and refinancing of debt as it matures.

There are a number of plausible explanations for why the longer maturity Treasuries yield more than the shorter ones, including perceived risk of inflation over a long period, deficit spending lowering the value of the dollar in the future, or even supply versus demand, as investors need a place to hold cash for a short while.

The first book I was told to read when I got to Wall Street was the Sydney Homer and Martin Liebowitz classic, Inside the Yield Book. The book explores the relationship between rates of various maturities, which was the basis for a 1982 structured finance invention credited to Liebowitz when he was at Salomon Brothers.

In 1982, the yield on the long bond was quite a bit higher than the yields for shorter Treasury Bills and Notes. Salomon Brothers created a trust to hold thirty-year Treasury Bonds. By "stripping off" the interest payments from the bonds, Salomon sold fifty-nine separate small bonds that were paid off by the twenty-nine and a half years of semiannual interest payments and one big bond that had a thirty-year maturity.

Salomon bought the undivided Treasury Bond at a high yield, much higher than the six-month T-bill, the one-year T-bill, and even the five-year and ten-year Treasury Notes. That gave them enough extra yield spread to give the first little bond a few basis points more yield than the six-month T-bill, the next bond a little more yield than the regular one-year T-bill got, and so on down the line. All the rest of the excess yield spread from the bonds was profit for Salomon, captured from the maturity spread.

It took some time for the market to realize that the price volatility risk was higher for the bonds that paid no interest before maturity than it was for bonds that paid interest regularly throughout their lives. At first, the market treated the new securities as a kind of free lunch. They were called Zero Coupon bonds, and sold for deep discounts, since the yield came from getting a single payment in the future. You can think of it as paying fifty cents today to get a dollar ten years from now, which is equivalent to getting a 7.05% yield on your investment.

Several other Wall Street dealers copied Salomon's idea, and soon there were a number of different private label bond issuance programs that bought long maturity Treasuries, and offered a series of smaller bonds that paid off when each Treasury interest payment was due.

Salomon's program was called CATS, or Certificates of Accrual on Treasury Securities. Soon, Merrill Lynch introduced TIGRs (Treasury Income Growth Receipts), and Lehman Brothers created

LIONs (Lehman Investment Opportunity Notes). We called them the felines, and they filled a purpose for anyone needing specific payments on specific dates.

Eventually the Treasury itself took advantage of this opportunity, and gave investors the ability to create their own zero coupon "strips." This saved some of the cost of funding for the government and didn't have the extra, albeit tiny, risk that the Trust might not pay the investors.

After the Treasury started to issue zero coupon bonds, it made no sense for investment banks to spend money to create special Trusts to hold Treasury Bonds and pay off the "feline" zero coupon bonds with their cash flows.

The investment strategies used by thrifts (Savings and Loans) and other investors also try to capture maturity spread. We call it "borrowing short and lending long."

A thirty-year mortgage pays a higher yield than the bank accounts and CD's the bank uses to fund itself, because those CD's and bank accounts have much shorter maturities. This worked just fine until the rates on CD's and bank accounts went up. Then the long maturity mortgages with their low yields were a problem.

The yield premium that an illiquid investment (like a mortgage or business loan) pays is another kind of spread investors like to capture. A bank spends money and time checking out each borrower before making a loan. However, if it wanted to sell its loans, any new buyer would want to perform due diligence of their own. Banks make loans knowing they may not be able to sell them easily or quickly.

Certainly if a bank wanted to sell its individual and small business loans quickly to raise cash, it would have to offer a substantial discount to the buyer. That lack of liquidity necessitates that borrowers pay a high enough interest rate to compensate for the bank's potential costs. The borrower pays what we call a yield spread for the bank's lack of liquidity, and the bank collects it.

If a bank can turn its illiquid, high-yielding loans into easily traded securities, it can monetize all the years of extra yield spread associated with lack of liquidity.

Securitization solved the problem, first by making mortgages into MBS that could be traded easily, and later by making all sorts of other loans – car loans, credit card loans, student loans and even corporate loans – into securities.

Borrowers benefited. By the time it was common to securitize mortgage loans in the 1980's, prime mortgage borrowers were paying a spread above bank CD rates that had dropped from around 300 to 400 basis points to just 150 basis points. Once there was a market to extract the liquidity yield spread premium from the loans, that premium began to shrink, just as happened with Treasury strips.

Still another way to capture spread is to lower the uncertainty and complexity. The more uncertainty or complexity, the more yield premium (spread) a bond investor will get. We can see this in the yields of Ginnie Mae MBS. Ginnie Mae mortgage bonds have the "full faith and credit" guarantee of the U.S. Government. That is exactly the same language that describes the guarantee on Treasury Bills, Notes and Bonds.

Because the payments of principal and interest in a mortgage come every month for up to thirty years, and because the amount of principal can vary as borrowers pay off their mortgages before maturity, Ginnie Mae MBS have to offer additional yield spread over regular Treasuries.

Part of the yield spread offered by Ginnie Mae MBS comes from their natural complexity. Another part comes from the option belonging to the borrowers of paying off their mortgages before maturity. We can call that second part of the yield spread the "option spread," or "option premium" which compensates an investor for the risk that borrowers might pay off their mortgages at any time.

As we delve more deeply into the concept of spread, we need to expand the definition of spread from a single rate comparison to a comparison with an entire family of related rates.

When I started in the business, every bond's yield was compared to the yield you could get investing in Treasuries. Doing so was easy if you had a straight five-year bond that paid interest for four and a half years, and then paid a final interest payment and the principal. We called those "bullet" bonds because the principal paid off all at once. A bond like this has a payment schedule exactly like a five-year Treasury Note, so comparing its yield to a government bond is easy.

To get the spread of the five-year bond over the five-year Treasury, just subtract the Treasury yield from the other bond's yield, and you have the spread. Treasury yields move up and down all the time, but the relative risk of a bond issuer versus the Treasury changes more slowly. The market adopted the convention decades ago of buying and selling all bonds based on a yield spread over Treasuries.

Calculating a price for most regular corporate bonds or Treasury Bonds is straightforward, but mortgages are different. That's because every month, homeowners make a payment that is part principal and part interest. In million dollar pools like Ginnie Mae's, if one of the borrowers in the pool pays off a mortgage early, there's an extra-large principal payment in that month, amounting to 5% to 20% of the principal.

One way to look at the spread in a Ginnie Mae mortgage pass-through involves measuring how much principal is paid each month, and multiplying that principal payment by the time it takes to receive the payment. Once all the payments are received, the sum of these products of time and dollars is divided by the dollars received. That leaves an average time, in years, that it took to get the principal paid back. Since each payment has a "weight" equal to the dollars in that payment, and because the result is measured in years, we call the result the "weighted average life" or abbreviate it to "average life." Using the average life gave us an easy single-point comparison between Treasury yields and mortgage yields – i.e., the spread.

The problem, of course, is that we don't know on Day One how fast a single mortgage loan, or even a pool of loans, will pay off. A very simple way to deal with this for a mortgage pass-through is to simply look at the history of millions of mortgages, and find the average for mortgages paying their principal, along with the fastest and the slowest meaningful samples (for example, the fastest 10% and slowest 10%).

By running various prepayment scenarios, a mortgage pass-through would show a meaningful variance in its potential average life. Returning to the average lives for these various prepayment speeds, we could measure the spread over Treasuries for several potential outcomes. If investors were satisfied that they would get a decent spread over Treasuries under most possible future scenarios, the bond was worth buying.

That was good enough during the time in which the thirty-year mortgage pass-through was the only available mortgage-backed security.

But when the mortgage market started carving the cash flows of mortgages into separate tranches, with rules about distributing principal payments, a more precise spread measurement needed to be developed.

It was a method to measure the spread over the entire Treasury yield curve, taking into account the variability of future payments of principal.

Research enabled us to predict prepayment behavior reasonably well. By using mortgage rates, yearly seasonality and general economic conditions as the main independent variables, the analytic groups I ran, and others like it, developed prepayment models to predict month-by-month prepayment behavior.

To be accurate about the future cash flows from the MBS, we had to correctly predict mortgage rates, seasonality, unemployment and inflation, among other things. The only one we consistently got right was seasonality, with slight variances from year to year depending on weather events like big blizzards or major summer storm systems, and where holidays fell.

The other inputs to the prepayment model were much harder. We did not know the future path of interest rates or the economy, but the method of calculating "implied forward" rates came to be accepted as a method of predicting the future for interest rates.

Here's how implied forward rates work: The Treasury has both one-year debt and two-year debt in the market, and each pays a different rate. Let's say the one-year bond pays 4% and the two-year bond pays 5%. The theory behind implied forward rates says that investing in U.S. Treasuries for two years should give the same return, whether you do it as a single two-year investment or as two one-year investments, one right after the other.

The 4% one-year bond would give the investor $1.04 at the end of the first year. The investor in the 2-year bond would have (approximately) $1.10 at the end of two years. In order for the two investments to be equivalent, the buyer for the one-year bond should be able to reinvest their $1.04 for another year to arrive at a total of $1.10 at the end of the second year.

To invest $1.04 for a year and end up with $1.10, you would need to get close to a 6% yield in the second year. Even though the rate for one year is 4% and the rate for two years is 5%, the "implied forward" one-year rate is actually almost 6%. As this example shows, the implied future short-term rate in an upward-sloping yield curve is higher than the rates anywhere along that curve.

Strong empirical arguments can be made that implied forward rates are not a reliable predictor of future interest rates. Still, any analysis of future investment performance needs a way to predict the path of future interest rates. Besides, if we can't agree on this method to predict future interest rates, what alternative do we have?

We all know that we can't predict the future of interest rates exactly, but if we have a way of predicting the future range of interest rates, we can analyze our investments in light of multiple future rate environments.

The option market can help with these predictions. The interest rate markets have options on future interest rates. Some of these are directly traded, and others are embedded in the rates that are part of interest rate swaps*. Because one counterparty in an interest rate swap makes payments of a short maturity interest rate measured multiple times in the future, the swap market includes an implied volatility of interest rates for years into the future.

Interest Rate Swap – Standardized contract in which one party pays the short maturity (floating) interest rate that resets periodically, and the other party pays the life-of-contract fixed rate. In practice, the payments are the difference between the floating rate interest due and the fixed rate interest due on each payment date.

From these markets, we have the volatility of rates that the market expects in the future. Volatility is simply the amount of up and down movement that can be expected. By using the observed volatility, we can create a family of possible future interest rates. If we put all the paths of rates on a single graph, they look like a "cloud" of paths that gets wider as time passes, the way a trombone's bell widens out from the body of the instrument.

By centering that cloud of rate paths around the implied forward rates so that half the paths are above the implied forward rate path and half below, we have a consistent set of future economic environments to use in our models to project future cash flows.

When we model these hundreds of future economic environments and cash flows associated with those paths in mortgage-backed securities, we fill in the cloud of future possibilities.

Calculating the difference in yield between an MBS or a CMO bond and the Treasury rates along each path, and then adding up the spreads along all those paths, we can arrive at a single average spread over the Treasury for the mortgage security.

Since this single spread takes the borrower prepayment option into account, we call the resulting spread the "Option Adjusted Spread," or OAS*. In times of more uncertainty or volatility, this spread tends to go up, and in times of more complacency and less volatility, this spread goes down.

OAS, or Option-Adjusted Spread – the average yield spread of one investment above another over a number of future interest rate paths that are constructed to reflect the current market's implied future rates and expected volatility of those rates.

When I entered the business, the Treasury issued many more "benchmark," or "on-the-run" debt instruments. We had issues of three-month, six-month and twelve-month T-bills, along with two-year, three-year, four-year, five-year, seven-year and ten-year Treasury Notes. We even had two regularly issued Treasury Bonds, the twenty-year and thirty-year "long bonds." In other words, we had a very full family of Treasuries to measure against. Today, that family of eleven members has shrunk to only seven.

As the Treasury eliminated its regular auctions of some of the benchmark Bills, Notes and Bonds, another strong shift was occurring in the market.

The interbank market (where banks lend to each other) was undergoing a revolution with the standardization of interest rate swaps.

Companies of all sorts were moving their funding to the LIBOR market.

During the 1990's, the U.S. Treasury yield curve lost its status as the benchmark against which all other interest rates were compared. It was effectively replaced by the interest rate swap curve, or LIBOR curve*, which measures the rates for LIBOR from overnight out to thirty years.

In just twenty-six years from the first swap (between IBM and the World Bank in 1981), the swap (or interest rate derivative*) market grew to a total face amount of $347.09 trillion dollars according to the International Swap and Derivatives Association 2007 mid-year survey of the major swap dealers.

* LIBOR Curve - A yield curve of the benchmark swap rates. Swap rates are available in the market for every maturity from overnight to thirty years, making it easier to reference than the much sparser Treasury curve.

* Derivative – A security whose price is derived from external asset prices or events. The most common derivatives are futures contracts, options, swaps and insurance policies.

Naturally enough, the mortgage market shifted its emphasis from OAS to LIBOR OAS, or LOAS. Since LIBOR is a bank rate and most MBS are better credit quality than most banks, LOAS for MBS can often be a negative spread.

So, what's the lesson in all this? First, that capturing spread nearly always involves taking on some kind of risk or eliminating a perceived risk. Second, that only speculators base their investment choices on the level of interest rates. Finally, that all financials live and die by the spread they can lend or invest at, and the spread they can borrow or use to finance their activities.

Put another way – if the spread on your portfolio or your borrowing goes up ("widens"), then times are bad. If your borrowing spread goes down, times are good. If the spread the market uses to value your portfolio "tightens," then your portfolio has gone up in value.

For investors that capture credit spread, most use less leverage than guaranteed MBS investors use, but they still use leverage of 4-1 or higher because the 2% or 3% per year in captured spread is not enough to get equity investors very excited.

Capturing maturity spread in securitizations can be profitable, but the spread is often very narrow after bets on the direction of the market are removed. For most of the past three decades, an investor in mortgage pass-throughs could only capture about 50 to 80 basis points of spread after hedging out the risk of rates rising or falling and after hedging away some of the prepayment option risk. With such a small potential profit margin, most MBS investors used leverage of 10-1 or more to increase their returns.

Capturing liquidity spread by securitization is even more levered, running 20-1 or higher. The only positive aspect of this kind of securitization leverage is that it usually does not require that the investor deposit more money when the value of the assets decline. We call that kind of financing "matched funding" or "term" financing, and it is inherently a less dangerous way to borrow because there are no margin calls.

It's a fact of life in the credit markets that when spreads widen, they widen for almost every kind of debt. The result can be large losses in value, even if the bonds in question have no fundamental problems. If leverage is involved, the losses can be magnified just the way the profits are magnified when times are good.

CHAPTER ELEVEN

The ABCs of Securitization

There can be little argument that securitization has revolutionized finance in nearly every market around the world. In essence, it enables lenders who know their borrowers to make and service loans, while letting investors without local expertise participate as capital-providers, with good risk-adjusted returns.

Securitization allows lenders to "recycle" their capital, extracting a substantial liquidity premium from the rates paid, and sharing that premium among the other participants in the process – the borrower and the investor.

By dividing the cash flows of the underlying asset among several or more investors, securitization caters to investors with distinct needs for assets, and varying appetites for risk.

In general, I feel that if you thoroughly understand something, then you can explain it to any reasonably intelligent person in terms they will understand. On the other hand, when something is inherently complicated, simplifying the explanation too much can have the same effect as intentionally misleading.

American fixed-rate mortgages are complicated. The day the lender pays out the mortgage in cash and takes back a lien against a house, that lender has given the borrower a call option*, good for the next thirty years, to pay off the mortgage early.

*Call Option – A derivative instrument that allows a call buyer to purchase a financial instrument at a defined price over a given period of time. In the stock market, usually the right to "call" 100 shares from the seller at a fixed price until a given date.

Before we get too deeply into the embedded call options in a mortgage, we need to back up and clarify who is the buyer and who is the seller in the basic mortgage.

Unfortunately, a widely repeated fallacy is that a mortgage lender sells a mortgage to a borrower. The exact opposite is true. A mortgage is a promise to pay principal and interest over time, secured by a piece of real estate. A lender pays cash for that promise. The homeowner has sold a mortgage in exchange for cash. Once we are clear that the borrower sold the mortgage to the lender, we can talk about the borrower's option to buy back the mortgage by prepaying the loan.

The right to buy a financial instrument at fixed terms at some point in the future is a call option. In the language of the option markets, the owner of that option can "call" the financial asset away from its owner. That's exactly what a mortgage borrower does when paying off the mortgage early ("prepaying").

If a borrower had a 9% mortgage and rates fell to 7% two years later, the mortgage lender would still like to keep collecting the 9%. Since most of the risk to investors from early payment of mortgage loans comes when interest rates fall, the call option in mortgages is usually thought of as an interest rate option.

This call option was exercised as borrowers took advantage of lower rates in the early 1990's, often refinancing so quickly that lenders never recovered their expenses from originating the loans.

As the flood of prepayments rose, investors in mortgage securities made from pools of those loans found themselves paid off in just two or three years rather than the ten years they had anticipated.

When mortgage bonds yielding 9% or 10% were suddenly called away in the early 90's, more than one insurance company or pension fund was left scrambling to find replacements for the lost yield. To obtain credit quality equivalent to that of the mortgage bonds they had held, they often had to settle for reinvesting at 6%. To obtain equivalent yield from anything other than mortgage bonds, they had to take a lot more credit risk, interest rate risk, or some other risk like political risk or currency risk by investing overseas.

It is possible to mitigate early payment call (prepayment) risk with specific CMO structures. For example, there was one bond structure a customer and I designed that actually extended maturity when the pool of mortgages paid off faster. But one of the difficult aspects of designing mortgage-backed securities is figuring out what all the future performance "paths" might look like and how likely they are to happen.

Once we arrive at a universe of potential outcomes for the cash coming from the mortgage loans, the next problem is deciding how much extra yield an investor should be paid to risk any negative outcome, and how much yield the risk-averse investor should give up to avoid the same risks. For the deal structurer, this usually involves working with both the risk-friendly and the risk-averse investor at the same time, "tweaking" the deal payment rules until the risk-friendly investor has enough reward given to them by the risk-averse investor.

Another way to address the cost of the early payment call (prepayment) option is to charge the borrower for it, in the form of a prepayment penalty. Prepayment penalties allow lenders to recoup the costs of originating mortgages. The elimination of prepayment penalties, while superficially easing terms for borrowers, ultimately results in harsher terms if it forces lenders to raise mortgage rates.

Since the meltdown, we are painfully aware of another option borrowers have that lenders gave them – the credit "put*."

After six decades of steadily rising house prices nationwide, lenders didn't take into account the fact that lending the entire purchase price of a house (or close to it) could tempt a borrower to stop paying the mortgage.

* Put Option – The option the holder has to sell (force another to buy) a financial instrument. Typically, the option seller collects a cash premium for giving the put option holder the right to "put" the stock or bond to the counter-party who wrote the option.

In effect, borrowers can "put" or sell their houses to their lenders in exchange for not paying back their mortgages. Lenders are then effectively forced to buy houses for the amount they lent.

There were regions of the country where house prices had fallen below the levels of their mortgage balances before, during periods of economic slowdown. But in those days, most of the low down payment lending had been to good credit borrowers who had the income needed to keep paying the loans. As borrowers with good credit records, they also had something to lose (their good credit score) if they chose to exercise their "put" option and have the bank take the house.

It was different when lenders offered 100% financing to subprime borrowers, and the risk of lenders owning the properties they mortgaged became even greater if borrowers withheld documentation of their income.

Now we see the first level of complexity: The lender/investor has given the borrower both a call (on interest rates) and a put (on credit and house prices). Evaluating those borrower options over a thirty-year horizon isn't as simple as valuing a stock option over a three-month window.

The next level of complexity relates to the asset itself. Every house is different, and so is every borrower. Standardization of legal forms, insurance, mortgage products and registration systems exists, but houses and the debt held against them will never be identical the way one share of XYZ Corp is the same as another share of XYZ Corp.

In a mortgage security, some of this variance is addressed by having thousands of loans in a single pool. By examining the characteristics and dispersion (stratifications) of the pools, a prudent investor can see how much variance there is outside the averages and evaluate the investment risk based on how many loans fall far outside the averages for the pool, and in what ways.

Investors can also get a wealth of data on dozens of different factors for every house and every borrower. The most precise method of predicting future performance of the loan pool would be to predict on a loan-by-loan basis. Unfortunately, that doesn't work because each borrower has a wide range of possible future actions.

The best predictions come from identifying characteristics which increase or decrease the probability of prepayment, home sale, or credit difficulties, and then breaking the pool of mortgages into sub-pools along the divisions made for those characteristics.

By modeling the performance of the high-LTV loans versus normal LTV loans versus low LTV loans, and then sub-dividing according to geography, verification of income, and credit score, we are able to divide a large collateral pool into manageable and predictable groups of loans.

The complexity that gets the most criticism from the press and others who are not directly involved in the mortgage market is the number of different tranches in a single deal (a typical deal has ten to twenty). Since the same pool of underlying loans collateralizes all the bonds, there is a dynamic relationship among the bonds that shifts over time as borrowers make monthly payments, become delinquent or default, or pay off their loans early.

Overlooked by the critics is the fact that the different tranches in a deal are specifically created to meet investor demand. The notion that investors don't know what bonds they are buying (and why) is held only by those outside the market.

Nevertheless, investors always take on some form, or many forms, of risk.

In a market with crazy demand like the one we saw through much of 2004, 2005 and 2006, investors risked not knowing as much as they might have wanted to about the bonds they were buying, but not because of ignorance. Rather, the reason was that they didn't have the time. Investors that wanted to take the time to examine the collateral closely were shut out from investing in deals because the deals were often oversubscribed minutes after announcement, long before there was time to do the analysis that used to be customary. There was simply no time to find the hidden gems or to avoid the hidden potholes.

A new dimension of risk had been brought into the securitization business. The overwhelming demand for securitized bonds forced investors who wanted to participate to make their decisions on limited analysis, and to rely on the credit ratings as a substitute for due diligence. Sloppy credit underwriting practices couldn't be identified and avoided. Aggressive performance assumptions based on a housing market that was unusually bullish for a long time may have also pushed aside prudent analysis of both the upside and the downside.

Those few long-term securitized product investors that tried to avoid the mania turned in lower performance statistics than their more optimistic competitors that were buying everything with a little higher yield. Those conservative investors experienced fund withdrawals as their performance lagged.

Some investors and speculators outside the securitization specialty could see that it had gone too far, and bet against the securitized bonds and the companies that relied on securitization for their funding, or on housing sales for their profits. Amazingly enough, these bets had no limits, or limits that existed but were ignored.

A limit that was ignored was the requirement that stock sold short on US stock exchanges must be delivered to the buyer, which means the short seller needs to borrow that stock from a genuine owner, and pay them to borrow that stock. That often didn't happen. One smaller mortgage lender was listed as having undelivered stock beyond legal limits for more than a year.

And there were no limits at all on the amount of bonds that could be sold short "synthetically" via Credit Default Swaps. Though CDS were introduced as a means of insuring or hedging against credit losses for bond investors or lenders, they became a very popular way for people to make pure directional bets on the credit markets. That use, pure speculation, became the dominant reason people bought them after the rules changed in 2006.

Until then, most CDS contracts required the holder of a CDS contract to deliver the defaulted bond or loan in order to be paid for losses on that credit. In that way, it was like car insurance, where you can't get the check for your "totaled" car unless you sign over the title to the insurance company. By the time the housing market was heading south, CDS speculators had bought "insurance" against BBB mortgage bonds that amounted to more than 100 times the face amount of those bonds.

It was this multiplier effect that made a correction into a crisis.

CHAPTER TWELVE

Zen Lessons

There's a reason why most reporters, politicians and even some investors think Wall Street uses complexity to hide larceny.

Securitizations are complex to begin with, and there's no way around that. It's not only the complicated mathematics and the specialized language. There are also the legal documents.

The "rules" for handling the money in MBS, which define how the cash flows from the mortgages relate to the bonds, are complicated for a reason, and the reason is not to hide larceny. The rules *have to be* complicated, because they have to be set up to deal with every future situation, no matter how unlikely. For example, what happens if all the borrowers pay off their mortgages early? What if none do? What if they default? What if they are called up on active military duty and Congress gives them a holiday on paying their mortgage interest? What if interest rates go to 25%? To 0%? And so on.

Today, virtually every kind of securitization exists, and the rules are pretty standardized. But it wasn't always that way.

Almost thirty years ago, when I was in my first job on Wall Street, securitizations were less commodities than they were trade secrets. The mortgage groups that invented a new kind of bond could make a lot of money before liquidity, in the form of multiple deals, and transparency, in the form of disclosure, made the market efficient and the profits thin.

Back then, the newest and most profitable thing in the mortgage world was the CMO, and my job at A.G. Becker was to write computer programs that helped our traders and sales people do their jobs. My goal was to figure out how the CMO really worked, not only so we could model it, but so that we could improve on it.

We were at a disadvantage when new CMO deals came out, because we didn't have computer programs to model the cash flows from new bonds. Since we couldn't calculate the prices for the bonds ourselves, we had to wait for the lead managers, typically Salomon Brothers or First Boston, to fax us copies of the price-yield tables they printed out for their own sales and trading groups. Of course, that usually only happened after all the big customers had already been offered all the bonds by those other dealers.

Because yields are based on time, the price-yield tables also became slightly incorrect the day after they were calculated, and they became more inaccurate as time went on. We needed to calculate our own price-yield tables. With the kind of approach that only the very young or very dedicated can pursue (I was both), I looked at the price-yield tables we got from Salomon Brothers and First Boston as a kind of Rosetta Stone, and believed that they held the key to understanding CMO deals.

I kept all the price-yield tables and worked on my computer model. If my programs were correctly modeling the CMOs, then my numbers would match the numbers on the printouts in front of me.

This approach almost worked. I started out by modeling the undivided MBS bonds, and ended up matching all the price-yield tables we had. Then I moved on to the first handful of deals which set up CMO bonds to be paid in sequence from the mortgages. When tranche A was fully paid off, then tranche B would begin to get principal, and so on. Soon, I could match the numbers on those deals, too.

But I was having problems with the newest twist on the CMO – the Z-bond*. Even though I could correctly model the mortgage cash flows, I couldn't figure out why I couldn't "tie out" with the numbers, and why the yield

*Z-bond – Also known as an accrual bond because the interest due is added to the principal balance of the bond in each payment period. That interest amount is used to pay down principal on other classes of the deal. Once those other bonds are paid off, the Z-bond begins to get both principal and interest.

would vary for a couple of the bonds under a few different scenarios.

It turned out that my problem with the Z-bond had nothing to do with my modeling. The problem was that I hadn't read enough. All I'd read was the one document which I assumed would tell me everything I needed to know to model the bonds. After all, most stock and bond deals are sold by providing investors with a single, long document full of warnings, legal definitions, and descriptions of the securities.

We called this document a "prospectus," since that was the most common offering document in the securities business. It became a generic term even though the Freddie Mac CMOs were described in Offering Circulars and state housing authorities distributed Offering Memorandums.

For CMO deals, the prospectus was a two-part document: a "base" prospectus that was a hundred to a hundred and fifty pages of small type, and a "prospectus supplement" that was another thirty to a hundred pages relating only to the specific deal being sold.

The base prospectus for the deal that contained the Z-bond told me that I needed to read another document: The Trust Indenture. This last document was where I discovered why an odd bit of cash kept cropping up here and there as I tried to model the Z-bond.

The Trust Indenture was a pile of lawyerese nearly four inches thick, that described how the Trustee was to handle all the cash flows from the collateral mortgages or MBS, and distribute them to the various bond holders and to the sponsor of the deal. It told me that the additional bit of cash came from reinvesting the mortgage cash flows before paying the bonds. Ah ha!

From then on, I read everything I could get my hands on for every deal. I found out that scattered among the thousands of pages the lawyers drafted were usually between five and twenty pages that described the actual formulas used to handle the money between bond payments, where the cash could be invested while waiting for the next bond payment, when it was due, what happened if it wasn't paid to the Trustee when due, etc.

It wasn't too long before I was inventing new bonds and giving the lawyers formulae and diagrams showing the relationship between them. It was up to the lawyers to describe in the prospectus and other offering documents how the cash flows were apportioned under any and all future scenarios.

The description of the bonds in the offering documents for these deals was like a Zen riddle. You couldn't speed read; you really needed to meditate. Unlike the terse but poetic Zen riddle, the riddles for securitized products came in the form of documents incorporating lengthy and nearly unintelligible text. Amazingly enough, the lawyers never wrote numbers as numbers, fractions as fractions, or algebraic equations in the formats we all learned in high school. Instead, they wrote everything in words, using dependent clauses and referring to definitions scattered throughout the document, all in long, run-on sentences.

Check out this single sentence describing the "waterfall" of principal payments in FHLMC Series 1167, issued in late 1991. I structured the deal, and it's hard to follow, even for me.

On each Payment Date:

(a) The Class 1167-C and Class 1167-D Accrual Amount will be allocated as follows:

First, to the payment of principal on the Class 1167-A, Class 1167-B , Class 1167-C and Class 1167-D Multiclass PCs, in that order (so that no payment of principal will be made on any such Class until the principal amount of each preceding such Class has been reduced to zero), until each such Class has received its Targeted Amount (as defined below) for such Payment Date;

Second, to the payment of principal on the Class 1167-H Multiclass PCs, until such Class has received its Targeted Amount for such Payment Date;

Third, to the payment of principal on the Class 1167-A, Class 1167-B, and Class 1167-H Multiclass PCs, in that order, until the principal amount of each such Class has been reduced to zero;

Fourth, to the concurrent payment of principal on the Class 1167-O and Class 1167-P Multiclass PCs, in proportion to their respective original principal amounts, until the principla amounts thereof have been reduced to zero; and

Fifth, to the payment of principal on the Class 1167-C and Class 1167-D Multiclass PCs, in that order;

(b) the Class 1167-F Accrual Amount will be allocated as follows:

First, to the concurrent payment of principal on the Class 1167-O and Class 1167-P Multiclass PCs, in proportion to their respective original principal amounts, until the principla amounts thereof have been reduced to zero;

Second, to the payment of principal of the Class 1167-H, Class 1167-C, Class 1167-D and Class 1167-F Multiclass PCs, in that order;

(c) the Class 1167-J and 1167-K Accrual Amounts will be allocated as follows:

First, on or after December 15, 1999 and only for so long as the Class 1167-H Multiclass PCs remain outstanding, concurrently (i) 99.9% to the equal and concurrent payment of principal on the Class 1167-E and Class 1167-H Multiclass PCs and (ii) 0.1% to the payment of principal on the Class 1167-G Multiclass PCs, until the Class 1167-E Multiclass PCs have received their Targeted Amount for such Payment Date;

Second, concurrently 99.9% to the payment of principal on the Class 1167-H Multiclass PCs 0.1% to the payment of principal on the Class 1167-G Multiclass PCs have received their Targeted Amount for such Payment Date;

Third, on and after December 15, 1999 and only for so long as the Class 1167-I Multiclass PCs remain outstanding, concurrently (i) 50% to the payment of principal on the Class 1167-E and Class 1167-G Multiclass PCs, in the ratio of 999 to1, and (ii) 50% to the payment of principal on the Class 1167-I Multiclass PCs, until the Class 1167-E Multiclass PCs have received their Targeted Amount for such Payment Date; and

Fourth, to the payment of principal on the Class 1167-I Multiclass PCs, until the principal amount thereof has been reduced to zero;

(d).1/20,001 of the Mortgage Security Principal Payment Amount will be allocated to the equal and concurrent payment of principal on the Class 1167-R and Class 1167-RS Multiclass PCs; and

(e).the remainder of the Mortgage Security Principal Payment Amount plus the remainder, if any, f the Class 1167-J and Class 1167-K Accrual Amounts (together, the "Remaining Principal Payment Amount") will be allocated as follows:

First, On December 15, 1991, to the payment o f principal on the Class 1167-A Multiclass PCs in the Amount of $1,580 (or, in the event of any proportionate increase in the original principal amounts of the Multiclass PCs as described under "General" above, such amount increase by the same proportion);

Second, concurrently (i) 99.9% to the payment of principal on the Class 1167-A, Class 1167-B, Class 1167-C, Class 1167-D, and Class 1167-F Multiclass PCs in that order, and (ii) 0.1% to the payment of principal on the Class 1167-G Multiclass PCs, until each of the Classes listed in subclause (i) has received its Target Amount for such Payment Date;

Third, concurrently 99.9% to the payment of principal on the Class 1167-E Multiclass PCs and 0.1% to the payment of principal on the Class 1167-G Multiclass PCs, until the Class 1167-E Multiclass PCs have received their Targeted Amount for such Payment Date;

Fourth, concurrently 99.9% to the payment of principal on the Class 1167-H Multiclass PCs and 0.1% to the payment of principal on the Class 1167-G Multiclass PCs, until the Class 1167-H Multiclass PCs have received their Targeted Amount for such Payment Date;

Fifth, to the payment of principal on the Class 1167-I, Class 1167-J and Class 1167-K Multiclass PCs, in that order, until the principal amount of each such Class has been reduced to zero;

Sixth, to the concurrent payment of principal on the Class 1167-L, Class 1167-M and Class 1167-N Muticlass PCs, until the principal amounts thereof have been reduced to zero;

Seventh, concurrently (i) 99.9% to the payment of principal on the Class 1167-A, Class 1167-B and Class 1167-H Multiclass PCs, in that order, and (ii) 0.1% to the payment of principal on the Class 1167-G Multiclass PCs, until principal amount of Class 1167-H Multiclass PCs has been reduced to zero;

Eighth, concurrently (i) 99.9% to the payment of principal on the Class 1167-O and Class 1167-P Multiclass PCs, in proportion to their original principal amounts, and (ii) 0.1% to the payment of principal on the Class 1167-G Multiclass PCs, until the principal amounts of the Class 1167-O and Class 1167-P Multiclass PCs have been reduced to zero; and

Ninth, (i) 99.9% to the payment of principal on the Class 1167-C, Class 1167-D, Class 1167-F and Class 1167-E Multiclass PCs, in that order, and (ii) 0.1% to the payment of principal on the Class 1167-G Multiclass PCs, until the principal amount of each such Class has been reduced to zero.

That's a deal from Freddie Mac and it has a credit guarantee. Believe it or not, it gets worse for deals without a credit guarantee. In addition to rules describing the payment of mortgage principal and interest like the one above, there are rules that allocate credit losses among the classes, rules that allocate recoveries from sale of foreclosed houses, rules that deal with paying for insurance and allocating insurance settlements, rules that pay for interest rate hedges and rules that allocate distribution of cash that comes from those hedges when interest rates move.

Remarkably enough, all the documents are called the "disclosure documents" by the lawyers who create them. Even a casual observer could tell that they were written to do almost anything other than disclose, especially in the early days when knowing how to model a CMO was a huge competitive advantage to a Wall Street firm.

It would be easy to jump to the conclusion that because of all this mumbo-jumbo and obfuscation that customers really didn't have any idea what they were buying. Especially if you didn't know about the "deal sheets."

Before the prospectus and all the other documents were written, customers got to see what we called the deal sheet, which was a single piece of paper. The deal sheet gave expected yields and prices for all the bonds and summarized how the bonds would perform under a wide range of future interest rate environments, along with a summary of the key characteristics of the mortgage collateral for the deal.

In fact, until fairly recently, most of the new deal structures were created to meet the needs of a specific customer who was often a participant in the structuring of the deal. Over the years, the models became standardized and the structures familiar, and innovation is no longer as important now that the profit advantage is missing from the equation. Accordingly, by the 1990's, scattering the whole story among several documents was uncommon, and it's almost unheard of today.

Before leaving the issue of documents behind, it's important to touch on the "Pooling and Servicing Agreement," or "PSA," which is at the heart of the controversy over mitigating losses in the mortgage market by forgiving some of the debt.

The PSA is a document for securitizations made directly from mortgage loans rather than from MBS. It lays out how and when the mortgage servicer is to collect the monthly payments and forward them to the Trustee, along with the procedure to follow in foreclosing a loan, how to determine whether to offer modified terms to borrowers, and how monies advanced to the Trust by the servicer will be repaid, along with a myriad of other specifics that define the relationships between and among the borrower, the servicer, the Trustee, and the bondholders.

A few overly simplistic bears would like the world to believe that pressuring servicers into modifying loan terms or forgiving some of the mortgage debt is breaking the most sacred of all business covenants – the contract between the borrower and the lender. *Not exactly.*

Most Pooling and Servicing Agreements provide for this kind of modification in the interest of the bondholders, but it is typically limited to no more than 5% or 10% of the loans in the pool.

A few investors arguing with a bias that supports their trading positions say loan modifications must be avoided at all costs, but cooler heads know that as long as the loans are dealt with one at a time under the PSA's, the contracts for servicing will not have been broken.

This controversy does point to a weakness in the process of securitization. By creating multiple classes of ownership in a single pool of assets, you can end up with future conflicts of interest among the participants in the deals.

That includes Uncle Sam, the guest that seems to invite himself to every financial repast. When Uncle Sam comes to dinner, he usually changes the rules of how the dinner is to be cooked and eaten. We'll see a lot of our Uncle's strange rules when we look at the unintended consequences of the tax laws in a later chapter.

There is also a specialized class of lawyers for securitizations whose sole professional goal is to keep Uncle Sam from taxing each interest payment twice. These lawyers are called the "40 Act" specialists. Each and every time we did a deal, we paid them handsomely to assure us that the Securities Act of 1940 did not apply. Their legal specialty is particularly Zen in its focus on not doing something.

Having traveled the path to creating new mortgage bonds, I left my own trail of Zen riddles that later financial pilgrims would ponder.

As my friend Martin Rosenblatt, Managing Partner of the structured finance practice at Deloitte and Touche, recalled:

"I remember spending about ten hours re-drafting paydown rules you sent to me on a UBS landmark deal and when I gave it to you, you simply said you didn't want it to be more understandable. I guess you didn't want to leave a roadmap."

That period at UBS (1988 – 1990) was a challenging time to be structuring bonds. The U.S. bond market had gone into an inverted yield curve*, and the structures that had worked in a "normal" (upward sloping) yield curve no longer worked.

One of the new deals we launched at UBS gave investors an interesting way to deal with mortgage prepayment variability. The bonds were arranged in several series, which shared a common mechanism for self-adjusting over time in order to get back

* Inverted Yield Curve – A market with longer term interest rates lower than short rates, as when three-month or two-year rates are higher than the ten-year rate.

to their original expected schedules as the interest rate cycle progressed. This deal was tremendously popular with investors and sold out very quickly.

The idea behind the deal was to make rules for distributing the payment variance rather than the payments themselves, with each group of bonds sharing a target paydown schedule and other schedules that defined their limits of variance. I thought I had come up with an elegant solution to the concerns our customers had about the variability of their investments over time, and the self-correcting feature brought our investors' bonds back to the original targets if they held them through a full interest rate cycle.

Unfortunately, that way of setting up the payment rules "broke" the computer models of our competitors by allocating principal paydown variance rather than the principal itself, so the competitors couldn't model the deal. The competitors wouldn't make markets in the bonds if they couldn't model the cash flows. We only did one deal like that because our customers needed other dealers' quotes on their bonds. It was the perfect Zen lesson.

CHAPTER THIRTEEN

Three Tools is All It Takes

This chapter presents an overview of the three basic methods of tranching for asset-backed securitizations, and provides a conceptual foundation for understanding how securitization allocates risk. For the individual or investment professional wishing to explore each method in depth, the overview is followed by an in-depth examination of each tranching technique. The text quotes extensively from a chapter I wrote for the 2006 <u>Euromoney International Debt Capital Markets Handbook</u>.

Overview

Securitization – the largest of all capital markets – caters to investors with vastly different risk appetites and investment needs.

When a deal structurer sets out to design a securitization to satisfy investor demand, that structurer needs only three basic tools, or operators, to create those new securities. Those ways of dividing, or tranching, the cash flows from the underlying assets are:

1. Time tranching
2. Credit tranching
3. Coupon tranching

Three operators are plenty. After all, every mathematical expression only needs the operators of addition, subtraction, multiplication and division, and those four are enough to make an infinite number of equations. *(Before the purists get upset, I freely admit that you can define multiplication as the repeated application of addition, and you can define subtraction as the inverse of addition.)*

Any securitization is fundamentally a form of redistributing risk; it does not lower the total risk embedded in the loans or leases that form the "raw material" for the securitization process. However, the portfolio effect of having thousands of obligors and the liquidity introduced by capital markets trading does lower shorter-term risk to an investor who might otherwise be investing in a small number of unsecuritized credits. After looking at the whole picture, securitization lowers the value at risk (VAR) for all but the largest investors for these assets.

Even the largest investors may find the liquidity and standardization of securitized bonds advantageous when compared to the cost of maintaining a staff and taking on the expense of purchasing loans separately in an unsecuritized form.

All multi-tranche securitizations involve setting up payment priorities among the classes, and a pre-defined set of rules for those payments. Since the rules cannot be changed later, the goal of the investor and the structurer is to weigh the potential outcomes while taking into account all the future events that might happen. The most successful investors do not allow a single bad scenario to drive their investment decisions, nor do they let themselves be drawn into an inappropriate risk posture just because they see a potentially very positive outcome.

Time Tranching

"Time tranching" divides cash flows into individual tranches (bonds) which may be paid sequentially, in parallel, or by defining variable proportion cash-flow allocation based on any number of factors. Such factors could be simple, such as the time since the deal closed, or more complex, through an algorithm driven by a calculated variable such as total pool balance, pool performance, or even some external independent variable.

Another version of the time-tranching technique involves setting a principal payment schedule for some bonds and letting other bonds, commonly known as "support bonds*," take the variance in principal payments.

The very first CMO, issued by
Freddie Mac in 1983, was a
sequentially paid, time-tranched
bond. In that deal, known as Freddie
Mac Series A, there were four bonds.
Only when the mortgage pool had
paid enough principal to retire the first bond, did any principal
payments go to the second bond. Then the second class received all of
the principal payments until fully paid, and so on through the fourth
and final class.

* Support Bond – A bond that absorbs undesirable characteristics like credit losses or prepayment variance so that other bonds are more attractive investments.

Since all the principal for the underlying mortgages was already
guaranteed by Freddie Mac in the form of pass-throughs, there was
really no change in the aggregate credit exposure for investors, except
for the fact that the first class to be paid had a shorter exposure to
Freddie Mac's credit guarantee. In the jargon of the business, this deal
structure came to be called "plain vanilla sequential," or "ABCD
sequential."

Later time tranching (or principal allocation) developments
included setting principal schedules for some bonds and giving them a
schedule of payment preference (rather than simply a payment
preference). By having a principal payment schedule, one group of
bonds in the securitization structure was less likely to be paid off
before the investor expected to be paid off, even if the underlying
mortgages paid off faster than expected. Though generally not as large
a concern, some market conditions, like interest rates going up, also
made investors worry about not getting paid as soon as they originally
expected. This "extension risk" is just the other side of the coin of
early payment. The unscheduled "companion" or "support" bonds*
also absorbed some of the extension risk along with the early payment
risk.

The scheduled bonds, called Planned Amortization Classes
(PAC's) or Targeted Amortization Classes (TAC's) gave their investors
less exposure to the borrowers' prepayment option. Investors in PAC's
and TAC's give up some yield in exchange for this lower maturity
variability, and that extra yield is available to reward the investors in the
classes that take on the extra risk.

Another common method of "time tranching" is the technique of allocating principal payments to different sets of bonds at different ratios as time passes. One popular bond structure started out using this variable principal allocation method as a way of protecting or "supporting" senior credit tranches. The senior bonds got a disproportionately high percentage of the principal payments for the first few years while the junior bonds weren't paid, so that the credit protection for the senior bonds grew over time. The technique was called "accelerating" the principal payments, especially when the senior bonds got 100% of the principal for the first three years.

When this time tranching technique migrated to the fully guaranteed Agency CMO market, the bonds came to be known as Accelerated Senior (or "AS") bonds. The other bonds, called "NAS," for "Non-Accelerated Senior" bonds, were protected from fast prepayment risk the first few years. The NAS bond takes a disproportionately low percentage of prepayments early in its life, and after a certain date, gets a disproportionately large percentage of the principal.

Credit Tranching

A different method of dividing the cash flows is through credit tranching. These bond structures are paid according to their credit priority, often using "time tranching" as described above on the most senior AAA rated bonds.

The typical way to allocate credit losses in these deals is to allocate any losses first to the reserve funds, excess interest cash flows, insurance policy or overcollateralization that might be included in the structure to provide support. If any such reserves, excess cash, insurance or extra collateral have been exhausted by covering losses already, then the credit loss is allocated to the lower priority tranches as principal by writing off some of the balance of the bonds. In other words, the investors in the junior bonds lose some of their principal when a loan defaults, while the money salvaged by selling the bad loan or foreclosed asset is allocated to senior credit tranches as early payment of principal.

Because of these dynamic credit protections, many bond deals can be more robust than they appear at first glance. For example, a bond that has only 4% subordination to protect it (sometimes called "hard" protection) might appear on the surface to have very little protection against credit losses.

However, if that deal also has 300 basis points of excess interest available to absorb credit losses, then 5% in losses in a year would only use up 2% of the subordination in the first year, because the other 3% in losses would be absorbed by the excess interest. If each foreclosed loan resulted in a loss of half the loan balance, the 5% in credit losses would come from having 10% of the mortgages going into foreclosure.

From this, we can see that despite the seemingly modest 4% credit protection for that bond, 20% of the loans in the pool would need to default in the first two years before any principal would be lost by the bondholders.

For a typical subprime mortgage deal in 2005 and 2006, the subordination level required to achieve AAA ratings was around 20%, meaning that 80% of the deal would be rated AAA, while the remaining 20% would have lower credit ratings. Using the same basic assumptions from the example above with 3% per year in excess interest available, roughly half the borrowers would have to default and losses on each default would have to run 40% or higher before the AAA bonds would lose any principal.

Among the bonds in credit layers beneath the AAA bonds, the credit markets have developed demand for every gradation of credit tranche, so the resulting lower-rated subdivisions of the bond structure are so "thin" that each specific bond will be very sensitive to small changes in credit performance once the initial buffers of excess interest and subordination have been used up.

Decades ago, the credit ratings were single letters (A, B, C, etc.), but now each letter grade is divided into three "steps." If the single A credit rating for a pool of mortgages requires a subordination of 7.5% while a double A rating requires 9%, then each step in the single A credit would only be 0.5% of the whole deal. Bearing in mind that the mortgages are paying 3% per year in excess interest, it might take actual losses of 13% to 15% over several years before the first dollar of loss is assigned to the A- (A minus) rated bond. Once that occurs, it only takes another half a percent in losses to wipe out that bond and begin to take write-offs on the A rated bond. Another 0.5% in losses would begin to eat away at the A+ rated bond.

If you were to analyze the collateral mortgages at the time a deal is put together, it might be difficult to determine whether the default rate in the third through the tenth year would be 8% per year or 8.25% per year, but that relatively small difference might make the very large difference between one of those A- rated "mezzanine" bonds paying all of its principal, or none of it.

Coupon Tranching

Dating back to the days when bonds were elegantly engraved and printed on paper, a bond that had regular payments of interest had small detachable "coupons" printed at the edge. As each interest payment came due, the holder of the bond would physically present the payment coupon for that interest payment to the bank that acted as Payment Agent for the bond issuer. Because of that tradition, we came to call all interest payments "coupons," even though the bonds themselves and their payments are now electronic entries.

Coupon tranching, the third method of dividing cash flows, is based on interest payments. Some tranches can be set up to accrue interest while paying that interest to other classes as principal. The first of these interest payment tranching structures in the MBS market was the Z-bond, or accrual tranche, introduced in Freddie Mac's Series C deal, launched in January of 1984.

The fourth class in that deal was a 12.1% bond that accrued its interest (added to principal) each semi-annual bond payment period, making additional principal available to pay off the three sequential classes which were time-tranched to be paid off before the Z tranche.

The Freddie Mac Series C Class Z bond compounded, or accrued, at the rate of 6.05% every six months, growing from an original balance of $80.2 million in 1984 to a peak of $211 million by July of 1992.

All of the interest that was added to the Z-bond balance was paid as principal to earlier classes in the sequential time tranching of the deal. The holders of those shorter maturity bonds had an extra $130 million in principal payments that did not rely on the underlying mortgage pools having early principal payments, so the shorter bonds in Freddie Mac CMO Series C got a much less variable principal payment than they would have otherwise.

Investors in the early classes in this $525 million deal had significantly lower exposure to the borrower prepayment option because of this innovation in interest payment tranching.

Some tranches are interest-only (IO) and principal-only (PO) bonds. The technique of dividing mortgage interest payments into IO's and PO's (interest-only and principal-only securities) became infamous in 1987, when Merrill Lynch's Howie Rubin took the PO side of the trade and Franklin Savings' Ernie Fleisher took the IO side of the trade in the billion-dollar deal known as Merrill Lynch Trust 13. Unfortunately, Howie paid too much, and Ernie made a killing.

Merrill took a very public $275 million loss on the deal. It wasn't all Howie's fault, though. Salomon Brothers, Howie's prior employer, decided to price a similar IO-PO deal, selling their PO bonds for nearly 20% less than Merrill was asking.

In Wall Street's revisionist history, Howie was blamed for making an "unauthorized trade," but I have to say that I never saw a trader getting a prospectus printed for a CMO deal. It was a deal, not a trade, and it required the involvement (and signatures) of a number of bankers and analysts, along with senior management.

Post-fiasco, Rubin got a nice "kiss goodbye" from Merrill, followed by a decade of huge paychecks at Bear Stearns, which was only too happy to have the young trader who featured prominently in the book Liar's Poker.

At about the same time, Goldman was also doing a variation of these IO-PO deals, much less publicly. Goldman's preferred trade of the time was to take GNMA 9's and create equal and parallel bonds, one tranche with a 12% coupon and one with a 6% coupon, extracting a nice profit from two sets of buyers. At the time, GNMA 9's cost around par, or 100% of their face amount. The 12% bonds that Goldman created sold for a higher price, and were called premium bonds, while the 6% bonds sold for a discount*.

If you were bullish on bonds you would want to own the discount bond, or a PO. If you were bearish, your preference would be the premium bond or an IO. The bullish buyer would want a discount bond because they would enjoy a higher return if prepayments come in faster than expected, while the bearish buyer will choose the premium bond, believing that prepayments will come in slower. In general, prepayments come in faster if mortgage rates drop, and slower when they rise, so a structure like Goldman's also allows investors to make a bet on prepayment rates.

* Premium and Discount Bonds – Bonds that are priced above and below par (100%). Since all bonds pay the face amount at maturity, a discount bond yields more than its coupon (interest rate) if held to maturity and a premium bond yields less than its coupon as it matures and the premium amortizes.

Another form of coupon tranching allocates most of the interest from the mortgages to create a series of fixed rate bonds that sell at par. The associated excess interest is allocated to another class with no principal. Those are called WAC IO's, or excess interest bonds, because they don't have a stated coupon, and only get the interest left over after their associated fixed rate par bonds* have their interest payments satisfied.

* Par Bonds - Bonds bought at par, so the yield approximately equals the coupon rate, no matter how long the principal repayment (maturity) may take.

Perhaps the most interesting and controversial coupon tranching technique has been to divide the payments of a fixed-rate CMO bond into a pair of bonds that have variable interest rates, with one group collecting floating rate interest payments referencing an external market rate like LIBOR, while another bond paired with it becomes an "inverse floater." The floating rate bond and its companion, the inverse floating rate bond, were introduced in 1987.

Taking the example of 9% GNMA MBS again, we could divide the bonds into three parts LIBOR floating rate bonds ("floaters") and one part inverse floaters to create two classes of bonds that pay in parallel to each other. If we let the inverse floater coupon go to zero if LIBOR goes high enough, then each floater can have a maximum coupon of 12%.

The LIBOR floater bond might appeal to a bank that funded itself at LIBOR, as long as the mortgage bond offered 50 or more basis points of interest above the bank's funding rate. When we used GNMA collateral for the deals, the banks only had to reserve 1.6% capital against their holdings of these bonds because of the U.S. Government guarantee on GNMA's, so a positive spread of 50 basis points on the funding produced a very high return on capital for investors.

The buyers of the other bond, the inverse floater, were getting a very high interest rate to start with. If LIBOR was at 6% and the LIBOR floaters were at 6.5%, the inverse floater was getting 9% (the rate on the GNMA's) plus three times the 2.5% difference between the GNMA rate and the rate the banks were getting on their floaters, for a total of 16.5%.

With an initial interest rate that high and no credit risk on the GNMA's, there will nearly always be a buyer willing to make the investment in an inverse floater despite the concentrated interest rate risk.

If LIBOR goes too high, the cost of borrowing at LIBOR could exceed the return from holding a bond that can only pay a maximum of 12%. That effectively kicks in when LIBOR hits 11.5%, since the spread in the bond will shrink from the original 50 basis points.

This has not happened in the twenty years these bonds have existed, but there have been times when LIBOR traded above 9%, and looked like it might go higher. When that happened, the holders of CMO bonds with effective caps at 10% to 11.5% suffered a loss in market value. If investors sold during those episodes, they lost money, just like holders of 6% Treasury Bonds lost money if they sold when Treasury rates were high. If the floater buyers held on, they continued to get their spread of 50 basis points over LIBOR and an attractive return on capital.

For the holders of the inverses, these episodes of high interest rates were much more dire. If LIBOR went to 10%, the holders of the floaters would get their 10.5%, but the underlying GNMA's were still only paying 9%. Inverse floater investors would only get 9% - 3 * 1.5%, or 4.5%. Needless to say, getting 4.5% when financing with Fed Funds and LIBOR in the 10% vicinity can be painful, or even financially fatal.

The inverse floater buyers of the late 1980's did well if they managed to hold on. Even though one-month LIBOR did go above 9% in 1989 and the coupon on those inverse floaters dipped below 7%, investors that kept their inverse floaters until the early 90's ended up with coupons that went over 20%.

Around the same time that the floaters and inverse floaters were gaining in popularity, I got to introduce the super PO bond in a private CMO deal, American Southwest Series 63. It was designed to provide huge upside if prepayments came in fast, and slightly positive returns (around 5%) if prepayments came in slow. When the mortgages in the pool paid off quickly a couple of years later, the buyer of that first super PO got $10 million back on a bond originally priced at only $1.4 million.

Over the years, literally thousands of unique structured deals have been launched in the securitization market, with almost every imaginable underlying source of cash flows "feeding" the various bonds in the structures. To date, every bond type and bond structure has been made by some combination of these three structuring operators: time tranching, credit tranching and coupon tranching.

The success of securitization and structured finance comes from the power of these three structuring techniques to custom-tailor investments for a wide array of investors.

Banks may need safe, short maturity fixed rate bonds that match up with CD's they've issued or they may need floating rate bonds to match up with their interest bearing checking accounts. Hedge funds need to offer the kind of high yields they can get from inverse floaters or from taking extra credit risk. Life insurance companies need bonds that won't get paid off too soon.

Each can get what they need when the securitization market is working the way it should.

CHAPTER FOURTEEN

Anatomy of a Deal

In the bond world, there are a few customers that have to feel like they got a better deal than anyone else, and they often ask to see the one bond class (not theirs) that's terrible.

Other customers really want to understand everything, so giving them lots of information helps them make their buying decisions.

When I worked as a deal structurer, I tended to avoid the first kind of customer and really enjoyed working with the second kind.

Some investors need to see the downside, and figure out how a bond they're considering can survive the stress. A few need to see that they will have big upside in a scenario that could reasonably occur, like people who bet on long shots at the racetrack.

Long-term successful investors tend to start with the structure of their liabilities, and look to capture a profitable spread over the cost of those liabilities under almost every possible future performance "path" for the asset (in this case, a bond) being acquired.

The other approaches, like avoiding risk at all cost, or looking for big upside, tend to be less successful over the long run, simply because you can't always predict either the best or the worst of potential future scenarios, except to say that neither is very likely.

In the late 1980's, most of our deals were done with Agency (Ginnie Mae, Fannie Mae, or Freddie Mac) guaranteed mortgage pass-throughs as the underlying assets that provided the raw material for the cash-flow engineering that was the domain of the deal structurer.

In structuring CMOs, the main risks that were divided up were interest rate risk and prepayment (maturity) risk. When we created bonds with principal payment schedules that had preference, we divided the prepayment risk among the various bond holders.

Structuring to address the risk of prepayments became even more important to investors after the surge in prepayments in 1986, when Ginnie Mae MBS got prepaid so quickly that they stopped being thought of as ten-year bonds because they behaved more like five-year bonds.

When rates went back up towards the end of that decade, mortgage investors may have felt like they had whiplash as prepayments slowed down again. By 1989, the ten-year bonds that acted like five-year bonds looked like they were going to act like ten-year bonds again.

The important thing to bear in mind when structuring a deal is that you have to set up all the payment rules today, and those rules can't be changed later as conditions change. Some investors want "short" bonds only, so they are sensitive to extension risk. Others want "long" average life bonds. Still others want floating rate bonds that they can finance at a profit whether rates move up or down.

The result of the prepayment whiplash between 1986 and 1989 led some investors to steer clear of mortgage bonds completely until they were assured that their investments would not vary even if prepayments came in twice as fast or half as fast as originally expected.

The most risk-averse investors decided they would only invest in mortgage bonds that paid on a fixed schedule. Part of our structuring job was to create CMO bonds that would give investors a way to avoid wide variance in the time it took to get their principal payments.

The deal structure described below and steps in creating it are an abbreviated version of the actual process we follow when we create CMO deals with customized bonds. The deal most similar to this one was JHM Acceptance Series E, launched in March of 1989. The collateral was GNMA 9's.

The diagrams in this chapter are stylized version of what it looks like when you "map out" the cash flows in a securitization. These are the same kind of diagrams I drew for salesmen, traders and investors when I worked as a deal structurer.

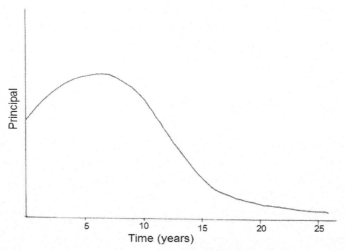

Diagram A: Principal payments at expected prepay speed

The diagrams also demonstrate, graphically, how the desires of many different investors are met in a single deal. Some investors could take the risk of maturity variance, while others insisted on relative certainty. One investor was looking for something special – a bond that didn't shorten in fast prepay environments, but actually lengthened, even though it did not adhere to a strict payment schedule.

I always worked closely with investors to meet their needs as I structured the deals. I was pleased when I could create great bonds for every investor, by making every tranche an ideal fit for the individual investor's needs. There was a great feeling of satisfaction when it all came together, the same kind of satisfaction a mathematician has when he writes an elegant proof.

First, I'd map out the expected principal payments, and then I'd run out the cash flows at fast and slow prepay speeds. That would give me patterns of principal payments under a number of different scenarios. The "rules" for how the cash flows are allocated are embedded in these diagrams, which show a "snapshot" of a deal and the range of behaviors of all the bonds in it, based on selected scenarios.

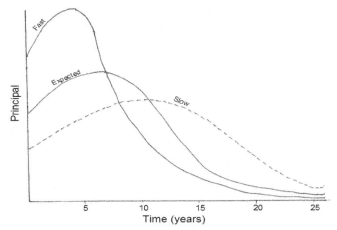

Diagram B: Principal payments at speeds twice as fast
and half as fast as expected.

Having mapped out the reasonable fast and slow principal
schedules, I could set up the tranches called Planned Amortization
Classes (PAC's) to satisfy the demand for stable bonds that are
protected from prepayment variance.

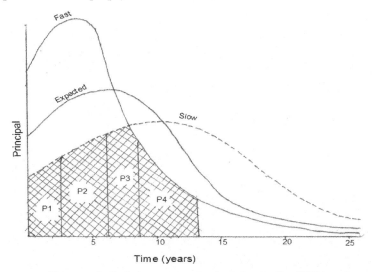

Diagram C: Defining payment schedules for the PAC bonds
using fast and slow speeds

As Diagram C shows, the PAC bonds are designed by setting their schedules as the minimum principal payment amount for both the fast speed and the slow speed. Because the PAC bonds have priority to hold their schedules, investors in the PAC bonds give up some yield.

The next diagram shows the "first cut" of the bond deal as it evolves. It has a short high yield bond (1.1 to 1.2 year average life) that gets some of the excess yield the PAC bonds give up, but absorbs the prepayment variance. If prepayments come in slow, that one-year bond might extend to being a three-year or four-year bond.

The big middle part of the deal is the "Total Return" or TR bond, which will eventually have the unusual property that it extends in duration when the mortgages prepay faster. To protect the TR bond from early payoff, it also has a schedule (set at the expected prepay speed), and initially a lower priority than the PAC bonds to hold to that schedule.

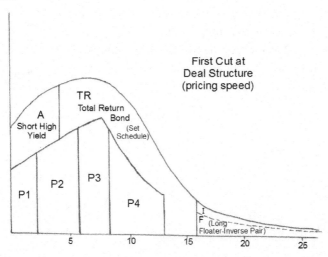

Diagram D: Laying out potential "companion" bonds to absorb the major variance in principal payments, we have a very short bond (Class A) that will be bought by an insurance company with short liabilities that wants the extra thirty basis points of yield, and will take the extension risk.

Now it's time to test to see if the TR bond and the long floater-inverse pair perform acceptably in a fast prepayment scenario. The floater and inverse floater together form a single fixed-rate bond, so they will always pay in parallel, in the ratio they began with. The new TR bond does expand to take the long cash flows, but in this deal structure, too much early principal payment comes to the TR bond, so it's not getting the duration lengthening that I hoped for.

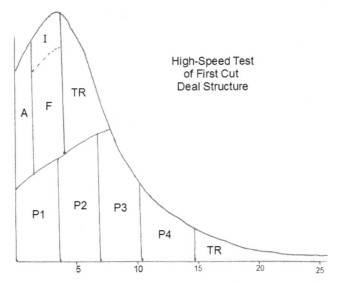

Diagram E – In the fast prepay test, we see that the TR bond begins getting paid in year 3, so even though it gets the later payments after all the other bonds have paid off, it does not extend its average life enough to get the customer the extension they want. The PAC protection needs to be less strong, beginning by removing the P4 bond, and changing the rules for P3.

Looking at the other bonds in the deal, it's not a problem if the floating rate bond's average life gets longer or shorter, because the investor who wants it is a bank that will be issuing CD's every month to fund the bond according to how much principal is still outstanding. Whether it pays off quickly or slowly makes little difference to this investor, as long as LIBOR stays below the 11.5% effective cap.

The inverse gets a yield of 15% to 16% if things don't change, and because it sells for a discount, it yields even more if it pays off quickly. Its main risk is if LIBOR goes above 9%, because that will cause the bond to have a yield of only 7.5% to 8%. If LIBOR goes to 10%, then yield will drop several hundred basis points more.

Now it's time to fine-tune the structure. Changing the PAC series to eliminates the P4 class and allows the five-year P3 class to take some of the prepayment risk that the TR buyer is paying to avoid. The back-end floater-inverse pair of bonds and the Class A bond still take most of the prepay risk. The short Class A bond is larger to help with the fast prepayment absorption.

Looking at the schematic below (Diagram F) at the "pricing speed" (expected prepay speed), we see that the TR bond takes some of the early cash flows and stops paying around year thirteen if the mortgages pay off as expected.

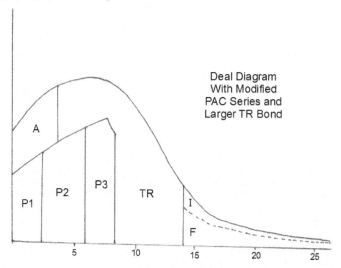

Deal Diagram
With Modified
PAC Series and
Larger TR Bond

Diagram F – The deal at the prepayment speed we expect the collateral to pay, also known as "pricing speed." The PAC series has been modified by removing the longest PAC (P4) and by changing the allocation of prepayments. The other three classes have all gotten larger.

The TR bond is now a bit larger (it's nearly 25% of the deal) and I've changed the payment rules to allow the TR bond to be the last bond paid if an "overflow" of principal needs to be allocated. With these changes, the Class A bond has grown to about 1.4 years' average life from the shorter amount in the earlier versions of the deal, and the TR bond and floater-inverse pair have each gotten a little shorter.

Diagram G shows how the bonds pay in a fast prepay environment. The Class A and the floater-inverse pair absorb a lot of the extra early principal, but the P3 bond also takes a small amount of early payment. The TR bond now extends to collect the entire last twenty-five years' of the mortgage cash flows, giving it an extension of about two years even though the underlying mortgages are paying off twice as fast as expected.

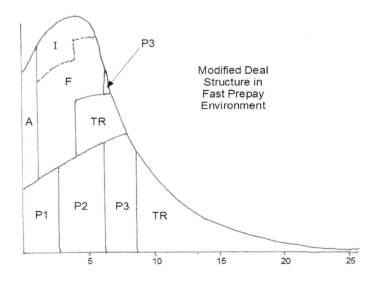

Diagram G – Here's the deal with prepayment speeds twice as fast as expected. Class A has shortened to 0.75 years from 1.4, the floater-inverse pair is just 2.2 years long, and the P3 bond has lost less than a tenth of a year in average life. The TR bond is now nearly 3 years longer than it was at pricing speed.

In designing the TR bond in the deal that's simulated here, I was working with a customer who worked so closely with me in the process that he actually served as co-designer. That investor bought the bond he co-designed, and paid approximately one percent more than he would have paid for a bond without its unique features.

The last set of changes in the deal structure results in a slight risk of shortening for the P3 PAC bond, but the amount it shortens under fast prepayment is so slight that the buyer will only need a couple of basis points of extra yield. We can provide that by lowering the price of the bond just one eighth of one percent.

The amount of average life extension the TR bond enjoys in the fast prepay scenario is significant. It now gets several years longer when the principal comes in fast, and the customer for this bond is willing to give up yield to enjoy that "option" behavior that counteracts the normal behavior of mortgage securities and callable corporate bonds. The yield the TR bond buyer gives up translates into higher yields available to reward the investors in the other three fourths of the deal.

We've just walked through the process of structuring an MBS deal that's far from plain vanilla, but not the most complicated of deals by far. This is an abbreviated version of the actual process that goes on. The real process takes days and dozens of iterations, with intervening conversations with potential buyers of bonds if they are affected by structural changes. Then there are the deal ideas that never go anywhere, or the deal structures that work one day, until the market moves, and they don't work at all.

Back at Pru, we called our deal structuring room the "War Room" for a good reason, because the team in there was constantly dealing with changing market information along with a flow of requests and reactions to deal structures. We kept a big white board covered with requests for bond characteristics, and tried to fit the requests into each deal.

At the end of the day, the deal structure described above gave an attractive investment to each buyer in the deal. Furthermore, the deal was innovative, containing bonds with characteristics that were simply not available in the bond market at that time.

Near the end of the 80's, after starting the Mortgage Finance effort at UBS, we were able to adapt the structures of the Agency CMO business to non-guaranteed "private label" MBS, and for a while we had very little competition.

At that time, the insurance companies Travelers and Prudential were major issuers of non-Agency MBS, as was the General Motors finance subsidiary, GMAC. We used the AAA senior bonds from these issuers as our raw material for new CMO deals, creating the same

* Agency Mortgage Securities – MBS or CMOs that are guaranteed by Ginnie Mae, Fannie Mae or Freddie Mac. Timely payment of principal and interest are guaranteed.

kind of complex CMO structures others were creating from Agency MBS*.

The mortgage loans behind these AAA bonds were also called "jumbo" loans. They were as good or better credit quality than the loans in the Fannie Mae or Freddie Mac deals, but they didn't qualify for Fannie or Freddie because they were above the upper size limits for Agency guarantees.

Since the cash flows from those "private label" MBS had very minor differences from those used in the loans backing Agency MBS, a deal that used AAA bonds as collateral had to capture those subtle cash flow differences exactly in order to comply with disclosure document legal requirements.

While the competition played catch-up, we had about 40 to 80 basis points of excess yield to work with to create customized investments in full-featured CMO structures built from "whole loan" MBS. By the simple act of combining the more complex structures from the Agency CMO business with the extra yield in the AAA piece of the whole loan deals, we could give our clients the same kind of tailored cash flow bonds they bought in Agency CMOs, except with higher yields. We could also pay the sellers of those private label MBS about a quarter of a percent more for their AAA MBS than the rest of the market.

We did it all using a single computer model as our tool. By another of the industry's historical accidents, most Wall Street mortgage departments had two sets of computer models (along with two sets of traders), one to deal with Agency mortgage bonds, and the other to deal with private label (whole loan) deals.

It took almost a year for most of the competitors to combine their two models to catch up to us. That year was 1989 and after only months in the business, our innovations led us to attain the number one position in the "private label" CMO bond business.

CHAPTER FIFTEEN

The Year the Prepayment Models Broke

The mortgage market had plunged to a bottom in 1986 and 1987 and was whipsawed from a sudden rise in mortgage rates in 1988 and early 1989. Investor concerns were centered on prepayments – how many people would pay off their mortgages before the terms of those mortgages (typically fifteen-year or thirty-year) ended? With the volatility of the market, investors shifted from worrying about early call risk from prepayments to worrying about whether their mortgage securities would extend in time as prepayments dropped.

These concerns were based on models for prepayments, which were based on observations of the behavior of tens of millions of mortgages over several economic cycles. The analytics groups I worked in, and others like them, had taken a wealth of historical data and built predictive prepayment models.

Prepayments always happen and there are many different reasons why they happen. Personal events trigger them. Regardless of what else is going on in the economy, some borrowers will sell their houses. There are also a myriad of specific life events and circumstances that can trigger prepayments, such as losing a job, getting a new job, having another child, getting divorced, suffering a major illness, or a death in the family.

Changes in the economy can also trigger prepayments. In fact, the primary reason for prepayment is that a borrower takes out a new mortgage. Borrowers usually refinance to get a loan with a lower rate, but they can also refinance out of variable rate loans into fixed rate loans to avoid the risk of having their payments go up in the future.

Homebuyers may need to draw additional equity from their homes in a high-rate environment, causing them to prepay even when rates are higher. They may be underemployed or disqualified for refinancing for other reasons, and therefore not exercising their "in the money" option of prepaying when rates are lower.

In fact, at any given time, a typical pool of thousands of borrowers will have some people prepaying no matter where rates are, and some not prepaying no matter how attractive the refinancing rate might be.

Collecting data on the behavior of a large group of mortgages forms the foundation for prepayment model-building. Looking at the data graphically can help identify "base functions" and external variables that might affect a mortgage borrower's behavior.

Statistical tools are used to compare the behavior of a mortgage borrower with external variables to see whether the movements in a variety of outside factors tends to lead or lag correlated movements away from the mean, or average, expected prepayments.

When my team and I built a prepayment model, the first external variable we looked at was the age of the loan. We called it the "seasoning" of the loan. Once we had an expected life cycle for an average new loan, we could study how other variables impacted mortgage borrowers.

There was also a seasonality to loan prepayments. There were enough homeowners with children to make the school year a strong effect. Winter weather in northern states tended to keep people home, not spending their weekends looking for a new house. The exception to this was resort and retirement areas, that sometimes showed a "reverse seasonality" when compared to the bulk of the U.S. housing market.

As you might expect, there was a clear correlation between falling mortgage rates and people paying off their loans and refinancing. Upfront costs like appraisals, fees, and commissions typically acted like a barrier to refinancing, so borrowers only got serious about this option when rates dropped by a couple of hundred basis points.

After factoring in the universal effects of seasoning, along with the time of the year, we could compare our "expected" prepayments with what actually happened, and see that over 70% of the variability in prepayments was explained by mortgage rates.

The next most significant outside variables turned out to be 1) employment growth in the immediate area, and 2) house prices. Those two variables seemed to be interrelated, which made sense – when employment rose, there was more demand for houses as new people arrived to take new jobs. More demand raised prices. Between these two variables, employment growth appeared to be the stronger "explanatory" variable.

The location of the loan was an important factor as well. In general, the East Coast, West Coast and Sun Belt showed greater housing turnover activity, so they had faster prepayments. Perhaps most striking within a single state was the difference between upstate New York (known for its slow mortgage prepayment) and the region closer to New York City, where mortgages pay off much faster, especially when mortgage rates drop.

We found that the coastal regions seemed to be more likely to take advantage of lower rates. We guessed that geographic areas with more concentrated populations were areas where more mortgage bankers set up shop, which then led to more refinancing.

Several additional variables were found to be significant as we combed through the data. One, we called "the USA Today effect." If mortgage rates hit a new low, the news media would run stories about it in the paper and on TV, and, like clockwork, two, three and four months later, we'd see a surge in refinancings. This made perfect sense, since at that time, it took between one and three months to process a new loan application, and then another month for the prepayment to show up in the mortgage bond.

Another surge in prepayments could be seen shortly after mortgage rates bottomed and then headed back up. We hypothesized that this effect was caused by borrowers waiting to see the bottom before committing, so they would avoid locking in a new rate only half way down.

We had literally tens of millions of mortgage "life histories" documented from the FHA's experience of guaranteeing mortgages.

Dating back to 1970, we also had detailed history for the loans that Freddie Mac and Fannie Mae guaranteed.

That gave us plenty of data to test against. By 1986, we already had models that would predict performance for mortgage "pools" to accuracies of 95% to 97%.

This research and the explosion of structuring techniques to divide up the cash flows in mortgage securities created a new kind of competition among Wall Street firms.

In the days before computers, investors and issuers of securities often chose their investment banks based on whom they trusted to give them good advice. It was all about the people, their relationships, their industry knowledge and their integrity. Now it was largely about which firm had the best models and market penetration.

In 1990, the bond market was coming off an unusual period. The shortest rates, for one month through six months, were at or above the longest rates, the rates for ten years to thirty years. This inverted yield curve was a rare occurrence, and nearly always led to a recession and dramatically lower interest rates.

The size and national scope of the Savings and Loan debacle had become clear. The overhang of so many assets needing to be sold, especially commercial buildings, had led the Federal Reserve to aggressively lower rates in an attempt to head off a recession. Mortgage rates came down, and people began to refinance their mortgages.

The government sponsored a new company to manage the liquidation of the assets of the failed thrifts, and called it the Resolution Trust Company, or RTC. I was working as Head of Analytics in the Mortgage Department at Daiwa and our group, along with our competitors, was very active buying mortgage loans of all types from the RTC, as well as structured bonds.

The most difficult to analyze bonds were the "residuals" from CMO deals. Even conceptually, residuals can be difficult to understand, as they are more than just the "left over" cash flow after paying the rest of the CMO classes. This unique tranche of CMO deals came into being as a consequence of the 1986 Tax Act. Legally, it is equity rather than debt, and serves as a way of providing the IRS with the taxes it requires which aren't being paid by the buyers of the bonds in a CMO deal.

If, for example, mortgages that yielded 8.5% were carved into tranches in a CMO deal, the government wanted to be paid taxes on that full 8.5% yield, regardless of which bonds were paying off when. The bonds in the deal might be yielding anywhere from 6% to 10%, providing taxable income either lower or higher than that the 8.5% that IRS wished to tax, and some would pay off before others.

Enter the residual, a nifty tranche to fix the problem.

Since the residual tranche was required to pay enough taxes to maintain the tax revenue from a steady 8.5% income, this created "phantom income" – the investor in the residual didn't actually receive this income but was required to pay taxes on it nonetheless. Over the life of the deal, this phantom income would be balanced out by "phantom losses" once the lower-yielding bonds had paid off and only the higher yielding bonds remained.

Needless to say, the fact that a residual bond might bring its owner five million dollars of cash flow in a year but generate six or seven million dollars of taxable income, made it both complex and attractive only to a select few investors. With its tax implications and its position as the remainder after everything else was paid, you can almost imagine the Greek chorus chanting "Toxic Waste! Toxic Waste!" next to the trading desk each time we bought one of these unusual illiquid bonds.

Our group at Daiwa started buying these residual bonds from the RTC at yields of 25% or more, even though the tax bite cut into our income. We did this partly because we thought the prepayment models based on history weren't predicting what we felt was about to happen.

Mortgage rates were coming down, and the process of refinancing mortgages had also changed. Automated processing and standardization of documents had reduced the costs and hassle of refinancing. You couldn't go to a party in Manhattan or Chicago (or lots of other places) without hearing people talk about how they had already refinanced their mortgages twice.

Most importantly, securitization had given banks a way to generate income from mortgage origination through the capital markets rather than through the fees paid by borrowers. If mortgage rates dropped to

7%, someone with an 8% mortgage could refinance into a 7.5% mortgage without paying any "points," because banks and mortgage brokers were getting their 2% commissions when the capital markets paid 102% to buy those 7.5% loans to securitize.

At Daiwa, we thought it was likely that prepayments would come in twice as fast as the models were predicting. That made the residual tranches of CMO deals very attractive. The amount of time we would pay taxes on phantom income would be drastically cut, and the day we got the benefit of phantom losses would come much sooner than the rest of the market realized.

Historically, we had never seen whole classes of GNMA mortgages pay off any faster than 35% per year. Since the prepayment models were based on historical data, 35% was the fastest prepayment rate the models could predict.

In the new mortgage environment, we thought mortgage pools could actually pay off at 40%, 50% or even 60% per year. Our CMO residuals were likely to get to the point where they would be tax-advantaged much quicker than the market predicted. The only real risk to our investment was if the mortgages paid off so rapidly that we only got to enjoy our tax-advantaged cash flow for a short time.

Our solution to this was to approach the big Wall Street firms and offer to buy PO (Principal Only) bonds from them. Our competitors still trusted in the prepayment models which we felt were now obsolete. Knowing we were hungry buyers, they pushed the price up, and thought they had taken advantage of us.

I had designed the "super PO" bond four years earlier to help investors exposed to prepayment risk hedge out that exposure. This time, we needed the hedge ourselves. Once we owned lots of PO's bought from other dealers, we did a series of CMO deals to create super PO bonds we could retain. We sold bonds that had fixed schedules amounting to two-thirds or three-fourths of the total PO bond principal, and kept a bond from each deal that would have a huge payoff if prepayments came in very fast.

The super PO bonds we kept helped us cover the potential loss of future cash flows in the CMO residuals. If the mortgages backing the CMO residuals only paid off a little faster than expected, we still got our 20% or higher return, and we still got a partially tax-sheltered cash flow from those residuals a year or two after buying them.

Taken together in a portfolio, these two basic types of investments performed very well if rates dropped, regardless of whether prepayments increased a little or a lot. That single trade idea was a big part of our $400 million in profit over the next two years, which came from a capital base of only $50 million.

When we tie ourselves to statistical models based on past performance, we can take unexpected losses or make unexpected gains when conditions that drive performance go outside the boundaries that existed in the past.

In 1990, automated underwriting, standardized documentation and very active capital markets made it much less expensive to process and fund mortgage refinancing. These changes rendered our historically based prepayment models obsolete, virtually overnight.

Predicting the shift in behavior due to radically changed market conditions or market operations can be a very rewarding (albeit risky) speculation. Given that the majority of the market is discouraged or even prohibited from speculation, episodes like these can be extraordinarily profitable for those few who can "throw away" history and bet against the crowd.

CHAPTER SIXTEEN

Unplanned Exit

In April of 1996, I was two thirds of the way through my three-year contract to build a securitization effort at Deutsche Bank. The business was growing and producing profits within 5% of what I had forecast in the business plan I had submitted when I had made my pitch to the Bank two years earlier.

The Bank had hired Edson Mitchell, who came from the sales tribe at Merrill, as Head of Global Markets (the Bank's name for investment banking). It wasn't surprising that he wanted a much bigger securitized products department than the one I was running. He also wanted to do the "generic" mortgage business, like trading Ginnie Mae MBS, and I was focused on the "exotics."

The Agency business, which we called "plain vanilla," came with a very expensive infrastructure and generally made little or no profit. But it did keep salesmen busy, and that would have been great had we been at Merrill, but it didn't fit into my plan for Deutsche.

I'd never wanted to compete head-to-head with the big Wall Street shops for the low-margin business, and that unorthodox strategy had been part of my pitch to the Bank. Now here I was, with the Bank's backing and there was Edson Mitchell, also with the Bank's backing. It wasn't clear whose side the Bank was really on when it came to the future of my department.

I kept to my plan while others planned my demise.

In the spring of 1996, a new Head of Fixed Income came in to be my boss, and I should have read the writing on the wall. He was a former partner at Goldman Sachs, and had recently run a hedge fund, rumored to be less than successful. Some said that Deutsche agreed to pay his hedge fund investors something on the order of $25 million to relinquish their interests.

My new boss was a real charmer – literally. When I checked him out with my sources before he started work, I heard that he had managed to get three women pregnant at the same time, including a current wife, an ex-wife and a current secretary. I concluded that he was really good at convincing people to do what he wanted, and that he was probably terrible at risk management. I never confirmed this, but it was just too bizarre to be completely fabricated, even for Wall Street gossips.

Soon after he started, he set up interviews with each of the people in my department. I wasn't present at any of the interviews, but a few people told me he offered them the position as head of their groups. According to more than one salesman, he would be the new sales manager…and according to more than one banker, he would be leading the banking effort.

No matter. He probably told all three of the women that he loved only them, too.

I wasn't spared his attention, either. He repeatedly told me how brilliant he thought I was, and how well I had put the group together. It really would have mattered to me to know that I was appreciated, years before. But my time on Wall Street had made me tougher. I knew what the game was about and it wasn't a popularity contest. He told me how much he "liked" me, while he offered the people working for me different positions than the ones I'd hired them to do. I told him I didn't care if he liked me, as long as we got to continue making money.

I didn't even take it personally when he started to rave about the skills of a young trader he wanted to bring over to "help me" run the department. Through the years, I'd also learned to pick my fights (I used to fight every one I could). "Keep your eye on the ball," I told myself, "Don't lose focus. Make money for the bank and you'll save your skin."

I asked to meet this Wunderkind who was ready to give me help I didn't want, but my boss insisted it would be too much of a risk for the potential new hire, who was in line for Wall Street's last Big Brass Ring – the Goldman partnership. Unless, that is, we could steal him away.

I offered to meet my potential assistant out of town or on a weekend, so his cover wouldn't be blown, but my offers were declined. I felt a little silly when I realized somewhat belatedly that the real idea was not for this person to *help* me at all. The real idea was for this person to *replace* me. My new boss, with the backing of his boss, had picked my replacement and there was nothing I could do about it.

I went to my boss' office with an olive branch and told him that I had no problem with him wanting his own people. I offered to stay through a transition period as long as he would like, provided we dealt with the contractual issues, which included the fact that I was to be the sole head of the department, or would be paid what was left of the compensation guaranteed in my three-year contract.

My boss vehemently denied that it was his intention to replace me, and assured me I would just love Kevin and really appreciate the trading prowess he would bring to the table.

April 15, 1996 was Kevin's first day. We spoke for a few minutes, and then I took him up to human resources. It was clear as all this was happening that I was indeed being replaced, but no one would say a thing about it. I think they expected that in order to keep my job, I would just nicely step aside and be grateful that I hadn't been fired.

But I had worked too hard to get where I was. I had written the plan for Deutsche's entrée into the business, and I'd delivered on my promises. I wasn't about to hand over the keys to the kingdom. Instead, I delivered a letter I had drafted over the weekend saying I loved my job, and wanted to keep doing it, but we needed to negotiate the appropriate changes in my employment contract.

As soon as the Head of Human Resources read my letter, I was asked to surrender my building pass, and building security was called to escort me out.

I had two concerns: How was I going to be compensated for breach of contract and how was I going to take care of my clients, one of whom had been working with us on a billion dollar deal?

So I went to my lawyer's office and called my client. I told him that I was "out," but that I thought our deal was still on track, and that it was far enough along that the new guy couldn't stop it even if he wanted to. That thought might sound strange. What firm wouldn't want to do a billion dollar deal with one of the biggest and smartest clients out there? Well, it makes sense if you think of Wall Streeters the way you think of tomcats, and realize they like spraying on someone else's corner.

By placing the call to my client before all my own legal issues were sorted out, I was taking a risk, because I'd stop playing the game according to the rules. But I've always felt that it was my clients that made my career, not the Wall Street firms where I worked. I knew it could hurt me, and I knew my lawyers wouldn't be too happy, but I didn't care. It would hurt me more in the long run if the clients who trusted me couldn't count on me to take care of them.

As it turned out, making that call was a good idea. The new guard at Deutsche didn't want to move forward on our billion dollar deal. How did I know? Strangely, I got a call, at home, from Deutsche's legal department to ask me whether I could help them show it was a renegade salesman's idea, a deal that hadn't been properly documented. They wanted me to testify on their behalf.

I reminded them that I had spent weeks getting this deal through the Head Office credit department and into the queue to be approved by the Board of Managing Directors in Germany (the powerful Vorstandt, as it was referred to even on this side of the Atlantic). They had absolutely zero chance of preventing Germans from keeping copies, and the client would find those copies if a dispute were to end up in court.

Unlike most banks, Deutsche had not spread its legal work around to all the top firms, so I was lucky enough to be able to get representation from what was perhaps the best securities litigation firm in New York, and have Harvey Pitt as my personal attorney. When we finally sat down with Deutsche's attorney about a month later, I was confident that my lawyer could beat up their lawyer. Later, I wondered if they all remembered that very meeting when Harvey became Chairman of the SEC.

I'm pretty sure they ended up regretting trading me for Kevin Ingram. Of course, it's Wall Street, so it's anybody's guess.

What isn't a guess is that after I left, the color of the bottom line in my department turned from black to red. Rumor had it that the department I had founded and built had hit the magic number of $100 million – in losses.

When it came time to fire Kevin, my replacement, he called on Jesse Jackson for support. Kevin's exit, under the veiled threat of racial discrimination, supposedly cost them another $20 million.

It also cost them much more publicity than they would have liked, even after he was gone.

An article ran in *The New York Observer* on September 30, 2001, with the headline "Kevin Ingram Pal Questioned About bin Laden."

> Like many of his brethren on Wall Street, Kevin Ingram, a top bond trader at Goldman Sachs and Deutsche Bank, had his share of career ups and downs. He had soared high at Goldman Sachs, moved on to a dream job at Deutsche Bank in 1996 and, like others during the bond-market collapse of 1998, was forced to resign.
>
> Looking for something else to do, he started his own Internet bond-trading firm, which was recently forced to shutter its doors following the dot-com wipeout.
>
> It was, for the most part, a typical Wall Street story—until June 21, when the U.S. Attorney's office for the Southern District of Florida announced that it had arrested Mr. Ingram and a Pakistani national, Diaa Badr Mohsen of Jersey City.
>
> The six-page affidavit supporting the charges went on to detail a plot straight out of Elmore Leonard.
>
> In a sting operation in a Fort Lauderdale hotel room on June 12, the affidavit said, Mr. Ingram and an associate had been caught taking two cases stuffed with $2.2 million in cash from government agents. A Lear jet waited, fueled and ready to take Mr. Ingram to Amsterdam, where the money would be laundered, the affidavit contended.
>
> Mr. Ingram was arrested as part of a broader sting operation on an alleged plot by Mr. Mohsen and another Pakistani national, Mohammed Rajaa Malik, to export arms, Stinger missiles and nuclear devices to an undisclosed foreign country.

After Deutsche, I was exhausted and disappointed and tired of building new departments that would be profitable and which I'd then lose as they became spoils for the pirates.

My personal life, which had increasingly diminished as I served the Gods of Wall Street, was in a shambles. My marriage was under stress. I didn't recognize the meaning of the word "fun." I was a Type A disintegrating into a *Type Who Am I Anymore?*

I decided if I was going to continue working (and I still loved the bond business), I was going to work for myself or for the clients I admired and whom I'd always been devoted to serving. My last day at Deutsche was my last day on Wall Street. I've never regretted the decision. And I'm glad I wasn't at some Wall Street mortgage department during the 2007 meltdown. It was hard enough on the buy side, where I saw what happened to the buyers of all those bonds.

CHAPTER SEVENTEEN

Going Head to Head with Wall Street

Wall Street has hundreds of pithy sayings that pass for wisdom. One is that the market is always right. If that were true, then value investing wouldn't work, and Warren Buffett wouldn't be a billionaire.

Another Wall Street saying is that the assets of an investment bank leave each night in the elevators. In 1996, I hoped that particular saying was true, because I thought that with the right people and the right amount of capital, I could beat the Wall Street firms at their own game.

While I worked on a business plan to raise capital for Howard B. Hill & Co., LLC, the core group of systems architects who had been with me since the Pru days came to join me, along with some talented programmers that I had worked with at Deutsche. We started to build the cutting-edge analytics that would be our trademark as well as our market advantage.

We had a vision of expanding securitization technology to new asset classes and new markets, and using the Internet as our way of supporting both issuers and investors with on-demand access to our models and deal structures, in real time. We'd always worked directly with clients when we structured deals on the Street, but we'd never been able to do so efficiently or easily.

Our group developed new systems to structure and analyze bonds, all on a Java platform that would enable our models to be delivered over the internet, so our clients could work right alongside us. Our idea was revolutionary and we thought investors would relish the new opportunity it presented.

Some of the smaller Wall Street firms proposed a strategic partnership, but we wanted our independence. A group of executives from Enron came to see us, but they made us nervous in their desire to move fast without being able to articulate their needs or goals. Institutional investors who had been our clients when we were on the Street wanted us to prove ourselves before they made a major commitment, offering us less than a tenth of the capital we needed to compete. More than one potential investor was interested in having us modify our plan, and turn ourselves into a hedge fund.

I wasn't ready to sacrifice my dream, which was to be the nimblest securitization group with the most advanced analytics and most personalized service anywhere. Although the fulfillment of this dream required a huge capital commitment, on the order of $100 million, we believed we could get the funding we needed once the business plan was finished and the systems well down the road to being finished.

I was intent on my vision of competing directly with Wall Street and my colleagues shared that vision. We knew we could run rings around the Big Firms if we just focused on the business and the clients, and didn't waste time and energy on Tribal Warfare.

Soon, we got our first big break, a chance to help one of Wall Street's biggest clients cut out the expensive middlemen. We were invited to present a plan to one of the federal housing Agencies in Washington, D.C., so they could become direct issuers of CMOs.

I sat down with people at the Agency who had known me since my earliest days in the business, so there was a foundation of trust on both sides. At the meeting, they confirmed the fact that we were fulfilling a need in the marketplace for clients to access deal structures as they were developed, in real time. They expressed their desire to move forward to an agreement, and we began to draft a contract.

A week later, they called and gave us the bad news: We were offering them everything they needed and wanted, and they could agree to our terms. They just didn't want to be our first client.

It was a let down, to be sure, but we didn't take it too hard. This big client had just confirmed that we were filling a niche that was desperately needed and that our fees made sense. The only reason they weren't working with us was that they were scared to be the first. No big deal.

Our company, now ten visionaries working without salaries, kept the dream alive. Five to seven days a week, we gathered on the trading floor that I'd converted from an enormous playroom on the third floor of my house – a twenty-two room, turn-of-the-century shingle style house attributed to Stanford White and overlooking Long Island's Oyster Bay harbor.

Over the next six months, we soldiered on. A few of my colleagues returned to Wall Street, and a few new professionals, their imaginations ignited by the same dream, joined us in their place.

That summer we got our first lucky break -- an advisory contract with one of the most esteemed and powerful firms on Wall Street, Lazard Frères. Lazard wanted to explore opportunities in the securitization market.

This was our big chance as a new firm to prove that the niche we'd carved out for ourselves did indeed need to be filled. We still didn't have the money we needed to do everything we wanted to do, but it looked like that would be a lot easier if our little securitization boutique could put Lazard on the map in our specialty.

Around this time, Collateralized Debt Obligations – CDO's – were looking like the next big thing. It seemed as if every group on Wall Street wanted to do one, with bank loans, junk bonds, even project financings. Lazard's emerging market desk thought this new structure could work really well in their specialty. They wanted us to help them craft a CDO out of a portfolio of emerging market bonds from all over the world, starting with the southern hemisphere and the former Soviet bloc.

At the same time, another group at Lazard wanted us to help them create securities from FHA housing project loans. Being advisors to some of the most respected advisors in the business was a real feather in our cap.

For the FHA securities project, we analyzed several portfolios, and helped Lazard's traders buy and hedge a portfolio of seasoned loans that had been held for their first seventeen years by a state pension fund.

These loans were unique in one aspect: When they hit their 20th anniversary, the FHA program that guaranteed them encouraged the borrowers to refinance. If the borrowers chose not to refinance within three years, they would pay a much higher interest rate for the following twenty years.

We came up with a securitization structure that matured in three years, complete with a backstop that would buy the loans at that time if the borrowers didn't refinance for some reason.

In the meantime, the emerging market desk at Lazard set out to acquire its portfolio of high yielding emerging market bonds. We modeled a trial portfolio and our preliminary work showed us that the deal would have a solid arbitrage.

We were all set to go on both fronts, when the French bank that was in line to buy the FHA bonds asked for one more week to finish the paperwork for a three-year interest rate swap. We re-ran all the numbers with a new settlement date.

And then, over the weekend, Thailand's currency blew up.

It's easy to see how that could stop an emerging market bond deal dead in its tracks.

But you might wonder what it has to do with a major French bank buying bonds based on U.S. Government-guaranteed apartment building loans. The answer is "everything."

Three-year swap spreads widened, and when spreads widen, ordinary hedges against interest rate risk provide no protection. The deal that would have made $4 million profit the week before now showed a loss of $2 million.

Lazard had a close relationship with the French bank that was the other party to the deal, so they let them out of the trade. We didn't get our million dollar structuring fee.

A week later I was on the phone with the Senior VP at Lazard who'd been my original contact. Alex and I were both bemoaning the fact that our deal had fallen through, and we bounced ideas off each other in an attempt to figure out how to rescue the situation. Lazard now had $450 million worth of FHA loans they didn't know what to do with.

We agreed that we were victims of plain bad luck (which reminds me of another pithy Wall Street saying: It's better to be lucky than smart). In an attempt to find some comic relief, Alex told me his wife had given him the monthly horoscope from *Town and Country*, which he wanted to share with me. He read me his horoscope, which focused on the fact that Saturn, the "taskmaster" planet, was in his sign and was retrograde, and that meant he would be taught a difficult two-year lesson, most likely about money.

Alex's sign was Aries. So was mine. So was my wife's. And strangely enough, Saturn had first come into Aries in April of 1996, on my last day at Deutsche.

At our company's weekly meeting I tried to cheer everyone up by telling them that the collapse of our first big deal may have been an astrological event, nothing more. That's when it turned out that all but one of the seven people sitting at the conference table was also an Aries. I had heard about the importance of diversification, but I didn't think that extended to asking job applicants, "What's your sign?"

We poured our energies into the other deals we had in the works. We were working with one of the Japanese "Big Four" brokerage firms, which had been approved by Fannie Mae to do its very first deal. We'd already matched numbers with Fannie Mae's analytic team, and it was all set to happen on the coming Monday.

That Sunday, the home of the President of the parent company was raided by the Japanese police, who charged him with securities fraud.

Another deal in the works was with a trio of Korean construction and finance companies looking to finance a CDO. We'd written a 180-page tome, <u>A Confidential Report on Creation, Structure and Issue of the First Korean Mortgage Backed Securitization Issue ("MBS")</u> and delivered it after receiving the first of three payments.

We had already demonstrated our systems over the Internet using their specific mortgage loan files. We had showed our clients how they could use the systems while they sat at their desks in Korea and we worked on the same deals and files as we sat at our desks on Long Island.

Our second scheduled payment didn't come. Suddenly, there were delays and evasions. We attributed part of the problem to the fact that our main contact was the eager but unsure young son of a powerful Korean who was instrumental in making the deal happen. The rest we attributed to a culture gap. The Koreans were nervous. They wanted more information. They needed more hand-holding. Then they just opted out of their commitment, reneging on their obligation to pay us.

Later, we found out that they had paid a fee to a Korean company related to one of the client companies instead of us and executed a similar but much less efficient deal. The document they thought they could use as a roadmap didn't serve them quite as well as they hoped without access to our system, but they got their deal done. We lost ours.

At this point, all the setbacks and disappointments and the fact that we still didn't have the capital we needed was too much for most of my original partners. Some of them wanted us to alter our strategy. Maybe we *should* become a hedge fund. Everyone else was.

Old members of our boutique left and new members took their place. I was still intent on my vision but found myself spending more time writing proposals than doing deals. We were a registered broker-dealer but struggling to survive on the fringe. Now I realize that it would have been easier to raise the money we needed if I'd called the company Bonds Dot Com.

My wife desperately wanted me to fold up my tent, go back to Wall Street or retire to Vermont "to build the perfect breakfront," as she put it. I refused to let go of the dream, even as the last of my partners left the company.

That December, I was alone on the trading floor in the third floor of my house, working after dinner again, when a call came in. It was someone I didn't know, from Refco, the powerhouse futures and commodities broker in Chicago, which was to fold some years later in an accounting scandal. They wanted to arrange financing for an equity deal, and they needed it to happen by the end of the year. It wasn't right up my alley, and the timing was really tight, but it was certainly something I could handle.

On New Year's Eve, I was on the phone with Refco. The deal happened. I thought it was a sign that there was still a future for Howard B. Hill & Co. My wife thought I had lost my mind.

Maybe I had. Several more months passed and I couldn't attract any new partners, any new clients or any new money. We sold the beach house and then the country house and finally, the big house with the trading floor. It was over. And so was any possibility of ever returning to Wall Street.

In presenting clients with a better, cheaper way to do securitizations, I'd declared myself an adversary. I was an enemy to Wall Street. Although I still had friends on the Street, I no longer belonged there. No Wall Street jobs were offered to me and I didn't go looking for any. I'd gone for broke and if Wall Street had its way, that's exactly how I'd end up.

My wife and I split up. She'd seen me through every phase of my Wall Street career, and she suggested again that I get a job on the buy side, as she had many times through the years.

I bought a small house in New England and she did the same, not far from where we had both met, at Yale. I traded stocks and planted flower bulbs and cooked. It was strange having so much time on my hands, but I was enjoying trading stocks and options again, as I had in my early twenties when I used to walk from Yale across the New Haven Green and down to the Merrill, Lynch, Pierce, Fenner and Smith branch to watch the ticker tape.

I had retired from Wall Street, but I hadn't given up my passion for the market. I was trading options again…and getting margin calls almost daily. My wife had given me some of her money to invest alongside mine and one day she called and said she was really nervous about the market and she wanted it back. I told her it was bad timing and she said, fine, she'd take my cars as collateral. I knew she was serious.

I sold everything the next day, took huge losses, and gave her back her money. As I was sitting there in the midst of trying to close out more than four thousand option contracts in a hostile market, the phone rang.

It was my friend Alex from Lazard. He had moved on after the FHA loan fiasco, and was calling to see if I felt like joining him and two others to help a Dutch bank deal with a distressed CDO portfolio they were finding out wasn't worth what they paid for it.

The date was October 8, 2002, the exact bottom of the bear market.

I drove down to Greenwich to meet the group for drinks, and it turned out that one of the people involved was a friend from the Pru days.

I had started my career on the buy side, as my wife had been urging me to for years.

Things were easier on the buy side; it was a lot more relaxed. I'd come out of retirement for this job and I found myself enjoying the nine to five. I realized I'd spent years fighting. Fighting for everything on Wall Street and then fighting for my dream of competing with Wall Street. It felt good to put down my gloves.

A couple of years later, we were making money for the Dutch, and had a growing asset management business. We even achieved the distinction of being the first CDO manager to sell bonds to the Central Bank in Beijing.

Then the Dutch pension funds that owned our bank put it up for sale. We read about the twists and turns of the proposed deals in the industry press and The Wall Street Journal, but none of the potential buyers ever came to our offices to check out our operation.

We were making almost half the money the bank was taking in as fees, and using only a sliver of the bank's capital, yet no one was interested in what we were doing. If we weren't even important enough to visit, our future after the sale wasn't looking too promising.

It was time for me to work with like-minded people, after all these years. I called one of the clients I'd worked for since the early days back at Pru – the same client I'd called the day I was fired at Deutsche, to give him the "heads up" on our billion dollar deal that was in jeopardy.

Soon, I was joining the Quantitative Management group at Babson Capital. It was part of the family of financial companies owned by MassMutual, one of the few AAA rated institutions left, with a 160-year history. I hoped I'd found a place where I belonged. I wished I'd done it years before, maybe when my wife first suggested it.

CHAPTER EIGHTEEN

The Year the Credit Models Broke

Although I didn't manage to build the business I had hoped to at Howard B. Hill & Co., I am proud of one of our innovations, which, in retrospect, seems portentous.

One of our modifications to existing technology was to model credit losses in a framework consistent with the prepayment and interest rate models we had developed. From this, we were able to create what we called a "Credit Adjusted Spread," or CAS.

For us, the Credit Adjusted Spread replaced the Option Adjusted Spread, or OAS, that had been used for years to measure the "cost" of borrowers' prepayment options in residential mortgages.

Both our proprietary CAS model and the OAS in use by other firms examined the cash flows of mortgages, bonds or portfolios under many (hundreds or thousands) of future economic environments. By measuring the return on the bonds or mortgages as an average across all these scenarios, we could arrive at a single expected spread above either swaps or Treasuries.

The OAS model had only been used for modeling interest rate or prepayment risk, but did not address securities or mortgages that also had credit risk. By extending the customary analysis to credit-impacted investments, we moved the technology of securitization a small step forward.

Our model calculated defaults on mortgages by taking a base "life cycle" of defaults, and then multiplying that base according to how inverted the yield curve became. This is because inverted yield curves are usually associated with times of economic stress, or even impending recessions.

Calculation of losses that might be incurred from defaults took into account the fact that defaults do not necessarily lead to losses. In fact, those who defaulted on their mortgage payments but whose houses were only 50% financed would nearly always sell the house, pay off the mortgage, and walk away with cash. If the mortgage was less than 80% of the estimated current value of the house, each default predicted by the credit model would show up as a prepayment in our system, rather than as a foreclosure..

While this all made sense, and even moved the art of predicting investment performance forward a bit, we did miss several key factors. The only meaningful data we had that showed actual declines in home values were in a handful of regional markets during a few episodes of local economic decline in the past.

For example, when the price of oil and gas declined precipitously in the 1980's, Texas, Oklahoma and Louisiana ("Oil Patch") home prices declined substantially. Similarly, big defense budget cuts in southern California led to a decline of 25% or more in housing prices in those local markets.

In accordance with classic supply and demand economics, most researchers concluded that loss in jobs drove loss in home values. Job creation (or job loss) correlated with defaults, and predicted credit loss to within 80% accuracy a full year in advance.

Examination of over three hundred separate Metropolitan Statistical Areas (MSA's) through several growth/recession cycles showed that if there was strong job growth in area metropolitan region, there were fewer mortgage defaults a year later.

All was well until 2007, when the credit models broke. Mortgage bond performance was declining and house prices were falling, even though unemployment was not rising.

Delinquencies and foreclosures rose to historic levels in 2007, from historic low levels in the two prior years, and kept on rising. There was simply no historic precedent for the trends in mortgage defaults, so the historically-derived models used to predict them were no longer valid, just the way the prepayment models had turned out to be invalid in 1992.

Unemployment was still under 5% nationwide, but troubled loans (loans that were delinquent by two months or more) were running twice the expected rate, and the trajectory was upwards from that.

Soon, every Wall Street research department that studied mortgages came to the conclusion that falling house prices were now the most important cause of mortgage defaults, rather than employment. Like everything else in the business, this new and critical factor soon got its own acronym, "HPA" for "House Price Appreciation." Before long, mortgage researchers began to project credit models with "flat HPA" and "negative HPA," which increased loss estimates for mortgage-backed securities.

When the models derived from historic data "break," investors find themselves in uncharted territory. They tend to look at trends, and then project that those trends will continue.

Unfortunately, simple extrapolation of trends rarely predicts the future accurately, no matter how popular the projection of the trendline might be. In the not-too-distant past, this was spectacularly demonstrated by Paul Ehrlich's 1968 bestseller <u>The Population Bomb</u> which predicted that hundreds of millions of people would die of starvation by the 1980's unless population growth was radically curtailed.

In a similar way, by the beginning of 2008, the market had extrapolated credit trends and come to the conclusion that 75% or more of all subprime loans were destined to default. Five years after subprime was declared "word of the year" in December of 2007, the actual losses to AAA through BBB rated subprime MBS issued from 2004 through 2007 were only around 7.5% of the principal amount issued, or $99 billion in losses among $1.3 trillion in bonds. Put in perspective, losses on the underlying mortgages was more than three times the expected levels, but roughly one tenth the amount the subprime bears said would come when making their predictions.

In retrospect, it seems obvious that years of rising housing values, especially the years of double-digit annual increases, had the effect of hiding the country's weaker borrowers, and keeping them from showing up as credit losses in Wall Street's statistical models.

While house prices were increasing at a rapid rate, borrowers could refinance into new subprime mortgages and take out cash to pay off credit card debt or simply to spend, thus sustaining the appearance of economic growth.

In this case, appearances were deceiving. Subprime mortgage MBS looked safer than they would have looked if borrowers who were spending more than they earned had been unable to refinance. In essence, refinancing "hid" the true credit problems of the borrowers, as borrowers consumed every dollar of available credit and focused only on covering their monthly debt service. This effect was compounded by the fact that borrowers who appeared qualified but really were not, were able to refinance at a lower rate and/or for a greater amount.

At some point, lenders had already lent money to all the good credits and responsible borrowers. But with virtually nonexistent losses to all kinds of borrowers and attractive financing from the capital markets, they kept lending.

As the volume continued to crank up, mortgage brokers just a few years out of high school were driving Mercedes. A lot of them didn't even recognize a bad loan when they saw one. Other mortgage brokers kidded themselves. And some didn't care, because making bad loans had lots of present positives and limited, distant negatives.

The negatives were that mortgage brokers or appraisers could eventually find their names on the blacklists kept by the most responsible lenders, those that tracked bad loans back to the source. Still, most bad loans take a year or two to go bad, and by then some of the individuals responsible for those loans would have already retired.

Similar to the children's game "hot potato," bad loans quickly passed from one hand to another. Wall Street conduits took a larger and larger percentage of the market. Wall Street ended up buying roughly 70% of all the subprime loans in the market, and bundling them to sell securities to an eager market.

For the Wall Street giants and a few other participants in the subprime market, the use of securitization went one step farther. There was a stream of excess interest – the 3% to 4% per year the mortgage loans paid over and above the cost of paying the subprime mortgage bonds. This was now pledged as collateral for yet another class of securitized bonds called NIMs, or Net Interest Margin Securities.

When the value of NIMs exceeded 5% of the cost of the mortgage loans in 2004 and 2005, the securitization equivalent of perpetual motion was born. By issuing NIMs, Wall Street dealers eliminated even the 5% exposure they retained in the initial securitization.

Securitizers could get all their money back, plus a profit, in a matter of months, and still own the rights to any excess interest after the NIMs paid off in two years or less. Since only about half the mortgages in a typical subprime pool of loans paid off in the first two years, that remaining "tail" of excess interest payments could be substantial, and owned for free.

By 2005, Wall Street "captive" subprime mortgage securitization companies were handling more than two-thirds of all subprime mortgage securitizations. The typical Wall Street subprime mortgage deal grew to $2 billion or more in size, and deals came every month or even more frequently from the largest issuers.

Subprime mortgages have been financed since the 1990's by issuing asset-backed securities that float over one-month LIBOR. Floating rate assets funded by floating rate liabilities like interest bearing checking accounts are typical for the ABS* market. These assets (loans) tended to have higher prepayments and higher delinquencies and defaults than conventional prime thirty-year mortgages.

ABS, or Asset-Backed Security - Bonds created by bundling financial assets such as car loans, trade receivables, credit card accounts or home equity loans together into a trust. Typically, these are floating rate bonds with shorter maturities than MBS.

In the world of subprime mortgages, even those with a thirty-year final maturity, prepayments by borrowers who refinanced or sold their houses gave the mortgage loans a three-year average life. That's why subprime mortgage bonds were grouped with other asset-backed securities like car loan or credit card bonds.

With interest rates low, lenders could make loans that were fixed at 7.5% for two years and then reset, eventually floating up to a full 5% or

6% over LIBOR. For nearly three years, Fed Funds were held at just 1%, so one-month LIBOR hovered just above that. High grade adjustable rate ABS bonds backed by subprime mortgages could be sold with interest rates that started out below 1.5% because money market rates were so low.

To guard against the risk that the Fed would raise rates, a securitizer could enter into an interest rate swap contract with a bank to pay a fixed rate of 2% to 2.5% per year and receive LIBOR floating rate payments in return. The banks that acted as counterparties liked this arrangement, because they collected the difference in rates, and only had to pay out money if one-month LIBOR went above the 2% or 2.5% fixed interest rate. Of course, the securitizers loved it, too, because they were able to lock in excess interest payments of 4% to 4.5% per year during the first two years of the securitization.

The only exceptions to this originate-to-securitize business model were the portfolio lenders, a handful of independent companies, and several large banks who originated mortgages in order to retain them in their investment portfolios. Banks would often cross-sell mortgage lending to their existing customer base. They "knew" their borrowers, and had room on their balance sheets to add portfolio investments.

But in the frenzy of the 2005/2006 market, lenders who chose to avoid dangerous lending practices risked going out of business. The mortgage brokers could always sell their loans to the Wall Street houses, or to large aggregator/securitizers like Ameriquest and New Century, who made their profits more the way Wall Street does and less the way traditional mortgage lenders do. They made their money by selling the loans into bond deals.

Among the loans that were hungrily consumed during this period were those that had no documentation and no verification of income or assets, along with the piggyback or down payment second mortgages. By carving up the loan into different categories and giving these categories different names, lenders could make it appear as if a loan was a prudent 80% loan-to-value first mortgage in circumstances where the financing totaled 100% (or even more than 100%) of the value of the home.

These loans were as dangerous for borrowers as they were for lenders and investors. For many borrowers, loans such as these looked like once-in-a-lifetime opportunities for wealth-building. But there was no margin for error. Borrowers couldn't afford to have their rates go up or their house decrease in value or lose their jobs or have any unexpected expenses. For borrowers living from paycheck to paycheck, these kinds of mortgages were potential winning lotto tickets. All that needed to happen was for the real estate appreciation trend line to continue.

Sharing the same unbridled optimism were the "flippers" who believed they would need to pay only one or two mortgage payments before they sold their investment property for a profit. Or they could spend a little longer improving the property and then really cash in. So popular was this last idea that many people left their jobs to become real estate speculators. Some became the stars of popular reality TV shows.

For other borrowers, the out-of-control lending environment created opportunities for fraud. After securing a mortgage, these borrowers simply didn't make the payments, essentially living rent free until foreclosure. The Rating Agencies have a category to describe the act of falsifying income or assets on loan applications to get into a house and live there as long as possible without ever making a mortgage payment. They call it "fraud for housing."

Some clever and unethical brokers and borrowers even hit a dozen lenders at the same time with loan applications for a dozen purchases, so the enormous burden of all those mortgages didn't show up in borrowers' credit reports until too late.

Ironically, the mad dash for home ownership backfired. Many formerly owner-occupied homes homes are now rental properties and some borrowers who never intended to become landlords find themselves as such. The financial crisis has created a plethora of renters from the formerly swelling ranks of home owners unable to make their payments.

Most subprime deals had pools of loans out of which about two-thirds were from refinancing rather than purchase. Weak borrowers who relied on cash-out refinancing to bail them out of the difficulties became the first to fall once the decline in house prices took hold.

Former renters seeing home ownership as a way to an instant nest egg got in over their heads with 100% financing. Some of them let their mortgages go into default while they stretched out the time they lived in the house they owned before becoming renters again, with a little more cash in their pockets from living mortgage-payment-free. Bad credit isn't all that bad if all you want is to qualify for a lease on a rental property.

As some housing sectors have recovered, especially the mid- and higher-priced homes, a huge fraction (estimated at one-third) of homes worth less than $100,000 have mortgages larger than their worth in the market, more than five years after the crisis.

The "good" subprime borrowers held on, and struggle to continue to do so. The more creditworthy borrowers had more lasting power and were largely worry-free early on in the financial crisis, but many of those borrowers are now feeling the pinch and worrying about just how long they can last. Few of the borrowers in even the riskiest categories would have turned into defaults in a market with steadily rising house prices.

Many of yesterday's investor-owned houses bought for resale have appeared on the rental market and many former homeowners are now renters again. It remains to be seen what percentage of the new landlords have the resources and wherewithal to take care of their rental properties and tenants, and for how long. The now swelling ranks of renters, many of whom are former homeowners, are no longer dreaming of building equity through home ownership and are unlikely ever to own a home again. Some may never be able to. Others will never undertake the risk again.

CHAPTER NINETEEN

The Great De-Levering

Levering means adding leverage; de-levering is the taking away of leverage. In the financial world, that means less money at work. And this can lead to a cascading downward trend that builds momentum as it goes.

The first quarter of 2008 brought even more signposts of the end of the financial world I believed in and helped to build. Chief among these were the signs of de-levering.

When everything was going well, it was easy to borrow as much as 95 to 98 cents on the dollar to finance high-quality securitized bonds. But when the market as a whole began to lower its exposure to leverage, investors who were borrowing money to finance their purchases had to come up with bigger down payments, just like home mortgage borrowers.

As the market turned south, borrowers with high leverage suffered a classic double whammy. Not only were their assets worth less, but secured lenders were no longer willing to lend them as big a percentage of the lowered values.

Let's imagine you were one of those investors. You'd been borrowing 95 cents of every dollar of value on your AAA MBS bonds from the friendly Wall Street firm that sold you those bonds in the first place. You watched your net worth plummet, as the bonds you thought were worth a lot suddenly became worth a lot less. Then you got "the call." It was actually a phone call but it was also a margin call.

If the value of your MBS had declined to 92 cents on the dollar, your Wall Street lender was now unwilling to lend you 95% of the lower value, because the asset you had (that MBS) could suddenly lose more than 5% of its value. Your lender never told you that they wanted a 20% cushion instead of the 5% cushion that used to be okay.

In a situation like this, you don't have a lot of great options. You can sell your MBS bonds at 92 cents on the dollar and still owe your lender three cents on the dollar. Or you can somehow come up with more money to give your lender. That bond you bought for 100 cents now only qualifies you to borrow 73.6 cents against it. Since you already owe the lender 95 cents, you need to come up with 21.4 cents per dollar, just to avoid having to sell your bond.

It was, and is, an ugly situation for investors. There were plenty of borrowers who couldn't meet their margin calls. The cascade was on, with lower prices forcing selling, which forced even lower prices, which forced more selling, in a continuous cascade downwards.

That's de-levering.

It has become clear that there are two kinds of participants in our leveraged financial world – the leverage users and the leverage providers. Even though most investors think of their brokerage firms as leverage providers, they are actually leverage users, borrowing more than they lend out.

When there are liquidations, prices go down, and that hits the capital base of the leverage providers (banks, insurance companies, pension funds), so less leverage is available to the leverage users (hedge funds, financial companies that aren't banks, Wall Street dealers). Bear Stearns was a huge leverage provider to customers and a huge user itself.

The only leverage provider that doesn't suffer loss of capacity when prices go down is the federal government. In March of 2008, the Federal Reserve offered a $200 billion credit line to the top twenty broker-dealers. It was the first time that the Fed had offered to lend Wall Street dealers Treasury securities in exchange for ordinary AAA-rated mortgage-backed securities offered as collateral.

That credit line didn't come in time to save Bear Stearns because it didn't become active until March 28, 2008. Bear Stearns ("the Bear") had been a giant in the mortgage business just a few weeks earlier, with monthly trading volume in MBS in excess of $1 trillion. Bear Stearns had been ranked the fifth largest Wall Street firm. In securitization, especially mortgages, it was even more important than that, ranked as Number Two in 2007.

On March 16, 2008, the Bear was mortally wounded when its hedge fund clients made multibillion dollar withdrawals. The firm was running out of liquidity. Its shareholders were crushed when the Fed decided that JP Morgan should take over, with no competition and a $29 billion loan from the taxpayers. The reason was simple: JP Morgan was the world's largest market marker in Credit Default Swaps (CDS). Bear was "only" the fifth-largest CDS market maker in the US market, though almost certainly larger than JP Morgan in the subprime MBS sector of the CDS market. Integrating Bear Stearn's CDS business into JP Morgan's was the easiest solution at hand.

Rather than forcibly de-lever the Bear, the taxpayers provided leverage to JP Morgan to take over. JP Morgan got the benefit of the spread between Bear Stearns' massive mortgage bond portfolio and the low cost of borrowing from the Federal Reserve. JP Morgan also got to take in some of the profit the CDS buyers had on paper, since they were now the only game in town when those hedge fund buyers wanted to cash in, so Morgan could set the close-out price as they pleased.

As you may recall from an earlier chapter, various kinds of MBS were used by investors to capture various kinds of spread. When spreads are tight, virtually every strategy to capture spread requires the use of leverage to provide adequate return on capital. In 2006, when spreads became very narrow, some Wall Street firms and Structured Investment Vehicles (SIVs) added leverage as high as 50-1 by issuing Asset Backed Commercial Paper (ABCP). Another large group of ABCP issuers were bank-sponsored conduits. These conduits were usually set up to finance bank clients or large producers of financial assets such as major mortgage lenders or auto finance companies. Unlike the SIVs, these ABCP issuers could move their assets to their sponsoring banks if they couldn't sell their commercial paper.

Leverage was a fact of life for the banks that remained the largest single ownership class of Agency MBS. It was true for the hedge funds, mezzanine CDOs and non-Agency mortgage REITs* that bought non-Agency MBS rated below AAA. It was also true for the banks, and

ABCP conduits and high profile mortgage REITs that bought AAA
and AA private label MBS.

Investors use leverage to magnify
profits, but that same leverage magnifies
losses. A particularly dangerous form of
leverage used by some investors includes
terms that mandate nightly valuations of
assets. If an investor was levered 19 to 1
(putting up 5% in cash and borrowing
95%) and the MBS in its portfolio

** REIT, or Real Estate
Investment Trust – A
company that invests in
real estate or real estate
debt, and pays no tax at
the corporate level as long
as it distributes 90% of its
taxable income to its
shareholders as dividends.*

dropped in value by just 2%, a margin call would come for more cash,
equal to 40% of the 5% cash they initially deposited. It gets ugly pretty
quickly when the de-levering cascade is in motion.

Throughout the summer of 2007, margin calls went out on a daily
basis for leveraged investments that relied on repurchase agreements
("repo") for financing. Among all forms of leverage for debt investors,
repo financing is probably the least forgiving.

It's a sale and repurchase, so the borrower doesn't legally own the
assets while they are pledged in the lending arrangement. This generally
helps the lender avoid lawsuits against the borrower, and in most cases,
even bankruptcy filing.

In a repo financing, the owner of the asset sells it to a lender and
simultaneously agrees to buy the asset back at a slightly higher price,
anywhere from a day to a year later. The difference in price is the
interest charged. Most repo financing in the MBS world is arranged for
up to three months at a time.

Repo agreements also allow the lender to assign new values to the
collateral held in the agreement at any time, and to request additional
collateral nightly – or even several times during a single day. Repo
lenders can also change the terms of the amount of
overcollateralization (the "haircut") they want – at their sole discretion.

While these strong lender protections enable even borrowers with
relatively weak credit to obtain attractive financing terms for good
quality collateral, it puts borrowers at serious risk in difficult markets.

Somewhat less dangerous is leverage that comes from maturity
mismatches. Using the attractive short-term financing available in the

commercial paper market, roughly $500 billion in longer-maturity asset-backed and mortgage-backed investments were held by issuers of ABCP in July of 2007.

Since Commercial Paper is short maturity, legally less than 270 days, the CP that funds five-year or ten-year average life assets has to be paid off and re-offered frequently. If investors didn't renew their subscriptions to the CP when it rolled off, the ABCP issuer would have no alternative but to begin selling assets.

When spreads widened and prices went down dramatically, the first kind of ABCP issuer to go under was the SIVs, or Structured Investment Vehicles. In place of bank support in the form of Letters of Credit or the liquidity arrangements that bank-sponsored ABCP conduits or programs used, the SIVs had a separate layer of debt in their capital structure, and rules regarding the market value of the assets.

For its AAA rated or AA rated assets, a SIV might issue 95% ABCP and 3% to 4% private debt rated BBB. That left only 1% to 2% of capital, which was considered equity in the SIV and levered between 49 to1 and 99 to 1.

While the SIVs did not have direct margin calls, they did have structural rules that required market value cushions over and above the outstanding senior debt (the CP). Among all the ABCP issuers, SIVs had the most direct de-levering risk because of this market value maintenance requirement.

A few of these highly-levered vehicles faced liquidation when the value of structured investments like AAA CDOs declined, and the news of those liquidations caused widespread avoidance of the CP issued by all ABCP issuers. This despite the fact that only a small fraction of the $1.2 trillion in assets held by issuers of ABCP was mortgage-related.

In 2007 and 2008, a number of ABCP issuers found themselves without buyers when it came time to auction new CP. Some dealt with these auction failures by extending the CP terms and paying the investors a premium interest rate during the extension period.

When the extensions began to run out, the debt market was in even worse condition. A number of ABCP issuers ended up having to liquidate their underlying AAA and AA assets into a hostile market. A few couldn't even pay off their ABCP because proceeds from the liquidations came to less than 95 cents on the dollar.

Investors began to question the quality of all types of underlying assets in all types of ABCP. The total amount of outstanding ABCP also began to decline as the renewals came up, which forced the sale or transfer of the underlying assets, whether they were questionable subprime bonds or not.

Over the period from mid-2007 to early 2008, aggregate ABCP declined from approximately $1.2 trillion to less than $800 billion, and those assets had to be sold or transferred onto the balance sheets of the sponsoring banks. Put in perspective, the assets being sold by these vehicles over a six-month period roughly equaled the record high 2007 Federal budget deficit.

The asset liquidations didn't make headlines because they happened gradually. Most ABCP in the market had various maturities spread out from one week to six months or longer. Because of this gradual selling, even investment professionals outside the fixed income arena weren't focused on the pressure that liquidation of top-rated structured bonds was having on the entire infrastructure of the debt investment world. But constant pressure was on the market.

The de-levering cascade was gaining momentum.

It is telling that as the cascade began, the Federal government's first attempt to stop it was to save the SIVs. Ironically, this initial government attempt at a bailout was almost invisible and did not involve subprime mortgages.

In July of 2007, Treasury Secretary Paulson tried to get a consortium of major banks to create a $100 billion "Super SIV" to finance the existing SIV assets for a full year without the risk associated with frequent commercial paper rollover auctions. At that time, SIV assets were estimated at a total market value of approximately $320 billion.

From the vantage point of the White House, there was a problem requiring action in the levered finance market nearly two months before the problems of home buyers had risen to a level that elicited government action.

For the general public, the news broke relatively slowly. Approximately two months after floating the Super SIV idea, the White House began to address the mortgage market when President Bush announced the "Hope Now Alliance" to mitigate the growing flood of foreclosures in subprime mortgages.

For the world of bond investors, the crisis had been getting worse daily. Things had been getting progressively tighter all year, but August had been extraordinary, with even quasi-government bonds like Agency MBS getting "push back" from Wall Street as the dealers refused to renew repo financing for anything except government bonds.

Large scale liquidations of the highest grade structured bonds naturally forced prices down and spreads wider, and that forced spreads even wider on bonds lower down in the "capital stack" of credit subordination.

For a leveraged holder of bonds on repo, a decline in bond prices will result in a margin call. An increase in "haircut" will also result in a margin call. An increase in lending margin (the rate) adds insult to injury. All three at the same time guarantees a bad day at the office.

As a broker-dealer and newly formed mortgage lender, e*trade Financial was susceptible to these pressures, and lost its ability to borrow against its subprime mortgage bonds in November of 2007. Forced to reduce its inventory, it sold a multi-billion dollar portfolio to a Chicago-based hedge fund, Citadel. Citadel took advantage of the fact that the prices for the ABX* index of subprime credit default swaps had raced downward ahead of the regular cash bond market and used that index to set the price it would offer. The trade was reported in the press as having taken place at an average price of just twenty-seven cents on the dollar.

ABX – A family of derivative indices that approximate the cash flows of bonds from twenty large subprime mortgage deals dating from late 2005 through 2007.

This was an important signpost on the road to victory for the professional gamblers who became the big winners in the crisis. For the first time a big trade of actual bonds was traded based on the "synthetic" index that was more a measure of market opinion than an actual value derived from projected cash flows and time value of money calculations. To put it in terms we all can understand, it would be like the NFL awarding the Vince Lombardi Trophy to the Las Vegas betting line favorite rather than having the playoffs determine the winner.

Some of the more brazen players that had bet on the collapse even seized on this trade as a reason to threaten to sue any auditor who *didn't* use the ABX or the other CDS indicators to value assets at any bank or fund that owned any securitized MBS.

Leverage and tolerance for risk spans an entire spectrum of fine gradations. At one end of the spectrum, a few leveraged debt investors have no exposure at all to margin calls or even to refinancing risk. Only the actual performance of the underlying assets determines the results for those investors. At the other end of the spectrum, a few investors are 100% exposed to nightly market valuations and associated margin calls. For those investors, the biggest factor in their results will be whether they can meet their margin calls. If they can't, the eventual performance of the underlying assets is immaterial, as it was with e*trade. Even within this group of highly leveraged investors, some use more leverage than others.

During the LTCM crisis of 1998, borrowers like Criimi Mae and the Ellington Management fund were almost entirely dependent on repo financing. The markdowns that hit their assets translated instantly into do-or-die margin calls.

In contrast, leveraged market participants like mortgage originators and banks who didn't have to meet margin calls for loans in repo lending arrangements (called "warehouses") may have felt stress but it wasn't life threatening.

Following the problems of the credit crunch of 1998, Wall Street and the investor community were searching for a way to finance longer maturity assets, without having to constantly refinance them, or suffer from margin calls if the assets dropped in value.

In a sense, the explosion of the CDO market in 2000 through 2006 was an attempt to address this need. CDOs offered an answer to the dual problems of margin calls and mismatched funding. A "cash flow" CDO allowed an issuer to put a collection of bonds or loans into a funding vehicle that matched the funding term to the asset term.

All went well as long as the underlying assets kept paying. However, if the underlying assets began to lose their ratings beyond certain limits, or if enough of the assets weren't able to pay the interest due, then the deal was likely to reach an "Event of Default," or EOD. If as few as five percent of the bonds in a CDO had meaningful credit downgrades, the CDO *itself* could have an EOD. When that happened, the entire pool of assets could be liquidated.

These EOD's came in a trickle at first, and then a flood. When the Rating Agencies downgraded MBS and ABS, many of the bonds they downgraded were in CDOs. Exacerbating the situation was the fact that the CDOs were designed to maximize return, which meant they maximized leverage.

In the first four months of 2008, CDO liquidations were running around the rate of $10 billion a month *despite the fact that they had enough cash coming to keep paying.* The situation was one in which only 5% or 10% of the collateral experienced downgrades but *not actual credit losses,* yet it resulted in a forced sale of 100% of the bonds that the CDO held as collateral.

The extraordinary force of these liquidations pushed even "bulletproof" bonds to spreads measured in the hundreds of basis points. In March of 2008, Carlyle Capital only had $670 million in equity, but its collapse precipitated the forced sale of nearly $22 billion in Fannie Mae and Freddie Mac floating rate CMO bonds in just a couple of days.

That was less than three weeks after a large hedge fund called Peleton Partners was forced to liquidate its AAA MBS portfolio. Peleton was actually a big winner in 2007, having taken a large negative bet in the ABX and CDS market against mortgage credits. In the beginning of 2008, Peleton went long after their big win on the short side bet the year before. They bought top-rated subprime and alt-A mortgage bonds rumored to total $30 billion. Less than two months later, those bonds were sold to meet margin calls, and Peleton Partners went bust.

Once the "riskless" (from a credit standpoint) residential mortgage bonds had been crushed to the point where they paid enormous spreads, it was inevitable that the storm of the century in bond markets would sweep over the whole fleet. Investors in corporate bonds, commercial mortgage bonds, emerging market bonds, bank loans and even municipal bonds all faced abrupt loss of value for their investments. If they were using leverage, they were likely forced to sell.

Eventually, the system-wide de-levering began to take hold in areas seemingly completely separated from mortgages. The municipal bond market had a "mini meltdown" when auctions for short-term municipal paper called Auction Rate Securities (ARS) failed to get enough buyers to refinance maturing ARS. Dozens of banks pulled out of the business of making student loans even though the government guaranteed 95% of the principal of those loans. Shipping companies began to cancel orders for new vessels even though daily charter rates for tankers, container ships and dry bulk ships were near all-time highs.

When we look at the de-levering cascade, we have to ask ourselves: Are subprime mortgages really the problem here?

When Bear Stearns collapsed, preliminary analysis of its assets and liabilities showed a mere $200 million in net exposure to subprime and subprime-backed CDO bonds in a $400 billion pool of assets (that's five basis points, or about one half of one tenth of a percent).

Bear Stearns was also shown to have $11 billion in capital supporting that $400 billion in assets. That's a 36 to 1 leverage ratio. And that's the real problem.

Banks also operate with high leverage. They can be leveraged 12 to 1 on loans they make to individuals or companies but they can and do carry leverage ratios as high as 40 to 1 for assets like the CMOs the Carlyle Group held at a leverage ratio of 32 to 1.

That explains why the Fed began aggressively lowering rates in 2007, even as the spreads on all types of loans kept rising, a trend that makes bank lending more profitable. The Fed was intent on recapitalizing the banking system by giving them enormous profits from holding high-yielding assets. The losers were people who depended on bank CDs or other short-term assets for income.

While bailouts, zero interest rates, taxpayer capital infusions and credit supports were the rule for the big banks and big investors as the de-levering took hold, there was almost no accommodation for households that were also forcibly de-levered.

Household de-levering didn't happen in the liquidity crisis after LTCM, or in the asset liquidation following the S&L crisis. Millions of households that had home equity lines of credit (HELOCs) or credit cards as an emergency source of funds received letters from their banks cutting those lines, even if those borrowers had never missed a payment. This put more and more families on the verge of going through their own personal de-levering spiral, a spiral that culminates with the loss of their single largest store of wealth – the equity they had in their homes.

On a small scale, all Americans suffered the same loss of liquidity as the banks, insurance companies and fund managers, but without the benefits that corporations enjoyed, such as carrying the losses forward to shelter all their income for years ahead or the massive support from taxpayers.

Leverage was the undoing of most of the non-bank mortgage lenders, a number of high-profile hedge funds, and even seemingly conservative special purpose companies that bought high quality debt and funded it by issuing commercial paper.

Banks, insurance companies, Wall Street dealers and even financial arms of industrial companies like GE and GM were all given additional credit lines when the market wouldn't lend to them. That came from the ultimate leverage provider, the U.S. Government, via the Fed's Discount Window*.

How the de-levering plays out for households won't be clear for years, perhaps decades. The largest impact will probably be in dramatically reduced lifestyles for Baby Boomers and the Gen X group that suffered a major loss in household wealth. But it isn't just the wealth tied up in their homes that suffered. Many responsible people decided to keep paying their debts even as their income dropped, so they cashed in stocks when prices got hammered, and paid tax penalties if those stocks were in their retirement accounts.

Discount Window – A repo lending facility the Federal Reserve provides to regulated banks that takes in Treasuries, MBS, ABS, or other collateral to give the banks short term financing. It carries the risk of margin calls for the banks, but has the promise that no bank will be turned away.

It all brings to mind one of the most cynical of Wall Street's aphorisms... "The purpose of a bear market is to return the wealth to its rightful owners."

CHAPTER TWENTY

Contagion

As the structured finance credit crisis unfolded, two of the most popular words used to describe it were "contagion" and "contained." Although both these words share the Latin prefix "con," meaning "with," the first word was used to throw gasoline on the fire and the second word was used in an attempt to throw water on the fire that was spreading out of control.

It was common throughout 2007 to hear business leaders, our Federal Reserve Chairman, and a stream of politicians all using the word "contained." By repeating the mantra "the subprime mortgage problem is contained," the containment team hoped they could convince the market and the public that it was only those little subprime people who had a problem.

Arrayed against the containment team were the reporters and hedge fund bears who shouted "contagion" every chance they got.

It was enough to make you wonder if either team knew how the capital markets really work. The belief they had in common was that creditworthiness (or the lack thereof) is contagious. The analysis was presented as if they thought that sharing an elevator with a person with poor credit might make a responsible person go home and default on their obligations.

The fact is that simple exposure to subprime borrowers does not make good borrowers turn into bad borrowers. Nor does one investment turn bad just because another does. That kind of contagion is an imaginary malady, like the "humours" doctors thought caused disease before they discovered bacteria.

The containment team looked to all the other classes of debt to assure themselves that credit problems were contained, pointing out that credit card bills, prime mortgages and car loans were still being paid on time. At the same time, the contagion team looked everywhere for evidence that other classes of debt were collapsing.

Meanwhile, the real contagion both should have been worried about was taking hold. The relentless focus in both the financial press and the general press on what they liked to call "the subprime meltdown" was leading investors to do everything they could to avoid any exposure to this sector of the debt market. Some investors automatically sold the stock of banks, insurance companies, mortgage lenders or any entity that might have exposure to subprime mortgage debt, no matter how small, and regardless of whether that exposure reflected any genuine risk or not.

Fire sales took place for financial products containing no genuine risk, such as a bond with top priority for payments and a huge percentage of the structured deal subordinated to it. We sometimes saw these kinds of bonds with 70% or 80% of the deal in junior positions in a credit "waterfall."

Let's see what actually happens in a deal such as this when a mortgage loan in the pool is foreclosed. After the house is sold, selling expenses, legal fees, repairs, etc. are repaid to the mortgage servicer who advanced those costs. Then the proceeds from the sale are forwarded to the Trustee for the securitization. Any loss is recorded as a reduction of principal ("write off") for the lowest priority bond in the deal structure. Finally, the money that is recovered is used to pay down principal on the highest priority bond. A bond with 80% of the deal subordinated underneath it could withstand having every single house in the mortgage pool foreclosed and sold at a small fraction of its former value. Where I was working, we called these bonds "bulletproof," because they actually get paid no matter what happens, and they could be paid off even faster if there are more foreclosures.

When investors avoid bonds like these, and force them to be sold for very high spreads, they essentially force every other bond to offer the same or higher spread. This is capital markets contagion, and it has nothing to do with creditworthiness.

Billions of dollars worth of subprime debt was being sold for a song, even the bulletproof stuff. The result was that borrowing became much more expensive. This affected both prime mortgage borrowers and foreign governments. Corporate entities also had to borrow operating capital at much higher rates than they would have otherwise.

Soon, investors who bought mining company stocks, agricultural companies or fast-growing foreign companies were disappointed by earnings that came in lower than expected. Lower earnings should have been no surprise, given the fact that the asset-backed commercial paper programs were among the biggest suppliers of trade financing used to cover the cost of metal ores or agricultural commodities until delivery.

When the market avoided buying that commercial paper, those who relied on that funding had to locate new sources of financing. Many good borrowers in the commodities business had to turn to bank loans for their short-term financing. That was already a more expensive source, but became even more expensive as the banks themselves paid higher spreads due to worries about mortgage exposure.

Selling good bonds dirt cheap and making all financing too expensive is the result of true contagion. It was a natural outgrowth of the avoidance of subprime mortgage bonds, no matter what the flavor or concentration. And it makes no more sense than wholesale slaughter of every livestock breed around the world following an outbreak of Avian Flu in chicken flocks in just one country.

One underlying cause for the eventual collapse of our debt markets was the policy reaction to the first recession of the new millennium – an extraordinary period of negative real interest rates.

We witnessed nearly unprecedented government spending increases at the same time that government revenues (taxes) decreased. The net result was huge inflation for assets that could be easily financed and exhaustion of savings to support current spending.

Trusting history, mortgage lenders believed the collateral value of the houses they lent against would not decline in any meaningful way, and certainly not nationwide. The capital markets enabled funding of mortgage loans, even subprime mortgage loans, only 30 to 50 basis points above LIBOR.

With LIBOR as low as 1.10% after the Fed lowered short term
rates to 1%, a subprime borrower was paying a full 5% premium above
funding costs even after taking expenses into account. Since the prior
peak for loss rates on subprime mortgage loans was only 2% to 3%
annually or 6% to 7% over the life of the deals, it seemed that there
was plenty of cushion against losses.

Homeowners responded to this environment by taking an
unprecedented amount of cash out of their homes, either by selling
them, or by refinancing. By 2005, "cash out refi's" were estimated to
have added as much as $600 billion a year to the American economy.
That was nearly 4% of the economy at the time.

The Federal Government was doing much the same, borrowing
about $400 billion a year from Social Security and Medicare payroll
taxes to spend on current projects, in addition to several hundred
billion a year in deficit spending. As a nation and as households, we
were trying to borrow our way to prosperity.

At some point, schemes that involve borrowing to support current
consumption run out of assets or future income to pledge, or run out
of lenders willing to lend. In the case of US housing, both effects
combined to help the market "roll over" precipitously.

Effects are often compounded when two unfortunate events
occur simultaneously. Virtually all the creditworthy potential home
owners (as well as many who weren't creditworthy) had acquired their
first homes. At the same time, the increase in home values came to a
halt and this latent source of future income to pay debt service
disappeared.

This latent income had actually bailed out many of the subprime
borrowers who paid their mortgages, credit cards and car loans by
taking out cash through refinancings as the value of their homes
increased much faster than the rate of inflation.

The open question is to what extent this latent income also made
prime and near-prime borrowers appear to be able to handle their debt
loads better than their earned income would allow.

The politicians and talking heads that fell into the "contained"
camp spent most of 2007 focusing on the good performance numbers
for credit card debt, prime mortgages, auto loans, and other debt. They

concluded that the rising tide of mortgage delinquencies was limited to the typical subprime borrower, a borrower who lived as little as one or two paychecks away from defaulting on their debts. The "contagion" camp was watching the same statistics, looking for an uptick in problem credits to justify their view of worldwide credit destruction.

For a while, the "contained" camp won the war of ideas, to disastrous effect. Nervous investors believed that if they could only contain the problem, they could preserve the value of their portfolios. So they tried their best to find anything that had any exposure to subprime mortgages. And they sold it at almost any price.

The great portfolio purge had begun. Investors were soon dumping commercial paper from SIVs that had pools of $400 billion in assets with only 2% to 3% subprime debt. Significantly larger asset classes in those SIVs were bonds and CDs sold by insurance companies and banks, prime mortgage investments, CLOs collateralized by bank loans to speculative corporate credits, and trade financing for commodities like oil, metal ores and agricultural commodities.

Unwittingly, in their rush to avoid subprime mortgages, investors were damaging market sectors that were supposedly insulated from subprime risk. The direct effect of the portfolio purge was to increase costs, cut funding capabilities and reduce profit in other market sectors. While its effect will not be seen for a while, and those commodities businesses are strong, they now have a need for new and more expensive funding for trade finance. This is Stage One of real contagion.

Ironically, the SIVs that were being forced to shut down only held about $8 billion of the subprime mortgage bond market, or about half a percent of the $1.2 trillion in subprime mortgage funding. Selling out of those positions made almost no difference to the subprime mortgage bond business but it made a big difference to the banks and insurance companies that had relied on the SIVs for funding. Those banks and insurance companies scarcely needed additional pressure on their capital bases or cost of borrowing, since they held most of the mortgage debt before the crisis began.

Banks under pressure had no choice but to tighten up on all lending, and to charge higher rates to borrowers. This is Stage Two of real contagion.

House prices were no longer increasing, but decreasing. Many borrowers needed rising house prices to pay their debt service. At the same time, the cost of debt service was going up with increased mortgage rates. The sell off in subprime mortgage bonds accelerated as investors anticipated that foreclosures and the losses on foreclosures would increase.

Some investors decided they couldn't ignore the attractive values available in residential MBS. However, because investors are nearly always fully invested, they have to sell something in order to buy something else. Selling one type of mortgage bond to buy another is the easiest choice within an institution, so commercial mortgage yield spreads widened as commercial mortgage bonds were sold so investors could take advantage of great deals in residential mortgage bonds. This is Stage Three of real contagion.

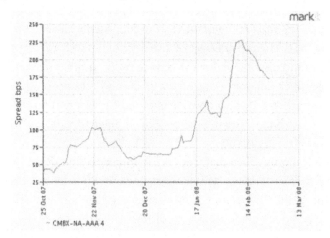

Source: Markit.com

Simultaneously, in 2008, commercial mortgage loans began to lose value, even though commercial properties had not been overbuilt to the same level they had been in prior economic cycles. Professionals in that specialty were dumbfounded, because fundamental credit performance was better than it had ever been. In January of 2008, securitized commercial mortgages recorded their lowest delinquency rate in history.

Even AAA-rated CMBS (commercial mortgage backed securities) were soon trading at 200 to 225 basis point spreads over LIBOR, up from 15 to 25 basis points a year earlier. Spreads for US Government-guaranteed Ginnie Mae MBS and implicitly guaranteed Fannie Mae and Freddie Mac MBS also doubled.

High quality corporate bonds from even top-rated corporations like GE and Berkshire Hathaway were soon trading at around 100 basis points over LIBOR, ten times the spreads they traded at in prior years.

Less creditworthy corporate borrowers experienced even harsher increases in borrowing costs and terms. The Markit.com chart below shows spreads for an index of 100 issues of high-yield corporate bank loans, loans to the same kind of companies that issue junk bonds.

Even though the subprime meltdown was well underway in October of 2007, the average junk bond was only trading around 220 basis points over LIBOR. That changed when the real contagion hit Stage Three, and investors began to sell other kinds of debt to raise money to buy more of the cheap mortgage bonds. The following chart shows the price and the yield spreads of the LCDX index, a proxy for CDS on bank loans for 100 corporate borrowers. As 2008 opened, spreads were around 3% over LIBOR and in six weeks, jumped up to 5.2% over LIBOR.

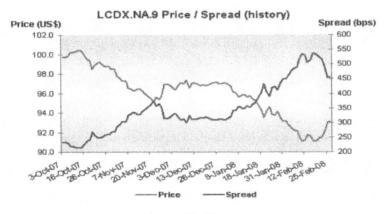

Source: Markit.com

The selling of debt instruments continued as more and more leveraged investors and special purpose vehicles were forcibly unwound.

There were subprime mortgage bonds in the market that would pay full principal and interest even if every single mortgage were foreclosed, and the houses mortgaged sold for circa-1988 prices. In spite of the virtually risk-free return of all principal and interest on these bonds, they traded in February of 2008 at spreads several hundred basis points over LIBOR.

This led rational investors to conclude that any borrower or debt would have to pay the same or higher yield spreads unless the "bulletproof" mortgage bonds started trading at lower yields and higher prices.

This was the fourth and final stage of real contagion, as the capital markets gradually became more difficult across all debt categories, no matter what the underlying asset or source of funds. The final straw was when subprime mortgage bonds with little or no credit risk could be bought at very high yield spreads, so all the other kinds of debt had to drop in value until they also offered high spreads.

A more insidious contagion was unleashed as we watched the weakening of the housing and housing finance market in the largest economy in the world.

The high credit scores of the alt-A borrowers indicate that they have more economic lasting power than subprime borrowers. However, it would be a mistake to assume that alt-A borrowers didn't see the same opportunities and take the same risks as the subprime borrowers did. This has proven to be the case, as we began seeing higher delinquencies and defaults among pools of alt-A mortgages as early as the second half of 2007.

Alt-A borrowers were simply the next group along the credit spectrum, and they, too were taking equity from their homes to spend, counting on further home price appreciation to fund their activities. The delinquencies and defaults showed up six to eight months later only because the alt-A's had more financial resources than the subprimes.

Actually, it's all a continuum. Every person and every family in America is constantly doing what they can to manage their cash flows and their obligations, and the results will always vary from those that can never pay all their bills on time to those that never miss a payment, even by a single day.

General economic conditions tend to push more of us up or down the scale. On top of that, at any given time, a decent sized fraction of us are dealing with large financial disruptions or setbacks such as divorce, a new job, tuition or medical bills, along with a myriad of smaller financial issues.

Lower house prices and poor real estate markets became a nationwide problem in 2007, so even the prime borrowers whose loans made up the core portfolios of major banks and the housing Agencies Fannie Mae and Freddie Mac were in trouble if they needed to sell their homes or refinance.

Even those prime mortgage loans and mortgage-backed securities became hard to finance by March of 2008. That's when the Fed stepped in, increasing its lending to nearly $400 billion, making the money available to the banks and directly to Wall Street dealers by resurrecting emergency lending authority not employed since the Great Depression.

Just a month later, in April of 2008, the effects of Stage Four of the bond market contagion struck the student loan market like a violent windstorm. Like the mortgage market, the majority of student loans are backed by government guarantees. Millions of families relied on these private loans to make up the gap between the government loans and the cost of college education.

Those loans had been securitized, just like mortgages, into asset-backed securities (ABS) and a market existed in both government-guaranteed student loan ABS and private label student loan ABS. When these ABS could only be sold at wide spreads, lenders were losing money on every loan. Dozens of banks had dropped out of the federal program by April of 2008. Virtually no lender would make the private loans, either.

By the middle of April, 2008, Congress was holding hearings to determine what sort of emergency action could be taken to bail out banks that were deserting the business of student lending, even with a government guarantee.

The question the market then faced was whether the extraordinary injection of liquidity into the bond markets by the Federal Reserve and the European central banks would be enough to keep the process of contagion from going on to Stage Five (no private credit at all; only strong sovereign credit accepted).

We got the answer in the fall of 2008. After repeated runs on the capital of AIG through margin demands by those holding CDS written by AIG Financial Products, the largest AAA insurance company in the world was suddenly insolvent. Sadly, the CDS insurance contracts AIGFP wrote were mostly held by banks, and insured only the top-rated AAA tranches of securitizations that contained some subprime MBS.

The banks and dealers that contracted with AIG were actually buying reinsurance* to limit the risk for the CDS contracts they had written, usually on the lower-rated BBB or single-A tranches of MBS or CDOs. On the other side of the dealers who wrote

Reinsurance – A form of specialized insurance used by insurance companies to lay off some of their risk to other "wholesale" insurance companies.

those contracts were the hedge funds that made the big bet. What surprised everyone is that the sheer volume of the cash claims meant that every large bank and major dealer was also insolvent unless AIG paid.

The economy of the whole world was threatened by Stage Five.

CHAPTER TWENTY-ONE

Invasion of the Profit Snatchers

Most of the people betting against the subprime mortgage bond market had not been traditional bond investors. In fact, most of them traded stocks for a living.

Strangely enough, many of them bet without even understanding exactly what their bets were.

I received an an eye-opening telephone call in 2007 from a bond salesman at a top Wall Street house telling me about a client of his who was an equity long/short hedge fund manager. The hedge fund manager had come in unsolicited earlier in 2007 to buy credit insurance on subprime mortgage bonds. My friend's firm had satisfied the request, and sold him Credit Default Swaps (CDS) on a basket of specific subprime bonds.

Shortly before he picked up the phone to call me, the bond salesman had received a call from this client. The client wanted to know when he was going to get the cash from his CDS. One of the subprime bonds referenced by the CDS had been downgraded by the Rating Agencies. Although his CDS contract had quite a bit of paper profit, the hedge fund manager seemed unaware that he wouldn't get paid unless the bond had a credit loss – a downgrade didn't count. While some corporate bond CDS contracts are written with a provision that defines default as a major credit downgrade, that's not true for CDS on subprime mortgage bonds.

Our hedge fund manager was on the hook to pay 2% or more per year in premiums until a credit loss actually happened. This pattern of paying cash equal to the bond's yield spread, and receiving cash equal to credit write-downs was radically different from the simple "on or off" payments in corporate bond CDS. It was remarkable to my friend the bond salesman (and to me) that anyone could put real money at risk without even knowing what it took to get paid on his bet.

It might have helped our hedge fund manager if someone had suggested that he think of his CDS credit insurance the same way he thinks of his car insurance. If there's a fender bender, collision insurance pays out something. It pays out even more if the car is totaled. Both the cost of the insurance and the payoff go down over time as the value of the car declines.

With his CDS, of course, he wasn't purchasing insurance on anything he owned. Imagine insuring *someone else's* BMW. That's what this hedge fund manager did when he took out credit insurance on those subprime mortgage bonds with a CDS. Now, if you knew that a bunch of people had taken out insurance policies totaling twenty times the value of your BMW and would get a big payoff if the car was totaled, would you be worried? The investors that owned those bonds should have been.

To understand a bit more about how credit default swaps work, let's look at the parties in the transaction. The buyer of insurance in the swap is the credit bear and we call that party the protection buyer. The seller of insurance is the credit bull, or protection seller.

If a credit bear buys protection on a bond that gets most of its principal paid off before foreclosure losses hit it, the protection buyer may end up paying more in premiums than the policy pays when the remainder of the bond finally gets written off. Even if the protection buyer bets correctly, the payoff can end up being less than the amount paid for the insurance. That's not to say that large profits can't be realized by the bearish trader who places a bet at the right time.

Under most CDS contracts until 2006, the credit bear who bought the CDS protection delivered the actual bond to the counterparty to receive its current face amount. This is how most corporate bond CDS contracts were written, as well as some subprime mortgage bond CDS.

Someone like our hedge fund manager could try to make a profit by placing a bullish bet in addition to his bearish bet. He was paying 2% per year on his original CDS. If the bond spread went up, let's say to 10%, he could sell protection (take the bullish side of the trade) for

10% per year. While paying out 2% and taking in 10%, he could lock in a profit of 8% per year until the bond matured or was written off by credit losses.

This activity is called "novating" the swap, and it creates two swaps that both run until the bond matures. In essence, it's one bet with an arbitrage. But the fact that there are two swaps helps in creating the huge numbers of swaps that make the swap market a significant risk to world financial systems. In fact, it's more likely that each swap contract is being counted four times, not twice, since the original swap and the novated swap were each reported by both parties to the contracts.

There is another way for the successful bear to realize a profit. If a distressed seller of mortgage bonds sells downgraded bonds in the market, the bear who wants to realize his profit on a CDS can buy the reference bond he holds insurance on and deliver that bond to the contract counterparty. To realize the profit without delivering the reference bond, the bear can buy a bond that is similar as a replacement.

If the credit bear buys the replacement bond for ten or fifteen cents on the dollar, he will get interest payments from that bond until it gets written off. That covers his obligation to pay out CDS premiums. In essence, he sold the CDS reference bond at par, and bought the same bond or its replacement for fifteen cents. He can now let the CDS contracts run to maturity and lock in eighty-five cents of profit.

In the 2007 meeting of the American Securitization Forum, one trader on a panel said he had sold the same defaulted subprime mortgage bond eight times, usually for five cents on the dollar. Each time the bond came back to him, it was still worth nothing, because other buyers were purchasing it simply to extinguish CDS contracts. Of course, the fact that he sold the bond eight times indicated just how many times insurance had been bought by speculators who didn't own the bond.

In 2006 and early 2007, taking the bearish side of the CDS market in subprime MBS was such a popular trade among hedge funds that the total outstanding CDS contracts ended up, by some estimates, being fifty to one hundred times larger than the total outstanding balance of the bonds.

In essence, investors placing these bets were allowed to buy or sell insurance on bonds that didn't exist. For normal insurance markets, that's fraud, but this kind of credit insurance has no regulation and no specific reporting. In fact, the only reporting at all is the aggregate total, by "type" – e.g; all CDS – for regulated banks, but not for their customers.

How can anyone buy insurance on something they don't own? Because the CDS market has no mechanism to require delivery. No one's counting. It's a case of intentional innumeracy.

The unusual situation we see in the credit default swaps market is prohibited in traditional derivatives markets by the Commodity Futures and Trading Commission (CFTC). And with good reason. Imagine a group of traders selling ten times as much wheat as the entire harvest, or ten times as much of a company's stock as existed. For a while at least, the price of wheat or the price of the stock would plunge.

The commodities markets require delivery, so a condition like that would make the price of wheat rebound. The short selling of stock also requires delivery, although the explosion in the number of failures to deliver (FTD's) for stocks that short sellers want to sell but couldn't or won't borrow also had an impact on the financial crisis. Needless to say, nearly all the stand-alone mortgage companies were on the list of shorted stocks. The SEC gave exemptions from delivery to some market participants, such as option market makers, and provided amnesty and extensions to others.

A few market manipulators were caught and fined by the stock exchanges for employing the exemption by creating "market maker" affiliates, and selling stock without delivering. Each time the last day for delivery approached under the exemption, they created new sham option transactions to reset the clock for the thirteen business day final deadline for delivery. Nobody went to jail and the fines were quite a bit less than the profits made on those manipulative stock and option trades..

The way it stands now, buyers of securities can pay for stock that doesn't exist, sellers can short shares that don't exist, and sellers and brokers can get their money even if delivery is delayed. It's an opportunistic infection that would be easy to remedy. Just enact a rule that buyers don't have to pay for securities until they're delivered. And then enforce that rule, with sellers receiving payment and brokers receiving commissions only when delivery has been completed.

The worldwide laxity of enforcement unfortunately coincided with short sellers of bonds and CDS employing the strategies and tactics commonplace in the equity arena. The somewhat stodgier world of bond trading wasn't prepared for most of them.

One of the biggest winners in the bearish bond betting club was a former Wall Street salesman named John Paulson, who manages a hedge fund from his eponymous fund manager Paulson & Company. In 2007, it was widely reported that Paulson had written to multiple regulators and was contemplating suing Bear Stearns because the Bear was modifying loans with borrowers. Paulson alleged they did so to limit losses on the ABX Index.

While it is true that modification of loans can help cut losses, Bear Stearns was actually required to do this as servicer of those loans, since it has a duty to protect the interests of the bondholders. Unfortunately, this kind of action also tends to limit gains for those betting against the bonds on the bear side of the trade.

Now, consider the fact that Bear Stearns only serviced the loans in *one* of the twenty deals in the index. It's as if someone betting against the Dow Jones Index of thirty stocks decided to sue one company for buying back a small amount of its own stock on the theory that it was manipulating the whole index.

In October of 2007, Mr. Paulson made a charitable donation of $15 million to the Center for Responsible Lending (CRL). With Paulson's support, the CRL was trying to stop or slow down foreclosures on subprime borrowers who weren't paying their mortgages.

According to the Mortgage Bankers' Association, the CRL encourages defaulting mortgage borrowers to declare personal bankruptcy. While the effects of personal bankruptcy do linger for ten years a bankruptcy filing can also extend the process of foreclosure.

If the CRL is successful in extending the time a lender must pay insurance, taxes and other expenses while borrowers don't, it costs the lenders more as they cover those costs. That cost ends up reflected in greater losses on subprime bonds, which in turn increases Paulson's payoff on the credit bet against those bonds. The profits from his bet were reported in early 2008 at a staggering $15 billion. How much larger were those profits, given CRL's nationwide effort to prevent and delay foreclosures?

Let's play "What if?" What if the decline in the subprime bond market was partially engineered as a trading strategy to maximize profits? Could we find other examples of leveraged trading instruments used to magnify profits?

Look at the first index of CDS on securitized bonds, which was launched in 2005 using twenty-five large commercial mortgage deals as its reference. That index, called the CMBX* 1, was used by real estate developers, lenders and others involved in the real estate market as a way to hedge spread risk during the process of negotiating and finalizing complex financing packages.

* CMBX – A family of indices of credit default swaps on bonds from 25 separate CMBS deals all originated in roughly the same nine months. Each index series has six different credit levels, ranging from senior AAA down to BBB- (triple-B minus).

In other words, the CMBX was used by professionals in the market the way farmers and cereal manufacturers had used the grain futures market for over a century. It traded very quietly for its first two and a half years, closely tracking the spreads for CMBS as they traded in the market.

That all changed in 2008.

In the first two months of that year, trading volume in the CMBX index experienced an enormous increase, with almost all new positions being short sales. Commercial mortgage investors reacted in disbelief as the monthly remittance reports trickled in with uniformly excellent news on the credit performance front. Their market had not been overbuilt in the last cycle. Occupancy was near an all-time high. Very little new construction was in the pipeline to put pressure on rents, which were stable or going up in most regional markets.

Other than observing a higher ratio of property values to income than in other real estate market peaks, investors couldn't see anything on the horizon to threaten the security of these mortgages. How then, could the index representing twenty-five deals from 2005 suddenly lose its value?

Shown below is the Markit.com graph of spreads on the Series 1 single A CMBS index. The spread on that index of commercial mortgage bonds quadrupled in a matter of weeks, even though the credit conditions for the owners of the properties had not declined in any meaningful way.

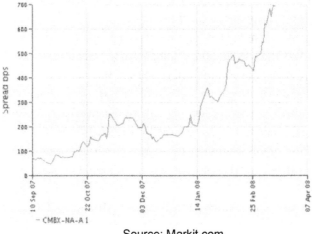

Source: Markit.com

If the index had simply kept its prior low volume and followed the cash market, we could have attributed the change in spreads to "contagion" and left it at that. Instead, the effect was to force holders of bonds similar to those in the index to re-value those bonds at drastically lower prices. A few were forced to sell by March of 2008, when bonds which had traded at LIBOR+60 just six months earlier were now going to buyers at LIBOR+700. For a 10-year bond, that can be a whopping 40% loss.

In February and March of 2008, right after the CMBX collapsed under overwhelming selling pressure, the financial press suddenly started releasing detailed articles about how the commercial property market was facing potentially catastrophic credit problems, in spite of performance data which indicated the exact opposite.

Almost like clockwork, the increased volume in the synthetic index and the drying up of leverage for bondholders was followed by a spate of articles cautioning investors that the commercial property rental market was on shaky ground.

Was the same playbook used in the residential markets also used on CMBS? Nobody wrote books lionizing a few smart traders for betting against commercial real estate, but the patterns are there. What we do know is that the commercial mortgage bond market was being negatively influenced by a synthetic index just as surely as the residential mortgage market had been.

The only saving grace for commercial property and mortgage investors was the fact that the originate-to-securitize business model never dominated the commercial real estate finance arena. Too many insurance companies and pension funds (those "real money" buyers) have too much experience lending directly against real estate and owning real estate to be scared away by artificially low mortgage bond values. That supply of money to finance purchases or refinance mortgages that came due did not dry up, though it certainly got more expensive.

That said, the commercial real estate CMBS and CDO business disappeared for years after the crisis. By 2012, the commercial real estate securitization market had revived, though not recovering to levels seen before the collapse.

More than a few real estate developers and levered commercial mortgage lenders and investors failed during the hiatus.

For all their reputation as smart, tough business people in tough markets, the real estate and bond market look pretty soft when they're up against the hedge funds.

As you'll see in the next chapter, those bare-knuckle "new players" in the bond market made their presence felt early on, shortly after the first ABX index was introduced in 2006.

CHAPTER TWENTY-TWO

Disastrous Insurance

In the summer of 2006, I was asked to write a chapter for the next years' edition of Euromoney magazine's International Debt Capital Markets Handbook. I chose as my topic the ABX, a synthetic index of US subprime mortgage bonds then in its infancy. That article was entitled "Synthetic ABS: New Players, New Opportunities, New Risks" and it explained how the new index enabled hedgers and speculators to take a long or short position on subprime MBS bonds.

"In January 2006 the first industry-wide index of Credit Default Swaps (CDS) on "benchmark" ABS bonds was introduced. Ahead of that announcement, spreads in the lowest rated investment grade single-name ABS experienced a sudden widening of spreads followed by a nearly equal tightening.

Several possible reasons for this unusual action come to mind. Perhaps the dealers that were going to be the market-makers in the upcoming synthetic index contract were getting short before the new index trading required them to take long positions. Perhaps large investors in similar bonds were locking in their spread profits from two years earlier, when they could invest at much wider spreads than were in the market by November 2005. The most likely reason, though, was a large influx of nontraditional MBS/ABS investors (equity and macro hedge funds) with a strong bearish credit bias. This is supported by the fact that a number of mortgage issuers' stocks were heavily shorted at that time, with some of them costing as much as 15% to borrow.

The subsequent tightening of the spread was caused by a large demand from traditional cash buyers such as CDO managers who found the yields of the synthetic bonds to be unusually attractive. The inherent leverage of the CDO structure sent the additional spread directly to the "equity," or unrated notes, with a handsome multiplier. This resulted in these income notes' expected yields jumping up from the 12% to 14% range to as high as 18% to 20%, without any change in expected performance of the collateral. ...

Whatever the actual reason, traditional ABS/MBS investors were initially taken off guard by the fact that the derivatives can drive the pricing of the cash instruments, which in turn can drive the prices of the underlying mortgage loans, and ultimately determine the health of the lending business. ... it is clear that origination, hedging and securitisation of mortgage loans has a new major influence on how it will price its loans to its borrowers."

What appeared to be going on was that hedge funds were swarming onto a bond industry hedging vehicle and creating an unprecedented amount of interest in it. The overwhelmingly bearish commitment moved prices down (yields up) so much that CDO bond fund managers were attracted to the higher yields.

I could imagine the conversations at the CDO shops: "If we buy the cash bonds, we make 13%.... If we buy synthetically by selling CDS, we make 19%. It's a no-brainer"

In the cash bond market, the CDO managers had been watching their profit margins get squeezed steadily for two years. Suddenly, the synthetic bond market (CDS) let them invest in the same risk but get a higher return. Unlike traditional cash buyers like insurance companies, mutual funds or pension managers, CDO managers were allowed to buy synthetic bonds by selling CDS.

The way that worked was that they would be paid the premium for the credit insurance on a bond or group of bonds, and in return they would have to pay out any losses that might come somewhere down the line.

To put it in a simple word chart,

Bullish on credit = receiver of interest payments and payer of principal losses

Bearish on credit = payer of interest payments and receiver of principal losses

That's how it worked for ABS bonds at the time the ABX index was designed, but it took a couple of major changes from traditional insurance before it got there.

The first CDS contracts were like traditional insurance for your car. As the buyer of insurance, you paid the monthly premium, and if you had a crash you got paid for the damages. If your car gets totaled, you get the blue book value of the car, but you have to give the wreck to the insurance company. Naturally, you have to own the car to buy insurance on it.

That all changed in 2005, when Delphi Corp (the auto parts maker) went bankrupt. Enough people in the market thought Delphi was going under that when it came time for the banks to settle up with the buyers of the credit insurance, there was more than $20 billion in insurance outstanding, but only $2 billion in bonds that could be exchanged to the CDS counterparty banks to get the payoff.

Since the credit bears (buyers of the CDS) had to keep paying the premiums until they turned in the bonds for payment, bonds that were trading for 60 cents on the dollar before bankruptcy reportedly began trading as high as 80 cents on the dollar after bankruptcy.

A complicated multi-dealer auction procedure was worked out for the Delphi Corp deal, so that the contracts were settled with cash rather than multiple iterations of delivering the same defaulted bonds (at an effective price of 63.375).

When Fannie Mae was taken over by the government, that was also a default event, and the same auction process set a price of 91.51, so each protection seller lost about 8.5% of the face amount of the CDS. The Freddie Mac CDS settled at 94 cents on the dollar.

Perhaps the most peculiar part of the event was that even though the government stepped in and continued to pay all of the two companies' debt, the CDS buyers still got their payday, estimated to be somewhere north of $50 billion.

With MBS, the situation was a little more complicated. Since they might get paid some principal every month, the face amount for which the insurance premium gets paid goes down as the bond gets paid off, and if enough principal gets paid off before the bond takes losses, the CDS buyer may never recover as much as they paid in premiums even though the bond eventually defaults. Just like you or I wouldn't get our premiums back if our car got totaled after it was 10 years old.

The standard adopted for the CDS that were nominally in the ABX index were called Pay As You Go, shortened to PAUG. I say "nominally" because the ABX index payments didn't even reflect the exact payments of the underlying MBS bonds.

The ABX index didn't actually pay the credit bulls dollar-for-dollar the interest payments of the underlying 20 bonds, but rather the average yield spread of the 20 bonds on the day the index was defined, multiplied by the balance of the 20 bonds. So the ABX was a derivative of a derivative.

Needless to say, there was never a way for the ABX index to be settled by delivering the bonds. So the big money gamblers were free to bet as much as they would like. By the time the January 2006 generation of the index was about to be replaced by the second generation (July 2006), the amount of open interest in the BBB and BBB- ABX had already grown to well over 100 times the total outstanding dollar value of the bonds themselves.

The CDS business as a whole also grew beyond all reason in a very short time. By the time the crisis hit in September of 2008, outstanding Credit Default Swaps totaled $55 trillion.

I've often wondered whether the hedge funds who were the winners in those bets could have paid their bets if they had lost. Since the banks they bought them from all tried their best to "lay off" the bets by buying re-insurance from AIG and a few AAA rated specialty insurance companies, would those banks have needed a bailout anyway? Even if the hedge funds defaulted on their payments, the banks would still owe AIG and the rest for the hundreds of billions (or trillions) in insurance they had bought.

After all, as powerful as they are, somehow I don't think the hedge funds who bet against the housing market could have actually paid hundreds of billions of dollars if they owed it to the banks.

I even heard, but can't confirm, that one major bank bought CDS insurance from a $50 million dollar hedge fund to cover losses on two Collateralized Debt Obligation deals, and that the insurance face amount was $2 billion. Not bad for the hedge fund if they never had to pay the claim. At the time, the going rate for that insurance on AAA CDOs was five basis points per year, or a very nice 20% return on that $50 million. AIG thought it was easy money too, but wrote hundreds of billions in CDS coverage on CDOs.

Reminds me of another couple of Wall Street sayings. First that comes to mind is "Heads, I win. Tails, you lose." And then there's the classic that got quoted in Animal House - "Hey, it's your fault. You trusted me."

CHAPTER TWENTY-THREE

Mark to Model or Mark to Myth?

As the credit crisis unfolded, the statement that "investors had no idea what they were buying" became a popular refrain. It was a plausible attempt to explain why so many MBS investments and so many investors lost money. But it was not based in fact.

While it is true that investors often had to act without performing the due diligence that had been customary before CDO managers turned bond buying into a race, portfolio managers did not simply rely on the Rating Agencies when deciding how to invest millions (and in many cases, billions) of investment dollars.

Traditional bond investors have used computer models to analyze mortgage bonds and the collateral behind them since there were primitive systems in place, when I came to Wall Street in 1984. I led the teams that developed some of the most robust and sophisticated of those systems in several big name firms. Companies like Trepp, Intex and Bloomberg sold their analytic systems both to Wall Street shops and buy-side investors. No one was guessing at the value of a bond. Everyone ran the cash flows and looked at the assumptions.

These models took years and cost millions of dollars to develop, and followed alongside the growth of the market itself. Some of the models were proprietary, such as the ones I helped develop for Prudential Securities, UBS and Daiwa. Others were available on a subscription basis for hundreds of thousands of dollars per year. Some firms used both kinds of model, but none did without any.

Despite claims by the innumerate that modeling cash flows for illiquid securities is some kind of make-believe, the primary models used to price bonds backed by large pools of loans are sophisticated computer programs for assessing value, and they are relied upon by investors for that reason.

One model includes statistically derived sets of probabilities for mortgage loans to pay on time, to prepay, to be delinquent, and to go into foreclosure. An additional model is used to predict the resolution of foreclosures along with the severity of loss at resolution. Yet another model takes the cash flows from the collateral generated using the models described above, and passes those cash flows to the tranches in the deal structure. The last step is to apply valuation models to the cash flows of the bonds.

In other words, the models exist to predict cash flows from the assets, and from that, cash flows of the bonds that are created from those assets. The models are derived from historical data which allow investors to derive probabilities regarding future performance. The models incorporate average or expected future scenarios as well as the positive and negative ends of the performance spectrum.

Recently, the common assumption has been that the models must be worthless since they were unable to predict the collapse of the mortgage market.

Of course, investors could have made a series of assumptions that would have led them to conclude that the mortgage market would collapse and the bonds that they bought were severely overvalued. In terms of analysis, however, those assumptions would have been pure conjecture, and any results derived from those assumptions would have been considered remote possibilities.

It's unlikely that any bond investors believed we would see the markets unravel as they have but if they thought that the performance of mortgage assets was going to radically change in the future, what should they have done? Disregard the historical data? Throw out the computer models that had served them well for decades? Would it be appropriate for the Rating Agencies or for pension and insurance company fund managers to value bonds based on personal opinions about what might happen in the future? Would we trust a system like that? Would we want those individuals investing our money based on a "hunch?"

Even if we did, managers of bond portfolios at pension funds or insurance companies have a fiduciary duty that overrides personal opinion. That duty, to act in good faith and with care, does not allow portfolio managers to arbitrarily decide to ignore decades of experience and make a contrary bet.

The fund managers who are the largest purchasers of MBS are also usually prohibited from short selling except within explicitly high-risk accounts, which many don't have and which are funded with a small slice of the overall investment pie. For the investors who really believed that MBS investments were a mistake, the only truly viable alternative was to avoid the mortgage market entirely, and accept different risks in the credit markets, or accept much lower returns in government bond markets.

Wall Street dealers and hedge funds are allowed to speculate that "things will be different this time," and make bets based on that speculation. Yet even most of these investors have models which they use to evaluate the worth and risk of their investments.

Through the years, a wealth of data has been accumulated regarding mortgage performance, broken down month by month and culled from the experience of tens of millions of American homeowners. We have enough data to know how those borrowers behaved when their properties gained or lost in value, how they behaved when the job market was strong or weak, what they did when they had the option of refinancing into a lower interest rate, how the cycle of the school year affected them, and even how they responded when rates declined and then reversed upwards, or vice versa.

All that data forms the basis for the computer models relied upon by bond investors. The initial and most influential models for asset behavior are the prepayment models, which correlate prepayment with various economic factors relating to those behaviors – factors such as house prices, unemployment, and even local variations like the time it takes to foreclose in different states.

When an analyst or trader is called upon to come up with a value for a bond quickly, they will commonly run a single vector of future economic conditions used to calculate expected vectors of prepayment and default/severity values. That is used along with a cash-flow model of the deal structure to create expected cash flows of the various bonds in the securitization.

The next step is to come up with a manageable set of scenarios to consider, anywhere from a handful to a dozen. These scenarios are run to highlight potential weaknesses in the future performance of the bond being examined.

When investors analyze bonds that are new to the market, they often have statistics on the individual loans backing the deal. The loans are grouped into cohort groups with similar characteristics, and then the primary analyses are run for the groups to project prepayment and credit behavior and the resulting expected cash flows.

As an extension to this static analysis, expected cash flows are often taken for each path in a set of future interest rate paths, since interest rates are the largest determinant of value in the bond market.

The bonds are also subjected to a variety of "stress tests." These include instantaneous shifts of the yield curve up and down by 100, 200 and 300 basis points. Another stress test incorporates modifications to the expected prepayment and credit performance vectors in order to test internal stresses in the deal structure and its collateral pool. Another very common stress test is to see how high the default rate needs to be in order to "break" the bond, i.e., cause the first dollar of credit loss.

One stress test that can find weakness in a deal structure and collateral composition is to move rates very high very quickly, while simultaneously accelerating prepayments on ARMs and slowing down prepayments on fixed rate loans. When combined with higher loss assumptions, this stress scenario quickly identifies potential weaknesses in the collateral pool or the bond structure. A bond analyst can then seek additional information on the underlying collateral, or possibly reconsider making the investment.

Sometimes, the standard analytic tests are used as an initial filter prior to examining sectors or subsectors of the collateral pools. Breaking down the pools in this way can illuminate risks which can then be examined more fully by requesting additional information from the bond issuer or Wall Street dealer.

Further stratifications of the loans underlying a given deal may steer investors away from tranches where everything has to go just right, or toward higher credit priority tranches in the same deal. On the positive side, careful due diligence can also uncover "hidden gems" in deals that have sufficient risk mitigants that more than offset troubling elements of collateral composition.

A good example of mitigants found by qualitative analysis and questioning can be seen in the Interest Only loans that received so much press in 2005, primarily because of the "payment shock" a borrower would have if the interest rate went up at the same time the loan began to be amortized with both principal and interest.

Some lenders were very prudent in their approach to these loans that gave homebuyers lower payments for the first two or three years. They underwrote the loans as if the borrower had to pay a regular amortizing payment at the higher reset interest rate, and capped the loan amount at the level they would lend for that more conservative loan. If they also arranged for rate resets and the beginning of amortization to be on different dates, they mitigated nearly all the risk of the "payment shock." This is the kind of information that can be used by a smart investor, and overlooked by those who perform insufficient analysis.

Some investors do the extra work to examine potential investments in depth and in light of many different scenarios. This may give them the ability to buy at slightly higher risk-adjusted returns. It may also help them avoid buying bonds that "look cheap" – bonds with a high yield but with risk elements that can hurt performance in a significant number of future scenarios.

Given the quality of models used by most serious bond investors and analysts, the standardized and specific analyses described so far would normally be performed in one to three hours, provided all the information required is available on the pool of loans and the deal structure.

Following that preliminary analysis, further risk evaluation and due diligence is performed. Building on the simple modeling outlined above, cash flows are run on hundreds or even thousands of economic scenarios, using a number of computers running in parallel (or a single computer running a very long time).

These multi-path analyses are most frequently described as "Monte Carlo" simulations, in which the scenarios have been constructed to be equally likely, and to have a distribution that fits the expected distribution of future interest rate paths and economic scenarios.

Within each path, the static prepayment and credit models are employed to help analyze performance. By taking all the paths together, a profile of expected returns and maturities is created. If all the expected returns are boiled down into a single average spread, we refer to it as an Option Adjusted Spread or Credit Adjusted Spread.

Automating these analytic tests can also be used to trigger "re-underwriting" for bonds already in position. Essentially, investors are forced to re-evaluate bonds in portfolio because analysis has highlighted potentially weak future performance. The value of such a process is obvious.

Another stochastic analysis may be employed which forecasts a change in price based on changes in the models. This "prepayment model duration" or "credit model duration" is an interesting way to see how a change in the assumptions might affect the value of bonds under consideration.

These analyses are especially valuable for relatively new mortgage-backed or asset-backed products, for which the models cannot be derived from statistical experience. When a new type of mortgage or loan is being analyzed, it is impossible to know how accurate a prepayment model or credit model will be over a period of ten years or more. A prudent analyst will vary the model predictions up and down, typically by 10% or so, to see how the performance of the bonds might vary under these scenarios.

The steps delineated above form an introduction to securitization modeling, and describe in basic terms how Wall Street firms and major investors like banks, large bond fund managers, insurance companies, large pension funds and specialized securitized products fund managers value and analyze their bonds.

At the end of the day, regardless of what analyses are run using the computer models, understanding the underlying assets is probably the strongest risk management technique a portfolio manager can use.

In looking at potential new investments, there are qualitative issues that need to be taken into account. For example, a new deal from a frequent issuer may show a change in the type of collateral or the underwriting standards. Such changes might include shifts in credit scores, types of loans, size of loans, documentation standards, or other characteristics.

The value of regular visits to lenders' offices provides a qualitative measure of potential future risks and rewards. Visiting with credit underwriters or loss mitigation professionals can give a sense of the workload per professional, the experience of the people doing the job, and the efficacy of systems in place. High turnover or sudden large expansion within these domains can affect the performance of a bond investment.

In addition to the computer models, investors make use of market intelligence. Naturally, if investors also have opinions about the quality of an issuer, this is one of the intangibles that color their investment decisions.

Investors may also make use of performance history, for those bonds that have history. Through conversation with the dealer community, investors may make use of recent auction prices for similar bonds. Investors may also arrive at yield spreads or discount rates to apply to the calculated cash flows through the indicated yield spreads of the ABX index. Spreads are adjusted up or down for "bad" pools or "good" pools, as needed, with pools that have heavier concentrations of risky loan characteristics or untested loan originators or servicers paying the higher spreads.

The bond market treats the ABX as an indication of market sentiment for a relatively poorly performing group of bond deals rather than considering the ABX as a provider of real prices (or values) for the bonds it contains. Using the ABX rather than computer models as a means of valuing bonds is an idea that could never be taken seriously by professional bond investors.

The unfortunate upshot of the development of the ABX index and its daily publication on a website everyone can see is that it facilitated the contention that using the ABX was the best way to determine the value of subprime bonds.

Short sellers and zealous commentators seized on the public ABX index as a measure of value. They wanted all holders of all AAA subprime bonds to immediately admit to losses based on "visible" prices of the AAA ABX index rather than their cash flow models.

They even began to suggest that accounting firms use the index rather than the values clients calculated. This flew in the face of logic and tradition, where each bond has historically traded on its own merits, and trades were done privately between institutions, without any publication. This lack of public disclosure, known as "over the counter" trading of bonds, and the evaluation by bonds by proprietary models always made some investors and regulators uncomfortable.

A number of companies and their auditors succumbed to the general panic in the market in the fourth quarter of 2007 and used the ABX to value their bond positions. This despite the fact that the audit practices of the major accounting firms understand the internal operations of the models in use by investors, and the audit process involves the analysts, traders and portfolio managers who use the models. The auditors are informed of all the assumptions used in the models, and are free to ask for alternate runs with modified assumptions. Perhaps the auditors, faced with potential criticism and a dysfunctional market, felt safest using prices they could get with the click of a mouse.

Some journalists, looking for a catchy phrase to support a dubious recommendation, soon branded the practice of modeling cash flows and calculating prices from market yields as "mark to myth."

This phrase would be far more accurately applied to the ABX. The bonds in that index have traded at prices as much as twenty percent lower than actual bonds could be sold in the open market. Traders who had profits in the short-biased trading instrument called the ABX could argue that it reflected "true" value, without ever having to buy or sell a bond.

It seemed evident that for many of these traders, there was a fundamental misunderstanding of how bonds are valued and why. A common assertion was that the price decline on AAA bonds was equal to credit losses. This was more than a misconception; it was absurd. For example, when the 07-2 AAA index traded down nearly 50%, it would mean that every mortgage in the pool had been foreclosed and every house sold for half price. The innumeracy went even further than that. I heard more than one person say that if AAA mortgages were selling for fifty cents, that meant the BBB mortgages were worth even less!

Nevertheless, when the markets seized up, the focus turned to the methods used by securitized product portfolio holders to determine the value of their holdings. The value of assets held in portfolio is especially important since most financial institutions are subject to capital adequacy regimes that include "mark to market" requirements for some or all of the assets held.

Even if the assets are not going to be sold, any bank, insurance company or brokerage firm subject to these requirements will reduce its ability to hold or buy assets as the value of their portfolio drops. They may even be forced to raise additional capital in a difficult market.

If the accountants and regulators accepted the synthetic ABX index values as the "market" for the portfolios held in traditional bond investors' hands, those bond investors would report large losses.

Under accounting rules adopted after the Enron scandal, a loss in market value of an investment company's portfolio would be reported as a loss when earnings are declared. That's exactly what happened when Merrill Lynch, UBS, Citibank, AIG and others reported multi-billion dollar losses.

For American Capital Strategies, the accounting rule that forced a "mark to market" valuation of assets reached a truly ridiculous level in the first quarter of 2008. A large commercial real estate CDO position held by the company was evaluated at $11 million using the new standards and the CMBX index. At the time, that particular investment was paying $8 million every three months. As the company stated in their quarterly report to shareholders, it was expected to pay out approximately $160 million over the coming years. Yet the auditors felt compelled to value the position at only $11 million.

When auditors use indices like the ABX and the CMBX as valuation tools instead of cash flow models, they play right into the hands of traders that hold bearish positions in the CDS, stocks or options of those companies that take large paper losses based on these flawed indices.

While the models in use are less than perfect predictors of future performance, are the valuations they produce inferior to valuations from a derivatives market like the ABX that consists primarily of bearish speculators trading among themselves? Should these models be tossed out, and replaced with a quick look-up of the latest price on Markit.com?

Before you say "yes," bear in mind that the Markit website only tells us what a limited universe of market participants will pay for a derivative that has roughly the same relationship to how actual bonds trade as the Las Vegas betting line has with the outcomes of the games played in the NFL. It's as if the snow was so thick on the field that the referees decided to score the game according to the betting. And while the betting line is usually pretty accurate in choosing favorites, or even predicting the difference in scores, it's just not the same as playing the game.

I'll make a wager of my own: Now that there is new data on the performance of mortgages and the bonds derived from them, the models used by investors to make their purchases will be more sophisticated and robust than they were before the crisis. As weaknesses in the system, from mortgage borrower to speculator, are eliminated, we will likely see investors building on, and relying on, the new and improved versions of the very same models which were in use before the crisis began.

CHAPTER TWENTY-FOUR

ABX – Mind the Gap!

The ABX was just six months old when I wrote about it in the *Euromoney* Handbook, introducing it to institutional market participants as a tool for hedging and speculating in subprime mortgage bonds.

A year and a half later, its use as a tool for speculators far outweighed its use as a hedging instrument. The hedge fund community loved it, and was able to exploit its fundamental weaknesses to short the subprime market and exert downward pressure on the holdings of traditional bond investors.

A twice-removed derivative composed of Credit Default Swaps, the ABX provided a way to buy and sell credit insurance on groups of twenty bonds from the largest subprime deals.

Approximately three-quarters of the issues were from captive entities owned and controlled by Wall Street firms. At the time the ABX was developed, the market for subprime mortgage bonds was in its heyday, so naturally Wall Street firms were maximizing their participation. There was a rush to purchase loans wholesale and securitize them and then to sell the resulting bonds as quickly as possible.

This business model is called "originate to distribute." It was condemned as an open invitation to fraud and poor underwriting by many observers, including Federal Reserve Chairman Ben Bernanke, the Rating Agencies, the President's Working Group on Financial Markets, analysts at the International Monetary Fund, and even by research groups who themselves work on Wall Street.

Two years after the introduction of this synthetic index, it could already be seen that the index was unable to serve as a stand-in for performance of subprime MBS securities taken as a whole. The eighty deals in the four ABX indices performed, on average, worse from a credit perspective than the average for the industry.

If anything, the opposite would be expected, since one might imagine that larger, more sophisticated operations such as those on Wall Street would have better quality control than smaller issuers.

In fact, the markedly better performers in the ABX were the handful of deals which were issued by portfolio lenders who originated the loans, serviced the loans, and took the first loss, even though they sold the rest of the bonds in their deals in order to finance their portfolios. As a rule, they treated the servicing of their loan portfolios as a key part of their customer relations rather than as separate profit centers, and that helped ensure the strength of their loans as collateral for securitizations.

These first tier performers included the Wells Fargo and JP Morgan Chase customer portfolio lending programs, and the formerly stand-alone portfolio lenders Accredited, NovaStar, and H&R Block's Option One, at least until late 2006 and 2007, when competitive forces led even portfolio lenders to lower their standards or go out of business.

Nevertheless, any of these first tier issuer's bonds from 2005 or before traded at higher prices than 2005 vintage bonds from the Wall Street houses or from the second tier market leaders Countrywide or Washington Mutual's Long Beach Mortgage, because these entities had consistently better quality control. In popular lingo, they all had "skin in the game," retaining credit risk that hit the capital in their portfolios before it hit the bondholders.

The weak relationship between the value of real bonds in the marketplace and the values represented on the ABX was especially visible in the AAA bonds in the index.

The AAA bonds selected for the ABX were all the last AAA bonds to be paid in time-tranched series, so they would naturally trade at lower prices than shorter bonds in the same series when spreads are wide.

The sponsors of the ABX index tacitly admitted this flaw when they added a new sub-index to the ABX family in May of 2008. They launched what was called the PENAAA (penultimate AAA) ABX sub-indices with a new set of benchmark AAA bonds from the same eighty deals in the original index.

The new sub-index included the AAA bonds that would be paid just before the AAA "last pay" bonds in the original ABX. The difference in value between these longer and shorter AAA bonds was striking. For example, on May 27, 2008, the 06-2 ABX AAA index closed at a price of 78.50%, while the 06-2 PENAAA closed at a price of 92.72%.

By acknowledging the existence of more than one kind of AAA bond, the ABX took a step towards closing the gap. The shorter average life of these bonds was far more representative of the general market than the smaller, riskier bonds that made up the original ABX AAA indices. However, the ABX was still far from representative of the tradable MBS market. Where were the first and second bonds in the series? Where were the AA+ and AA- bonds? How about bonds issued by solid community bank lenders that know every borrower? What about the hundreds of billions of bonds issued before July of 2005?

Regardless of the bonds in question, there was an even more fundamental reason why the ABX failed to function well as a synthetic vehicle for participating in the subprime market: There were plenty of sellers of the ABX but there are almost no buyers. And this was not due exclusively to market sentiment.

When the index was introduced, the only significant ABX buyers were fixed income hedge funds and CDO managers. By the end of 2007, a number of fixed income hedge funds had taken large losses and folded, and the CDO business had evaporated. The sellers, on the other hand, were growing in number and strength.

Hedge funds that had made the bearish bet against subprime mortgage bonds using CDS and the ABX index were making headlines with their extraordinary profits from the trade. As with most money-making trends in financial markets, the bears kept "pushing" on the trade.

After the introduction of the ABX index in early 2006, the most active trading was in the lowest rated indices, the BBB and the BBB-. Less than six months later, Goldman Sachs estimated that trading in those two contracts alone had reached $75 billion. That kind of volume was amazing. After all, this was not only a brand new instrument, but that $75 billion was more than 125 times the total face amount of the bonds it referenced.

There were many reasons why traditional bond investors avoided the ABX index. The large insurance companies and pension funds who might have been potential buyers (the traditional "long" investors) were effectively locked out of participating. After years of negative commentary on derivatives, many states issued outright prohibitions on direct investment in such instruments by insurance companies or pension funds, and these institutions were traditionally the largest investors in MBS. Those few institutional investors who could participate in the derivatives market were subject to much heavier scrutiny of those positions than almost any other investment they might make.

If this handful of institutional investors was really convinced that there was an important opportunity, they could take a small portion of their assets and invest it with outside hedge fund managers or create special purpose companies in order to make the investments. For those market participants, even indirect investment often involved creating or investing with a third party manager through an instrument like a hedge fund. Even then, derivatives investments drew heightened scrutiny from regulators.

By investing in the ABX, these investors could theoretically take advantage of pricing disparities between the cash and synthetic markets, but it was difficult to justify the expense and effort to make a synthetic bond trade if it involved several months of time and a significant allocation of human and financial resources.

Not many institutions made the commitment. There were too many questions to be answered. Was the synthetic market deep enough? Could it absorb meaningful amounts of buying interest? Would the pricing disparity between the synthetic and cash markets be there by the time a new special purpose entity was set up and running?

These institutions had seen what happened with an earlier synthetic way to trade securitized bonds. Called the CMBS Total Return Swap, this older form of synthetic instrument had traded at slightly tighter spreads than the cash market for more than a year by the beginning of 2006, when the ABX was introduced. On top of that, it was so illiquid that even a $25 or $50 million trade could move the market.

As a result, even though the new ABX indices were trading at prices that could give an investor a higher spread synthetically than they could get by buying regular bonds for cash, the traditional buyers of subprime bonds, especially the AAA bonds, simply weren't getting involved.

The AAA bonds in typical subprime deals were between 75% and 80% of the whole deal, so the bulk of the capital that supported the subprime mortgage boom came from those traditional investors. Institutional investors like Fannie Mae, Freddie Mac and insurance companies bought subprime mortgage bonds only after extensive due diligence.

If serious investors wanted to get the extra yield spread they could theoretically get in the ABX, they weren't going to invest in all twenty bonds in the index, because a number of the bonds came from issuers with poor credit performance records.

They could get extra yield by going long the index. But avoiding the weaker bond deals within the index was very expensive because it involved paying Wall Street dealers their asking prices on CDS for those individual bonds.

If the time, expense and additional scrutiny weren't reason enough for institutions to avoid the ABX as an alternative investment, the lack of information on the trading volume of the index simply added to the reticence of institutional buyers.

The final, essentially fatal, flaw in the ABX was that there was no way to buy the index as a way to get delivery of the bonds. With other indices, options, or futures, this delivery option is what forced derivative securities to behave consistently with the cash market.

In the commodities market, if wheat futures for a month from now are trading at too high a price, you can buy wheat today, store it for a month, and deliver it later.

If the put and call options for a stock can be bought or sold at prices that vary too far from the market value based on the stock price, investors will take positions in both the options and the stock to make a risk-free profit.

Because the ABX index had no mechanism to require or accept delivery, trading in the ABX index became a way to express an opinion about the subprime market rather than trade on the market value of twenty specific bonds. The only exception was for investors willing to buy or sell the separate CDS that formed the index and hold their positions to maturity in which event they would pay out or receive cash flows that mirrored buying or selling the twenty bonds.

When the Wall Street dealers first set up the ABX, they thought they would have a new source of profit, with much wider bid-offer gaps than they had in ordinary stocks and bonds. Trading desks were quoting spreads of two points – unheard of in institutional markets, but accepted in derivatives. A buyer who wanted to go long the BBB-index might buy at 96% of the face amount of the index, but if they wanted to sell, they got only 94%. By comparison, a buyer for individual bonds at the time might have paid 97.5%, and a seller might get paid 97.25%.

Setting up trading desks for mortgage CDS in 2005, Wall Street dealers reached into different specialties to staff those operations. Some dealers chose to take experienced CDS traders from the corporate market, and convert them into mortgage CDS traders. Others decided to move "cash bond" mortgage traders to the synthetics.

It made for interesting conversations for those of us on the buy side. The converted corporate traders looked at everything on the basis of correlation of defaults from their days trading individual company credits. If they could have sufficiently uncorrelated long and short positions with higher spreads collected on the long (CDS selling) positions, and lower spreads paid on the short (CDS buying) side of their portfolios, they felt they had a guaranteed winning strategy.

Old line mortgage professionals studied the individual bonds, and developed relative value opinions, so they would happily take in slightly lower premiums writing a BBB CDS insurance policy on a tier one issuer's bond than they paid for buying a CDS insurance policy on a weak tier three issue, even at the same BBB rating.

For a while, as a customer, I could hear proponents of both theories, and see them quote different prices for the same bonds. The wide bid/offer spreads didn't quite make it possible to simultaneously buy from one dealer and sell to another for a profit, but the gap between the yields quoted for identical bonds was much wider – up to 20 basis points – than I'd ever seen in the cash market. We were each trading in our own individually defined range of values and valuation techniques, unaware that our entire market was about to be devalued beyond anyone's range.

In early 2008, Markit.com began the preparatory work to launch two new indices, one based on alt-A mortgage bonds and another on auto loan ABS.

At the time, the bid/offer spreads on the ABX were wider than ever, suggesting that Wall Street dealers were making good profits. For example, some of the BBB- indices from the ABX were quoted at 12% bid and 14% offered. If one customer wanted to buy and another wanted to sell, then the dealers stood to make a 17% profit (2 point markup on a purchase at 12%) by simply standing in the middle.

However, standing anywhere was deadly. In repeated waves, the bearish selling of the ABX kept coming in, and the dealers reacted by selling the index at ever-lower prices, especially compared to the cash bond market. Even that didn't help. More and more selling drove the prices down, again and again.

The Wall Street dealers who had supported the ABX index with nightly price quotes had thought they would make a fortune trading in these things. What happened instead helped them lose more money than their firms had ever lost, and cost many of them jobs.

When Markit suggested new indices following the model of the ABX, Wall Street dealers responded with a resounding "Thanks, but no thanks."

CHAPTER TWENTY-FIVE

Bad News Is Good News

Within five minutes of the space shuttle Challenger disaster, Wall Street traders were in competition over who could be first with the latest joke. In the middle of the Crash of '87, when I was working at Pru, I heard a new joke every five minutes, even after a customer had burst into one of our firm's own branch offices and shot one of our brokers.

I saw bets escalate into the mid five-figures over stunts that were dreamed up to cause distress and humiliation for one or another among us. The stakes quickly escalated when target practice on the trading desk became a contest to see who could hit the bald "bull's eye" on one of the salesmen's heads with a crumpled piece of paper. One of our group's salesmen at Daiwa got $20,000 for shaving his hair off. Shortly thereafter, a woman in the systems department came up and offered to shave her hair off for only $10,000. She had nice hair, too.

Some call it tension release. Others think that Wall Street trading desks just attract obnoxious smart people who make too much money.

My pat answer to the assertion of "too much money" was always that there was a chair near mine for anyone who could do the job, because we could use the help. Now that I'm older and, I hope, wiser, I agree that Wall Street might be a little more honest if the pot of gold at the end of the rainbow didn't get paid out every year. I never had a retort to the accusation that Wall Street is populated with obnoxious smart people, since I believe it does have more than its proportional share.

Still, from my very first job until now, some things on Wall Street never change. How you did or how the market did last month or last year doesn't matter. The Street turns against its own if it senses weakness. And the only thing that makes traders happy is making money.

It should not surprise anyone that a world feeling generalized misery can be a reason for generalized happiness, if the trading desk is making money.

I saw this most starkly one Friday in the mid to late 90's. It was 8:30 a.m. on the first Friday of the month, when the Department of Labor released its employment report for the prior month. For the first third of my investing career, the Money Supply had been the king of all numbers, and everyone acted as if the markets would live or die on the change in M3 when it came out. Then the money supply number faded, and Wall Street waited for the employment report to feel the pulse of profit for both stocks and bonds.

On that particular Friday, I saw the reality of Wall Street happiness in a way that I hadn't before. The monthly jobs release showed much higher unemployment than had been predicted. The trading floor I was on was suddenly filled with a chorus of cheers as traders hooted and hollered and threw their fists up in victory, and then furiously bid up the price of bonds of every maturity and every type.

I headed into my office to see how the structured deals I was working on had changed with the new lower bond yields, but I felt like a visitor to another planet. Maybe it was because I wasn't raised with a life of privilege. I was the oldest of seven children. My father was a Master Sergeant in the Army and my mother helped take care of the children in the neighborhood to supplement our income. I went to Yale on a full scholarship. I'd always supported myself. I knew that the employment number represented real people who'd lost real jobs. When you include the families of those workers, at least a million more Americans were reported to be suffering hard times that day.

Whatever the reason on any given day, it is an overriding fact that bond traders really do like bad news. Luckily, traders can almost always find bad news to be happy about. When the economy is in the dumps, demand for credit drops, and rates drop. That makes bond traders really happy.

If rates drop, so the logic goes, there will be more companies looking to raise capital and pay nice commissions, so that makes corporate bond traders happy. When more people are buying houses or refinancing their mortgages, that creates more raw material for the securitization machine, and that makes mortgage bond traders happy.

This all works when things are "normal," but breaks down when fear takes hold of the market. When rates go up on corporates and mortgages and muni's because of fear, then the traders of those bonds get hit hard, both coming and going.

Not only are the bonds in their inventory losing value, but the cost of hedging with Treasuries they sold short goes up, so they're losing money on their positions and losing money on their hedges. Worse yet, if it gets bad enough, business coming from the companies and homebuyers could start to dry up.

That's what happened when the Great De-levering took hold of the credit markets in early 2008. Still, some stock and bond traders found a reason to be happy because of the rise in unemployment, even though the people losing their jobs were former colleagues and competitors.

As thousands of people were fired in mortgage finance operations all over Wall Street and in mortgage companies across America, stock and bond traders were focused on whether the Fed would cut rates again and by how much. The bad news for the families of all those people losing jobs and homes was good news for traders whose profits would go up if the Fed cut rates.

When traders look at numbers like the unemployment number, it doesn't matter that the number is likely to be adjusted the following month, or that the Bureau of Labor statistics make enormous adjustments even before releasing the number. All that matters is whether traders think they can make money off the number if it comes in above or below expectations.

Wall Street is a place of expectations, and when expectations are met, or fail to be met, everything is translated into money. Company earnings can come in at a record, but if analyst expectations were higher, the stock trades down. Companies can come out with bad news, but if the news is not as bad as what was expected, the stock goes up.

If the economists are predicting that 100,000 jobs will be added, and the number turns out to be only 50,000, that's bad news (which is good news for bond traders).

Sometimes even great news is bad news, if expectations aren't met. This is especially true when it concerns the personal paychecks for the denizens of Wall Street. One year, I gave one of the salesmen at Deutsche Bank a really great bonus – $800,000. He looked stricken rather than happy. Then he explained that if he added his salary to his bonus, his total pay was under a million dollars a year, and he told me that he needed to feed his family. He was depressed as he left my office.

On Wall Street, days that could be very happy can easily turn into days of anxiety and stress. Bear Stearns was legendary around the Street for their annual bonus day meeting for Senior Managing Directors. It would start off with Ace Greenberg, Chairman, standing up and announcing how much of his bonus was going to be donated to the UJA-Federation. Then every other person in the room was expected to follow suit.

Wall Streeters may be happiest when rewarding themselves but they often feel some happiness in sharing their wealth. Our group at Daiwa used to pick a children's charity to support each year at bonus time, and the donations were significant. The salesman who was paid $20,000 for shaving his head donated the money to charity.

In my experience, small stock investors can be even more generous, given their generally more limited means. From 2003 until I took a job in 2005 that did not allow me to participate, I was a regular poster on a Yahoo! Finance "message board" for one of the subprime mortgage lender stocks I followed. The company was tiny, with less than 2% market share. It was one of the most heavily shorted stocks on the New York Stock Exchange, and the constant target of attacks in the media. Many of those attacks were based on innumeracy and/or outright misstatement of fact.

I thought I could make a difference to individual investors by explaining the fallacies in the various reports on the company, and I took it upon myself to dispel some of the misinformation. More than a few of the supporters of the stock offered to send money to a charity of my choice as a way of thanking me for the informal, free course in structured finance I provided over the Internet. By 2006, over $100,000 had been given in my name to Justice for Children (JFC), an organization that provides legal advocacy for abused children.

When I was invited to join JFC's Board of Directors in April of 2006, I broke my company's rule against posting on message boards in order to thank those generous anonymous donors. My message was several paragraphs in length, and contained one sentence stating that I felt more optimistic about the sector and the company than I had for almost a year. <u>Mistake.</u>

The *New York Times* extracted that one sentence and quoted it in two different articles, insinuating that I was posting on message boards to "hype" the stock. Needless to say, a lot had changed for the subprime business (and for that company) between April of 2006 when I posted my comment and the publication of the articles in July and November of 2007, but the newspaper's readership was conveniently spared that fact.

Although that tiny company's stock had already collapsed by the time the articles appeared, it didn't seem to matter to the small investors who frequented the message boards and who kept donating in my name. By early 2008, the total of those donations exceeded $200,000.

Wall Street and the investing public do have a charitable side. It's just that it doesn't show on the first Friday of the month, when most are hoping that unemployment will go up.

It's easy to come to the conclusion that Wall Streeters only care about making money. What is true is that we are incredibly focused on our jobs, often to the detriment of our marriages, our health, or even our safety.

Once, during an intense day at Daiwa (and they were all intense days) fire alarms went off. We were busy, so we stayed at our desks and kept working, even when the fire and rescue teams showed up with their big yellow suits, breathing apparatus and axes.

The Fire Marshal didn't find this amusing, and went to our senior management and said he'd levy a $2,000 fine for each person who didn't leave his or her desk. We found out later that it was one of our group's own bankers who had set off the alarms. He was celebrating a deal closing by smoking a Cohiba he had brought back from Europe.

Some of the intensity of our jobs came from the rules we followed and the technology we used. For example, when we priced a new bond deal, we had seventy-two hours to deliver printed prospectuses to the buyers.

That could be a monumental effort, especially if we were introducing a new kind of bond or a new issuer to the market. The financial printing companies all had catered meals set up around the clock, fully equipped locker rooms, and lounges with open bars so clients, investment bankers, lawyers, analysts and accountants could all physically be there as long as it took to "get the books out."

In those days, bond certificates and prospectuses were delivered by hand, and designated people waited at the teller's cage at each bond purchaser's bank and the Wall Street underwriters* to see that the money, the prospectuses and the bonds had been delivered before the banks closed. Then they would telephone back to their firms that the deals had been officially completed.

Underwrite – A commitment by a securities dealer to purchase a stock or bond issue from its client. These issues are meant to be sold to the public, but the investment bank will buy the securities even if the public does not buy the offering.

More than once I was waiting for that call, watching the hands of the clock creep toward 3 PM hoping nothing went wrong. If we failed to deliver the bonds on time, we had to pay the full bond interest overnight without compensation, which was a big enough mistake to cost people their jobs.

It was after just such a successful closing call that our commercial mortgage securitization banker was enjoying his cigar the day the NYFD paid us a visit on the trading floor at Daiwa.

Today, the seventy-two hour rule is gone, the bonds and prospectuses are all electronic, and most deal documents are following templates. Commemorative "lucites" – the desk ornaments that bore the name of the deal, the issuer and the underwriter – are a thing of the past. We don't even have closing dinners any more.

When I talk with today's investment banking Associates, I realize that I sound like my father talking about the three hours he spent delivering newspapers each morning before school. The young Wall Street professionals of today don't even do a single all-nighter, much less two or three in a row. What's the world coming to?

Kidding aside, the lesson to take away from Wall Street traders' interpretation of bad news is that the entire credit system is interconnected. Tough times in the housing market leads to lower interest rates, which is good for companies that are not having tough times, at least up to a point.

That point was reached in the mortgage market when even "bulletproof" mortgage bonds were being sold for deep discounts. Other bonds, from other markets, had to compete for investor dollars with the super-cheap mortgage bonds. When that happened, bad news for mortgage bonds became bad news for other bonds.

CHAPTER TWENTY-SIX

Is Securitization Dead?

The quick answer is "no," unless lending itself is dead.

Back when the subprime collapse was making the news at least several times a week, securitization was an easy target. Even the President's Working Group on Financial Markets targeted the "originate-to-securitize" business model as a factor in the credit crisis.

Does that mean that the process of securitization is the problem? Should securitization be eliminated as a technique, or securitized bonds eliminated as a market? Is it possible they will be?

I don't think so. Our financial system needs securitization, almost as much as people need access to credit. Investment managers need high quality investments in debt, and it makes no sense for them to try to know each borrower individually. Local banks can no longer safely hold the long-term debt families need to buy houses. Efficiency, diversification, standardization and liquidity have been successfully provided by securitization.

Many people are lobbying for change in the mortgage market and the failures we've seen are powerful evidence that it needs restructuring. But some of the approaches are misguided.

One very popular idea is to return to a community-based lending model, a romanticized view of banking and mortgage lending personified in Frank Capra's holiday classic "It's a Wonderful Life" in which George Bailey runs his Building and Loan solely for the good of the people.

Certainly, a community-based mortgage lending system would be more trustworthy, as local lenders would know their borrowers and hold the credit risk of the loans they issue until maturity. Unfortunately, the problem faced by community-based lenders is mismatched funding. The primary reason for the development of the Freddie Mac and Fannie Mae securitization programs was to offload the long duration risk of thirty-year fixed-rate mortgages from savings banks which were unable to fund themselves with equally long duration deposits.

There are obvious and serious risks when a bank concentrates its credit risk in a local area. An event that hurts enough local borrowers almost guarantees that the entire area will be affected. At that point, a locality or region under stress will need better access to credit, not worse, just when a bank is least able to provide it.

These issues become even more meaningful for subprime credits. While there may be local areas with higher concentrations of subprime borrowers, prudent bank management requires that banks limit their exposure to higher risk credits. When a region has a downturn in economic activity, the last thing we want is credit providers to fail.

As we look at the problems in the mortgage market today, we have to be careful that by fixing one problem, we don't create another. Equally important, any changes we institute have to make sense for all the participants in the market.

When the impact of the financial crisis was at its peak, some people said we should let all the borrowers go broke and save the banks. Others said we should punish the lenders for tricking hundreds of thousands of borrowers into committing fraud or making loans the borrowers didn't understand and couldn't pay. Other people said we should just alter the terms of the loans, and force investors to take lower returns.

The reactionary solutions that were offered up are reminiscent of the string of Savings and Loan "fixes" that were instituted during the 1980's. That's when the seeds of our last national financial disaster were planted, only to be nurtured and grown through the next decade before presenting taxpayers with the bill.

Back when I began my career on Wall Street, the institutions known as Savings and Loans (or "thrifts") got the least respect of all institutional accounts. I was told that running a thrift was a 3-6-3 business. Management borrows money at 3%, lends it out at 6%, and hits the golf course by 3 pm.

That wasn't too far from reality at a time when Regulation Q still determined the rate that savings banks could pay on savings accounts. Through the 1960s, Regulation Q, which was passed as part of Glass-Steagall in 1933, gave Savings and Loans a stable source of inexpensive funds to lend to borrowers as thirty-year, fixed-rate mortgages.

Thousands of local banks supported their communities (and themselves) with mortgages. The thirty-year, fixed rate mortgage was affordable, and America became a nation of homeowners. Bank presidents all across America made a comfortable living. Life was good.

Then came inflation.

Big commercial banks started offering CDs (Certificates of Deposit) and interest-bearing checking accounts, and people started to move their accounts out of the S&Ls. The flow of accounts away from savings banks and into commercial banks reached its peak when Federal Reserve Chairman Paul Volker fought inflation by dramatically raising short term rates in the late 70s.

This "fix" helped the commercial banks attract deposits. The big banks offered higher and higher deposit rates. The deposit rate at the Savings and Loans experienced faster and faster attrition. And the S&Ls could only pay 3% on passbook savings accounts.

That situation led to a new "fix" -- the Monetary Control Act of 1980. Now S&Ls could offer competitive interest rates, take in large ($100,000) deposits from brokers outside their communities, and pay hefty commissions to get the money. *Here comes Wall Street!*

As Savings & Loans lost deposits, they lost money. They were paying out higher rates, but most of their investments were those 6% mortgages from the 1960's that could run for another twenty years.

In came the third "fix" – The Depository Institutions Deregulation and Monetary Control Act of 1982. Now thrifts could attract "hot" money with high deposit rates, offer credit cards that charged high rates, make loans to businesses, and even take ownership "kickers" in real estate deals when lending money to developers. Hundreds of S&Ls became major funding sources for real estate projects as they attracted hundreds of millions, even billions, of dollars of deposits through Wall Street firms and independent brokers who specialized in selling "jumbo" CDs. Management teams at the S&Ls convinced themselves that they were going to make such good returns on their lending and investing activities that they could afford to pay out very high CD rates.

Federal insurance made sure nobody lost money. Of course, risk-free money with high returns always attracts fraudulent as well as high risk behavior. In the early 1980s, one of the most common scams was for developers to take cheap raw land and put together outlandishly expensive commercial development plans that high risk investors and lenders found irresistible. A friend of mine who used to take regular trips from Texas to the Cayman Islands told me that he met a number of people traveling First Class and carrying briefcases full of cash that were filled by taking design fees, management fees, consulting fees, commissions, and land sale profits from the loans they got from the thrifts.

Developers could easily put together deals without using any of their own money. The tax laws gave large depreciation benefits to equity investors in commercial real estate. Developers could assemble investors to put up equity cash for down payments to thrifts issuing land development mortgages. Tax benefits became so large that for many of the equity investors, it didn't matter if the commercial real estate in question ever got leased or ever got sold.

In 1986, the new tax law eliminated those tax incentives that guaranteed commercial real estate investors would receive tax benefits several times the size of their investment. This was the fourth "fix" to the S&L problem and it backfired. It left hundreds of thrifts holding mortgages on properties that no longer made any economic sense. When the mortgages defaulted, the S&Ls owned the buildings or condo developments, and the guarantees on the high rate CDs were the taxpayers' problem. The whole experiment and those four "fixes" that seemed to make sense at the time, cost us $400 billion, about 0.6% of GDP.

Let's not make the same mistake again, even though securitization, not commercial real estate was the arena where the lure of quick profits without risk or responsibility once again led to poor lending.

Without securitization, however, community bankers have no way to balance their assets and liabilities, manage their risks and diversify their investments. In today's economy, you can't have one without the other.

When we look at the risks of securitization, we must examine where those risks truly reside, without deciding that the whole process is a problem. We have to look at the numbers, and at what really happened, and avoid being unduly influenced by the popular press.

In first level securitizations, the diversity of credit performance of the borrowers is passed through to the bond investors. As time passes and the economy goes through its normal ups and downs, some borrowers default and others don't. The risks are not amplified beyond this simple variability. CDOs that are backed by bank loans and commercial mortgage loans fall into the category of first level securitizations.

First level securitizations deserve to have a place in the market because the risks are quantifiable and unlevered. As the crisis shrinks in the rear-view mirror, non-conforming mortgages are once again being securitized outside the Freddie Mac, Fannie Mae and Ginnie Mae Agency programs, and institutions are buying the bonds that result. One ironic development is that the same houses that were foreclosed in the subprime crisis are now being financed in a new kind of securitization as rental homes.

Second level securitizations or "re-securitizations" are a different story. Those second level deals take a "slice" of performance from the first level deals, and use that as collateral to make new securities. CDOs collateralized by a collection of BBB-rated ABS and SIVs collateralized by a collection of AAA and AA bonds are examples of second level securitizations.

The inherent problem with these securitizations, which have largely been eliminated from the market, is that the effect of very small shifts in credit performance is magnified because of the smaller variability of the underlying collateral. Had the overall credit risk of these structures not been underestimated, mispriced and unaccounted for in the credit ratings of the resulting securities, the credit crisis surely would have been less severe. The rating agencies now know that the same conditions that cause one BBB mortgage-backed bond to go bad will affect all BBB mortgage backed bonds, so these second level securitizations are no longer executed as profit-making arbitrage transactions.

Similar risks exist in any securitization that is structured with collateral equally susceptible to market movement. If one piece of collateral fails, that shouldn't mean that all the collateral backing the bonds should be affected. That's the problem in such securitizations as CDOs backed by commodities derivatives contracts, and bonds collateralized by loands to hedge funds. Securitizations that take leveraged risk in one market sector and lever it again are imprudent investment vehicles to have in our marketplace.

Well structured securitizations make prudent investments, regardless of the taint attached to these investments during the financial crisis. In 2012 and 2013, seasoned, formerly AAA subprime mortgage bonds were the best performers in the entire US Dollar bond universe. Investors realized that not every mortgage made to a subprime borrower was going to default. Even houses in foreclosure produced cash that paid the existing MBS.

In 2012 and 2013, in a very small way, the residential private label MBS business showed signs of life with several "super prime" deals. Opportunistic institutional investors raised money during the worst of the credit crisis and began buying up foreclosed houses in bulk. Now they're renting them out to families, and boosting returns by issuing securitized bonds. The CMBS (commercial real estate) securitization market revived in 2011 and 2012. Even corporate bank loan securitizations showed signs of life.

The residential single family home is still the grandaddy of all securitization asset classes and the largest single asset in most families. While Fannie and Freddie (and Ginnie) continue with their explicit guarantees, new risk-sharing bonds are gaining acceptance in the market, a good sign that Fannie and Freddie may soon be weaned from anything other than a credit backstop from Uncle Sam .

Securitization isn't dead, because it simply makes sense for the capital markets, offering opportunities for investors and for our citizens.

CHAPTER TWENTY-SEVEN

The Market is the Solution

The fundamental reason the mortgage market exists is to facilitate home buying and safe investing. Reforms must serve investors as well as borrowers, because it is through their investments that capital is provided to mortgage lenders.

A myopic focus on the risks of subprime lending will only result in restricting homeownership to the wealthy. Requiring lenders to hold more capital (5%) against anything other than "plain vanilla" loans may make sense from a systemic point of view, but it means that potential homeowners who don't qualify for the safest loans may not have the option of buying a home at all.

Defining loans to less creditworthy borrowers as "predatory lending" and legislating or regulating them out of existence is regressive, serving only to return us to a time when the only people who could dream of owning a home were those with a big downpayment. If we truly want to turn most of our working class and middle class into permanent tenants throwing a third or more of their income into an after-tax dustbin, restricting mortgage borrowing to a few strict alternatives will do just that.

Looking at loans without looking at the market only means we have forgotten how to let the market do its job. For more than twenty-five years, borrowers have been saving approximately 2% in interest on their mortgages because of securitization. That 2% translates into a savings of approximately 1% of the GDP, while the outstanding balance of mortgage bonds has averaged about half the size of the GDP. If home buyers spent their savings on other goods and services, the securitization market effectively stimulated the economy by over $100 billion a year for more than three decades.

It isn't just subprime borrowers who benefited from the securitization market when it worked; the direct savings to American homebuyers in every credit range has been substantial. Each new kind of deal structure which appealed to investors tended to raise the value of the mortgages used in securitization, which in turn lowered the interest rates paid by the borrowers.

By far the bulk of the money provided to home buyers comes from institutional investors, in both the government-sponsored MBS and the private label MBS markets. These institutions, especially the ones that purchase AAA bonds, aren't a group of rich people looking for a vehicle to increase their personal wealth. They are, in general, funds managed for the benefit of ordinary people. They are pension funds, insurance companies, banks and mutual funds, all of whom are looking for safe investments to earn a return until employees retire and get their pensions, families receive compensation for medical claims or death benefits, banks pay off maturing CDs, and small investors withdraw money from their mutual funds.

We should let the market work, and give investors a reason to trust their money to private funding of mortgage loans, even loans that don't fit into neat definitions of "safe" borrowing. Let investors decide what expected return they need for taking the risks they take. In order to properly evaluate those risks, we need full disclosure and independent verification, at every stage in the process. In a word, transparency.

It was under a cover of darkness that most of the problems of greed, fraud or unwarranted optimism went unnoticed and unchecked. What investors didn't know definitely hurt them, and by extension, all of us. Areas of shadow persist, from loan origination through pooling and securitization, and finally to trading.

Achieving transparency in the market has been slow and incomplete. For example, investors will now have more information on individual loans in securitized bond deals and more time to verify that information, but only on "public" deals. A giant loophole was left in the rules when the SEC backed off from making the same disclosure requirements for quasi-public but technically private placement bonds issued under its Rule 144A. To get a sense of why this matters, nearly all CDOs and a huge proportion of CMBS were and are issued under this rule.

Most of the transparency we need will occur if investors insist on more and better information, and reward the lenders and securitizers who provide it. Enhancements could be made to our private information reporting systems to let investors see track records for individual mortgage brokers, appraisers, and others associated with the origination of each mortgage loan. Investors would pay more for deals originated by the better loan officers and appraisers, and could avoid untrustworthy originators.

There are several nationwide systems already in place that can facilitate full disclosure about the ongoing status of any mortgage loan. Investors make use of them, as do Fannie Mae, Ginnie Mae and Freddie Mac. Enhancing them to include information on the people involved in the transaction is a relatively minor change. Investors (and borrowers) should be able to see the track records of mortgage brokers, mortgage bankers, and bank loan officers, including how many loans those professionals make, and how many complaints and loan defaults there have been.

Transparency is also needed in the structuring and rating of securitized deals. If investors demand them, enhancements in disclosure will likely be adopted by investment banks as well as by the Rating Agencies.

When rating bonds, the Rating Agencies should follow standards similar to those used by stock analysts. Any rating should incorporate a history of the results of identically rated bonds in the same sector. That history should be clearly described, along with the number of comparable bonds outstanding, and any changes that have been made to the ratings, year by year. A period of up to ten years of rating history and subsequent performance should be sufficient for most investors.

Investment banks could enhance their standards of disclosure in the offering documents provided to investors. Currently, these documents describe the change in duration and yield of bonds based on a range of prepayment assumptions. They provide very little discussion of credit assumptions and associated calculations of investor returns when credit assumptions vary.

Without great difficulty, a matrix of results could be provided for each bond, reflecting future prepayment and credit performance. In the language of the market, the expected prepayment vector would be the "pricing speed," and the expected credit performance vector would be the "pricing default curve." Together they would make up the "pricing scenario." In order to give the pricing scenario validity, the offering documents should include past performance data on similar loans, ideally from the same lender and servicer.

Investors should be able to examine a number of scenarios showing the investment results of the loan pool prepaying and defaulting as expected, and also at half the expected rates, 1.5 times the expected rates, twice and four times the expected rates.

Changes adopted by the SEC in August of 2014 finally mandated that loan-level information (rather than potentially misleading averages) will be part of the disclosure for each public deal. This is a step in the right direction, but still just a snapshot in time. Investors need to know how the underlying collateral backing their bonds performs over time.

Ongoing collateral performance could be expressed as a percentage of the originally expected prepayment speed, default rate and credit loss rate. This information could be added to the monthly remittance reports from the Trustees of the bonds, which already include data on the loan pools and the bonds, including what percentage of the pool is at various stages of delinquency, along with how much money is paid to each class of the securitized deal and paid out or received from interest rate hedges.

It would be helpful if monthly bond remittance reports incorporated the information supplied in prior remittance reports, so trends could be easily observed, and the actual loan performance could be viewed in comparison to the expected cumulative total prepayments, defaults and credit losses for each month as the deals age.

The recent financial crisis has given us the opportunity to examine the problems inherent in the existing home mortgage system and fix them. Although changes should be directed at preventing another crisis, if they are forward-thinking and not reactionary, they they are also likely to make the system more efficient.

The changes I've proposed are all aimed at making the mortgage market more transparent, and therefore more honest. They would do a great deal to restore trust to the housing finance system. This matters to US investors, and to all investors in our financial system, all over the world.

Unfortunately, all the reforms to the securitization market won't keep the world from having another global meltdown. Massive leverage in that global system and the hidden way risks are transferred through the system virtually guarantees that another crisis is coming. Borrowers, investors and the global capital markets remain unsafe, as long as the current unregulated, leveraged betting on the market goes unchecked.

CHAPTER TWENTY-EIGHT

Finance Monsters

Dr. Frankenstein didn't set out to create a monster when he began experimenting with reanimation, and neither did JP Morgan when they created the first Credit Default Swap contract in 1997. The idea was simple – to enable a lender or investor to buy insurance against the default risk they held with their loan or bond.

CDS were a welcome addition to the market for lenders that held customized corporate loans in portfolio. Such loans could be harder to sell than corporate bonds, so insurance against default might be the best way to protect against a loss if the borrower's condition looked sketchy.

It wasn't long before bearish investors discovered they could achieve higher returns on their capital if they bought credit insurance on a target company than they could get by shorting stock. With $10 million in cash, a speculator could make a $20 million bet in the stock market or a $200 million bet in CDS. No longer primarily a hedging instrument, CDS became a straight bet with a huge potential payoff.

Because the CDS business is unregulated and the nature of the contracts hidden, the size of those bets against the market were potentially unlimited. The only limit, in fact, was the amount of exposure the banks were willing to sell to the hedge funds and investors. Like any kind of monster, the CDS market was big, powerful and scary.

At first, it seemed that the amount of debt a company issued set some limit on the amount of CDS that customers would demand. Each contract was written with a specific bond (the reference bond) as the insured item. To collect on the insurance after a default, the holder of the CDS had to deliver the bond to their counterparty to get a payoff, much the way you have to give the wrecked car to the insurance company if your car gets "totaled."

The idea that the amount of debt might limit the amount of CDS evaporated in 2005 when Delphi, the auto parts maker, declared bankruptcy. They had $2 billion in bonds outstanding, but to everyone's surprise, there were $20 billion in CDS outstanding. *Big, powerful and scary.*

In a $15 trillion economy, the CDS market was estimated at $55 trillion, a monstrous imbalance. The counterparties to the CDS bets were the big banks. Clearly, as big as they were, their balance sheets were dwarfed by the monster size of the CDS bets. Like King Kong with Ann Darrow in his grasp, when the squeeze was on, the King Kong of CDS would crush the big banks and leave havoc in its wake.

And that's exactly what happened. When it came time to pay out the winning CDS bets, no one knew which banks could remain solvent. None of the banks were considered creditworthy anymore, because all the banks were playing the game, but none of the positions were disclosed to regulators or the public. Every thing the major banks guaranteed was suspect. The commercial paper issued by thousands of companies no longer meant anything. Companies couldn't get their working capital, or use their letters of credit to make shipments, or fulfill their payroll obligations. Tens of millions of people in America had their economic lives ruined, and tens of millions more lost their jobs around the world as thousands of companies failed.

Some of the biggest CDS bets were against subprime mortgages. A nearly constant flow of scary news articles, many with blatant numerical falsehoods, helped the CDS winners' bet look better, and fanned the flames of panic in the market. In fact, there were so many such articles in 2007 that the American Dialect Society chose "subprime" as the Word of the Year.

By the end of that year, most people, and even most investors, were convinced that subprime borrowers were going to get to the end of their teaser rate period and have to pay twice as much or even more. The fact was that the 7% to 8% subprime teaser-rate loans had limits on how much the rate could rise, typically only 2% or 3%. The other fact not being publicized as the crisis gained momentum was that Fed rate-lowering had ensured that most, if not all, subprime borrowers were going to have their mortgage rates reset *lower*, not higher, in 2009 and beyond.

Another commonly misreported number was the percentage of foreclosures that would render subprime BBB bonds worthless. The frequently-cited figure was 7% to 8% . Those familiar with the cash flow rules knew that this number needed to be much higher -- somewhere in the 20% to 25% neighborhood -- before BBB bond holders took losses. The deals were set up with additional protections like excess cash reserves, which typically built up to 8% to 10% of the bond balances over the first few years when borrowers paid the teaser rates. When the foreclosed homes got sold, bondholders would also get paid.

Roughly three times as many foreclosures as were repeatedly cited in the press would be needed to render the BBB subprime bonds worthless. Where did those journalists citing incorrect numbers get their information? We don't know. But we can guess that it wasn't from the people who knew how the bond business worked or who ran the numbers, or who didn't have a stake in a negative outcome.

Threats are a classic part of the monster's repertoire, and the Street was abuzz with threats during the mortgage meltdown. There were reports that accounting firms were likely to be sued if they didn't use the ABX -- an approximation of 20 CDS priced differently than the actual traded prices of bonds or mortgages in the market. Did accountants feel as if they were being threatened by monsters if they audited correctly, and fear being sued for using real prices paid for real assets?

The rating agencies also received threats of lawsuits and calls for jail terms. It's true that the rating agencies blew it when they created CDO ratings for deals that held BBB and BB rated bonds which themselves were carved from the cashflows of thousands of borrowers. Still, the ratings on the subprime MBS bonds themselves *had to be based on historical statistics*. To do any differently would have meant the rating agencies were not, as one of the answers on my Securities Series 7 Examination specified way back when, Nationally

Recognized Statistical Rating Organizations (NRSROs). Why in the world would statisticians be threatened with time behind bars for correctly using statistics on the wealth of historical data they studied?

Although the CDS market operates behind closed doors, we have gotten to see inside at least one $2 billion deal, as the Goldman Sachs presentation of ABACUS 2007-1 is now part of several academic case studies and even a Federal Reserve study.

I went through the pitch book and what I found most revealing was how small the actual bonds in this deal were, and how the deal multiplied the exposure to those bonds. Goldman and John Paulson, who was reported to have made $15 billion or more on his play in the CDS game, chose 90 bonds to reference in a deal made entirely out of CDS, with a face amount of $22.222 million for each bond. Yet the bonds themselves were typically much smaller, on the order of $10 million. So that one deal more than tripled the losses of those bonds that the market had to absorb. How many other deals, and how many CDS that weren't parts of deals, also multiplied the effects of losses in those bonds?

Paulson chose to let the world know he was making money betting against the housing bubble. He also got lots of press coverage of $15 million in (tax-deductible) contributions to the Center for Responsible Lending, a liberal group who you might think never saw a mortgage they didn't think was predatory lending. The CRL was actively helping borrowers stay as long as possible in foreclosed homes while paying nothing, which maximized the losses in the very mortgage bonds Paulson was betting against.

Behind the scenes, Paulson was also instrumental in the last-minute shift in strategy for the TARP bailout of the major banks, when the $700 billion got re-directed from buying up the soured mortgages and bonds into recapitalizing the lenders through preferred stock purchases. The provision for buying that stock was almost an afterthought as the law was written, taking up just three pages among hundreds of pages of negotiated terms for buying bad loans or bad bonds. I was gobsmacked when the bill was signed into law, and then none of the $700 billion actually bought "troubled assets." Not coincidentally, that shift in US taxpayer investment allowed the avalanche of mortgage foreclosures and bond losses to continue unabated, since the banks wouldn't fail with all that new capital.

Strangely, even the losers in the big bet didn't lose very much. Wall Streeters who pumped up the bubble market and didn't bet against it kept the millions they took home in bonuses, and didn't go to jail. Many of them didn't even lose their jobs.

Most famous were the Wall Streeters who were selling bonds to investors while simultaneously betting against them, as we found out when $85 billion of AIG's CDS margin calls were covered by taxpayers and immediately wired out to major Wall Street firms and international banks.

The infamous "Magnetar" trade by one hedge fund worked exactly like that, with the hedge fund approaching all the Wall Street CDO dealers saying they would buy the riskiest "equity" pieces of new issue CDO deals heavily laden with subprime MBS, or, more frequently, CDS on subprime MBS. As it turned out, that same hedge fund was buying enormous dollar amounts of CDS bets against those and other deals. They made a fortune.

Maybe the most egregious case of losers who didn't lose was the crew at AIGFP. They bankrupted the largest AAA insurance company in the world, but the government overseers who took over in late 2008 somehow came to the conclusion that they had to pay retention bonuses averaging over $1 million apiece to every AIGFP employee. No mention at all was made about trying to recover some of the hundreds of millions in bonuses those same employees were paid during the years before the meltdown when they were setting up the deals that lost so many billions.

What about the losers who really lost? How much did they lose? A recent academic study that covers 90% of the universe of subprime MBS through December of 2012 showed about $100 billion of bond losses for AAA through BBB MBS through the end of 2012. The Financial Crisis Inquiry Commission estimate of $350 billion in actual mortgage losses once all is said and done seems about right, if not a bit high. That would translate into about $200 to $250 billion in MBS bond losses. Putting these huge numbers into perspective, the subprime mortgage losses and the MBS losses associated with them are smaller than the taxpayer-funded losses during the Savings & Loan crisis a generation ago, and only about one third as big when viewed as a percentage of the GDP.

The big difference between these two crises was that the mortgage crisis losses ended up almost entirely absorbed by working families. Homeowners and at-risk borrowers took the largest losses relative to their net worth, and many lost everything. Homeowners who didn't lose their homes lost substantial value in those homes. Pure mortgage lenders lost their businesses. The biggest banks lost several years of profits and their capital shrank to dangerously low levels. Bond investors lost a few percentage points in their diversified portfolios.

No problem for the finance monsters. There was no need to bail them out, because they took home the spoils.

We still don't know what the bets were, who held them or how big they were. We do know that it was a monster-sized feast, we're stuck with the leftovers, and we're still cleaning up the mess.

CHAPTER TWENTY-NINE

Detoxing Derivatives

Though the credit derivatives market has the potential to be toxic to the global financial system, it also serves a useful purpose for those who need to hedge or insure their positions. The CDS market is here to stay, but it can be difficult to discern the difference between legitimate hedging and gambling. The only rational choice we have as a society is to do what we can to keep a small group of gamblers from making bets that can ruin all of us.

The housing bubble in the US created an opportunity for profit for those who took leveraged bets against that market segment. Their counterparties in those wagers were the biggest banks and Wall Street dealers. When it became clear that trillions of dollars of winning bets might be out there, every investor charged with taking care of large sums of money took the same action at the same time, and tried to limit their exposure to *any* bank that might be facing insolvency.

The same thing happened throughout the global economy. Without a global credit system, grocery store shelves were going to be empty, not just in America but in New Delhi. Gasoline stations were going to run dry and tens of millions of workers might not get their paychecks on time. At that moment in the fall of 2008, global economic collapse and even mass starvation wasn't just possible – it was inevitable – unless drastic action was taken.

Only a few governments can be trusted to pay their debts. That's why, in October of 2008, I sat in an investment committee meeting where it was decided that a limit, even for cash deposits, would be placed on any bank. The banks provided the backstops to money market funds and Commercial Paper, so that was not an alternative. We

decided to buy Treasury Bills with our remaining cash after reaching
our limit for the handful of banks we felt could and would survive.
And so did everyone else. The T-bills we bought that quarter had a
negative yield. That's right – we decided to lose a small amount of
money in exchange for the US Government promise that we would get
99.97% of our cash back three months later.

As much as most people hated it, governments and central banks
saw no choice but to bail out and prop up banks and financial markets.
That's why preventing a recurrence isn't simply a matter of forcing
banks to make better mortgage loans or hold more capital aside when
they make those loans.

With just a short stroll down memory lane, we can see multiple
instances when our taxpayer guaranteed banks have been the facilitators
or direct participants in crises and scandals that were excused as "once
a century" events. LTCM in 1998. Enron in 2001. The subprime
mortgage crisis in 2007. The LIBOR rate setting scandal in 2009. JP
Morgan's "London Whale" CDS losses in 2012. In each case, the
losses were hidden or billions were borrowed that couldn't be repaid,
and undisclosed swaps were the vehicle of choice to hide those losses
from the market (and even from their own management teams).

The potential for another, smaller meltdown came again in 2012,
when Greece faced a grave financial crisis. The workout by the rest of
the EU was unnecessarily complicated by the need to refinance the
country's debt in a way that wouldn't trigger a CDS payoff. Once
again, no one knew exactly how many Euros worth of CDS were
outstanding, nor which banks might have inordinately large exposures.
Once again, a problem in one place, a country with roughly the same
GDP as the state of Missouri, threatened to metastasize throughout the
global financial system.

So what has been done?

Some steps have been taken, including the crucial establishment
of central clearing parties, like the exchanges where options and
commodities are traded. However, the age-old game of choosing the
easiest regulator by changing legal jurisdiction or form of business
hasn't stopped. AIGFP was legally a Maryland savings bank with a
London subsidiary doing its CDS business, even though the office

where the people who ran the operation was in suburban Connecticut.

All across the world, regulators and governments are trying to get their arms around the issue, mindful that today's capital markets allow those with serious money to pick almost any location as their legal place of doing business. The business is so large that it comes down to a couple of dozen financial giants to provide the credit that is at the heart of the business. Though they are resisting mightily, the global banking giants seem to have accepted that there need to be controls and capital requirements beyond their internal systems and procedures. But they keep trying to protect some of their most profitable derivatives business from disclosure, no doubt because they think they will make less profit if it's all done in the light of day.

The current battle lines are centered around what kind of derivatives trading might continue without being cleared with a central counterparty or allocated capital reserves, or how small a participant can be in order to escape examination entirely. This discussion of loopholes has already gone on for several years, and it looks like it will continue.

For example, when the Commodities Futures Trading Commission (CFTC) and the SEC released their initial rules for swaps, they proposed that participants in the market would be exempt from capital requirements and examination if they used $100 million or less in swaps. That classic loophole was widened to $8 billion during subsequent discussions, an exemption so large that someone who wanted to take on $100 billion in exposure could easily afford to set up thirteen separate companies to execute the trades.

The requirement to clear the contracts through the exchanges was waived for complex, unique, or difficult-to-value derivatives. Those contracts are exactly where some real damage might be done, so that's the last place we should ignore. It would be much safer if two parties who want to enter an "exotic" contract simply agree during their negotiations how to value their contract over time, and provide the model for valuation and capital margin calculation to the exchange. Both parties do it anyway to calculate their mutual payment obligations and their internal risk. So why not put it where the status can be seen and verified?

Perhaps the most needed change would be to "drill down" into the actual names that have CDS written against them. As the central clearing parties register the contracts, they should disclose the total exposure (both long and short) for any credit or index, and inform each "target" entity that its credit capacity in the global system is being used by third parties.

And that brings us to the last problem that hasn't been addressed in the CDS market. When Delphi was struggling in 2005, it couldn't find a place to refinance its $2 billion in bonds. That may be simply because it was failing. But the problem was complicated by the fact that the banks and Wall Street dealers had an additional $20 billion in Delphi credit exposure on their books, even though Delphi knew nothing about that exposure.

Did Greece deserve to pay more than 25% per year when it looked like they might default on their debt? Maybe, but who can dispute that the rate was higher because of the CDS market and the speculators who piled into the big trade of betting against Greece?

It's clear that the global financial system will remain inherently unstable as long as unlimited risk can be created and transferred with little or no personal or institutional cost to those who create and trade that risk.

The derivatives market is dominated by the largest banks and virtually unregulated hedge funds. The dollar amount of those derivatives are still far larger than the economy or any other financial market. And the derivatives aren't just side bets on mortgage bonds.

Those bets can be on commodities, interest rates, corporate loans, energy prices or even hurricanes, earthquakes or national debt for any country. In other words, the next crisis may come from almost part of the economy, but the mechanism to turn a sector loss into a global disaster is still in place.

****

Glossary

ABCP – Asset-Backed Commercial Paper. Short maturity (less than 270 day) debt sold in regular auctions to money market funds and other investors seeking safe places to hold cash. Secured by trade receivables and other assets, ABCP pays slightly higher returns than conventional CP issued by top-rated corporations.

ABS – Asset-Backed Security. Bonds created by bundling financial assets such as car loans, trade receivables, credit card accounts or home equity loans together into a trust. Typically, these are floating rate bonds with shorter maturities than MBS.

ABX – A family of derivative indices that approximate the cash flows of bonds from twenty large subprime mortgage deals dating from late 2005 through 2007. The first ABX series referenced bonds from the second half of 2005, the next series referenced bonds from the first half of 2006, and so on. Each had bonds rated AAA, AA, A, BBB and BBB-, so each series was really five separate indices.

Agency Mortgage Securities – MBS or CMOs that are guaranteed by Ginnie Mae, Fannie Mae or Freddie Mac. Timely payment of principal and interest are guaranteed. These organizations are also called GSE's, for Government Sponsored Enterprises.

Bonus Pool – The money allocated to pay bonuses, the once-a-year paychecks that usually exceed the "base salary" of those on Wall Street, often by millions of dollars. Top producers often get 90% of their annual pay in a bonus check. Even clerks and administrative assistants can get six-figure bonuses, so "Bonus Day" is a yearly exercise in mass hysteria

Call Option – A derivative instrument that allows a call buyer to purchase a financial instrument at a defined price over a given period of time. In the stock market, usually the right to "call" 100 shares from the seller at a fixed price until a given date.

CDO – Collateralized Debt Obligation. A securitized bond deal that uses bonds or loans as its collateral for a new multi-class bond deal. Initially executed with junk bonds by Drexel in the 1980s. Used to fund bank loans from its balance sheet by NatWest Bank in 1996, and adapted to become an "arbitrage" transaction in the late 1990's.

CDS – Credit Default Swap. A contract executed using standard swaps documents that specifies one party will pay regular payments equal to the yield spread of the bond, in exchange for the other party paying credit losses on the same bond.

CMBS – Commercial Mortgage Backed Securities. Pools of loans secured by income properties provide the cash flows to pay these bonds.

CMBX – A family of indices of credit default swaps on bonds from 25 separate CMBS deals all originated in roughly the same nine months. Each index series has six different credit levels, ranging from senior AAA down to BBB- (triple-B minus). The fifth CMBX (CMBX 5) series was launched in May of 2008.

CMO – A multi-tranche mortgage bond deal that distributes the cash flows from pools of mortgage loans or MBS to the bonds according to a set of rules for that distribution. The mortgage loans or MBS are said to "collateralize" the bonds.

CMO Derivative – The tranches of CMO deals that had unusual characteristics that made them unlike the underlying mortgage loans. Examples included Principal Only (PO) and Interest Only (IO) bonds, inverse floating-rate bonds, and bonds that had special payment rules, such as the "jump Z," a bond that took a different place in the payment order for the deal if a pre-defined trigger event occurred.

CMO Residual – The additional mortgage cash flows, usually excess interest, that is left over after the CMO bonds are paid their principal and interest.

Conduit – A legal vehicle set up to buy financial assets for the purpose of selling or financing them shortly thereafter. Used as "warehouses" for loans before securitization or as off-balance-sheet financing vehicles, conduits are sponsored by banks, lenders, or Wall Street dealers.

Coupon – The interest payment for a bond. The word comes from the time when bonds were engraved paper certificates that had small detachable "coupons" around the edge of the paper, each of which was cut off and presented to the payment agent to receive each interest payment.

CP – Commercial Paper. Short maturity debt issued by a highly rated company or special purpose vehicle on a regular basis for short term funding. Typically bought by Money Market Funds, CP has to have maturity of 270 days or less.

Credit Underwriting for Commercial Real Estate – Assessing properties for their current and future income potential, evaluating them in comparison to similar properties in the same area, and examining them for any deferred maintenance issues.

Deal Structure – How cash flows from mortgages are allocated to multiple tranches of bonds in a securitization. The tranches are divided by maturity, interest rates, principal payment schedules or credit priority to divide the risks among different types of investors.

Derivative – A security whose price is derived from external asset prices or events. The most common derivatives are futures contracts, options, swaps and insurance policies. All derivatives are contracts in which one counterparty pays the other based on external references, which can vary as widely as stock or commodity prices or even weather events like storms or rainfall.

Discount Window – A repo lending facility the Federal Reserve provides to regulated banks that takes in Treasuries, MBS, ABS, or other collateral and gives the bank term financing. It carries the risk of margin calls, but has the promise that no bank will be turned away.

EPD – Early Payment Default. A mortgage that defaults in the first few months after it was originated. Occasionally legitimate, as in cases where the primary breadwinner dies immediately after closing the loan, but more frequently a loan where the borrower never intended to pay.

Factors – The monthly update of the amount of principal remaining in a mortgage pool or CMO bond. By subtracting the new factor from the prior month's factor, you can determine how much principal was paid off in each month.

Fixed Income – The generic name for all bonds. In spite of the name, adjustable rate and floating rate debt is also the territory of the Fixed Income Department.

GNMA – Government National Mortgage Association. A government agency that issues and guarantees mortgage securities based on pools of underlying mortgages insured by the FHA (Federal Housing Administration) or the VA (Veteran's Administration). GNMA mortgage securities are the only mortgage securities that enjoy the explicit credit guarantee of the U.S. Government. Very small Agency with fewer than two hundred employees, in most years since it began guaranteeing MBS in 1970, GNMA (Ginnie Mae) has paid hundreds of millions of dollars in profits to the Treasury.

GNMA 9 – 9% mortgage pass-through security (MBS) backed by 9.5% FHA and VA mortgage loans. The investors get all of the principal and 9% in interest, while the bank keeps 0.44% (44 basis points) to service the loan and GNMA takes just 6 basis points for its guarantee of principal and interest.

Goodwill – An accounting entry put on a company's balance sheet to categorize acquisition cost for which no tangible book value is received, for example, a brand name. If the asset becomes impaired, as a brand name would if the product were no longer sold, then the goodwill entry is written off and charged against earnings.

Interest Rate Cap – A specialized form of interest rate swap that pays one counterparty (the purchaser) the difference between a fixed interest rate and a floating rate index like LIBOR, but only pays if the LIBOR rate is higher than the fixed rate. The purchaser of the cap pays a single upfront premium for this interest rate risk protection.

Interest Rate Swap – Standardized contract in which one party pays the short maturity (floating) rate that resets periodically, and the other party pays the life-of-contract fixed rate on a notional amount. In practice, the payments made are the difference between the floating rate interest due and the fixed rate interest due on each payment date. Since it is a contract, the way to close out a position is to enter into a new swap with mirror terms.

Inverse Floater – A CMO bond that is paired with a floating rate bond in such a way that the interest of the two bonds equals that of a fixed-rate bond. Some people refer to the fixed rate bond as being the "parent" of the floater and the inverse pair.

Inverted Yield Curve – A market with longer term interest rates are lower than short rates, as when three-month or two-year rates are higher than the ten-year rate. Since banks generally fund themselves with short term obligations and make longer duration loans to borrowers, inverted yield curves can cause stress throughout the financial system.

Leverage – Investment where the purchase is made by using some of the buyers' own money and the rest by using borrowed money. Often expressed as a ratio, a buyer paying 10% and borrowing the remaining 90% of the purchase price is said to have 9 to 1 leverage.

LIBOR – The London InterBank Offering Rate. Set each business morning at 11 A.M., London time, it sets the interest rates at which various top-ranked banks lend to each other. Established first by the British Bankers' Association, it now incorporates rates from a larger group of international banks. LIBOR is the basis for most corporate bank loans and most subprime mortgages.

LIBOR Curve – A yield curve of the benchmark swap rates. Swap rates are available in the market for every maturity from overnight to thirty years, making it easier to reference than the much sparser Treasury curve.

LTV – Loan-to-Value. The amount of a loan expressed as a fraction of the value of the asset that secures the loan. For most home mortgages, the standard was 80% LTV or lower until the housing bull market of 2001 through 2007.

Margin Call – a call for additional capital to protect a lender that has financed a stock or bond. The owner of the asset that is "on margin" is asked to deposit additional cash when the value of the asset falls so the lender is not exposed to a larger fraction of the value of the asset than they agreed to when the asset was financed.

Matching Numbers or Tying Out – When analysts at dealers, accounting firms, issuers or other transaction participants each run multiple sets of assumptions about the assets and liabilities of a deal structure through their computer models, and compare the outputs to be sure that all cash flows and calculations are identical.

Mortgage Pass-Through – A security that takes the monthly principal and interest payments from a pool of mortgage loans and pays them out each month to the investor. For guaranteed pass-throughs, the guarantor pays the monthly payments when they are due even if the borrower is late, and pays off the principal balance if the borrower defaults.

Mortgage Underwriting – The process a lender goes through before approving a loan to a borrower, which may include employment verification, credit checks, appraisal, clearing the title, search for liens and lawsuits, and review of tax returns.

Negative Real Interest Rates – When short-term rates, or the cost of funds, are lower than the rate of inflation. This policy quickly recapitalizes banks and other lenders by ensuring profits from almost all lending and fixed income investing.

Notional – The face amount of the underlying bond, stock or currency that is referenced by a swap contract. The huge numbers we see of "notional" swaps outstanding includes all the closed-out trades, which are double reported, even though they have no economic impact.

OAS, or Option-Adjusted Spread – the average yield spread of one investment above another over a number of future interest rate paths that are constructed to reflect the current market's implied future rates and expected volatility of those rates.

Option ARM (or Pay-Option ARM) – Adjustable Rate Mortgage that offers the borrower the option of several payment amounts:
1) Interest only – the principal stays the same;
2) Fully amortizing – the principal and interest are paid off over time, similar to the conventional mortgage, except the payment amount changes when the interest rate changes; and
3) Minimum payment – a low (or very low) interest rate paid that doesn't even cover the interest due, with the extra interest added each month to the balance of the loan until the loan balance grows to a limit, usually 15% higher than the original balance.

Par Bonds – Bonds bought for 100% of their face amount, so their yield approximately equals the coupon rate, no matter how long the principal repayment (maturity) may take.

Pass-Through – The simplest form of securitization, in which a pool of financial assets is created and each investor gets a pro-rata share of the principal and interest payments on each payment date. Pass-throughs may also have credit guarantees, such as those provided by the mortgage Agencies.

Piggyback Loan – A second mortgage simultaneously originated with the same borrower on the same house for a borrower who did not have the 20% down payment. Used to create 80% LTV loans that looked good on paper for most of the purchase price while actually lending more money to the home buyer.

Premium and Discount Bonds – Bonds that are priced above and below par (100%). Since all bonds pay the face amount at maturity, a discount bond yields more than its coupon (interest rate) if held to maturity and a premium bond yields less than its coupon as it matures and the premium amortizes.

Primary Dealers – SEC registered broker-dealers that provide the Federal Reserve with distribution for U.S. Treasury auctions. As of 2008, there were only twenty such Wall Street firms.

Prime Broker – A broker that executes trades and holds a portfolio for hedge funds or other institutional accounts. Providing margin credit, lending securities for customers to sell short, and clearing trades of all types for these accounts is one of Wall Street's most lucrative businesses.

Put Option – The option the holder has to sell (force another to buy) a financial instrument. Typically, the option seller collects a cash premium for giving the put option holder the right to "put" the stock or bond to the counter-party who wrote the option.

Rating Agencies – The companies that independently judge the credit quality of debt issues. The ratings range from "triple A" (AAA) through D for default, with gradations in between. Some of the Rating Agencies vary in the system of letters and symbols they use.

Reinsurance – A form of specialized insurance used by insurance companies to lay off some of their risk to other "wholesale" insurance companies. Often used to spread risk caused by having too many policies in place in a single geographic area or one business sector, reinsurance contracts are known as "treaties" between companies.

REIT – Real Estate Investment Trust. A company that invests in real estate or real estate debt, and pays no tax at the corporate level as long as it distributes 90% of its taxable income to its shareholders as dividends.

Repo – Sale and Repurchase Agreement. The way the bond market sets up short term financing of bonds. The holder of the bond sells the bond to the Dealer and simultaneously agrees to buy it back later at a higher price, with the price increase being the interest charged for the financing. The Dealer only advances a portion (often 90% to as much as 97%) of the value of the bond. Every day the Dealer can determine the value of the bond, and make margin calls for cash if the value of the bond has dropped. This is the kind of financing that put Orange County into bankruptcy when their Treasury bonds dropped in value.

Retail Brokers – Stockbrokers in the branches of a securities firm that deal with individual customers. They were paid an average commission of 40% of the firm's gross sales charge, while institutional sales people were paid 8% or less.

Securitization – The process of creating new securities by combining a pool of similar financial assets into a trust or other legal entity, which then issues the new securities. Especially common for residential and commercial mortgages, but used for almost any asset that has predictable cash flows, such as car loans, bonds, building or equipment leases, or even legal settlements or royalty payments.

Senior-Subordinated – The technique of creating two or more levels of credit safety in a securitization. The senior bonds only suffer credit losses if the subordinated bonds have absorbed enough losses to be completely written off.

Side Pocket Investments – Investments defined by hedge fund managers as "side pockets" are not subject to mark-to-market disclosure, even to investors in the funds. Originally created for investments in private companies, some managers designate almost any difficult to value investment as a "side pocket."

SIV – Structured Investment Vehicle. A special purpose entity that buys very highly rated (AAA or AA) structured securities and issues short-term debt called Asset Backed Commercial Paper (ABCP) to fund 95% or more of the purchase. Additional debt with ratings of BBB supplies more of the funding, with only 1% to 2% of the investment put in as equity by the sponsoring bank or lender.

Subordination – Protection against credit loss created by allocating loan default losses to the lowest-rated bond in the "credit stack" and using the salvage proceeds from selling that loan or foreclosing on the property to pay off additional principal on the highest rated bond then outstanding.

Support Bond – A bond that absorbs undesirable characteristics like credit losses or prepayment variance so that other bonds are more attractive investments.

Swap Rates – also known as LIBOR, or London InterBank Offering Rates. The rates that top banks charge each other when lending to each other. Today, most bank loans to companies, many bonds, and even home mortgages refer to swap rates to set and reset their interest rates.

Tranches – From the French trancher, to cut. In a securitization, tranches are prioritized (cut) by maturity, allocation of interest, or in order of credit priority. When divided by credit gradations, some deals will even take the most senior AAA rated bonds, and prioritize the credit one more time to create "super senior" AAA tranches.

Treasury Yield Curve – The family of tradeable obligations (Bills, Notes and Bonds) of the U.S. Treasury that span the range of maturities from three months to thirty years and are regularly auctioned to fund the U.S. Government's current deficit, and refinancing of debt as it matures.

Underwrite – A commitment by a securities dealer to purchase a stock or bond issue from its client. These issues are meant to be sold to the public, but the investment bank will buy the securities even if the public does not buy the offering.

"Private Label" or "Whole Loan" MBS – MBS or CMOs that have mortgage loans rather than Agency guaranteed mortgage pass-throughs as their collateral. Without the guarantee, the only source of payments is the loans themselves, so rules are set up to allocate delinquencies and defaults by the borrowers rather than assuming all payments are on time as they are when a guarantee is in place.

Z-Bond – Also known as an accrual bond because the interest due is added (accrued) to the principal balance of the bond in each payment period. That interest amount is used to pay down principal on other classes of the deal. Once those other bonds are paid off, the Z-bond begins to get both principal and interest.

About the Author

HOWARD B. HILL was one of Wall Street's original "rocket scientists."

He worked at AG Becker Paribas, Prudential Securities, the Union Bank of Switzerland, Daiwa Securities, Deutsche Bank and MassMutual Financial.

His innovative bond structures helped lower the cost of home financing on three continents, and the analytic techniques he pioneered have become essential for investors and risk managers in many of our largest financial institutions.

Howard is credited with an unequaled number of industry "firsts" in the securitization market, including the Z-PAC, super PO, ACE and re-REMIC bond structures. His teams executed first-time securitizations that lowered financing costs for apartment buildings, equipment leases, mobile home parks, nursing homes and life insurance policyholder loans.

After working at investment firms for 25 years, Howard started his own firm. He now trades for his own account and writes the popular blog mindonmoney.wordpress.com.   He lives in New Milford, Connecticut.